Congratulations a[nd] wishes to a very fine girl, - Kim; always keep your eyes on the "SON" and you will never have to walk in the Dark"

Presented to Kim Hoover by Rev. & Mrs. V. E. Inman
oct 8, 1975

LOVE
IS MY MEANING

LOVE
IS MY MEANING

An Anthology of Assurance

COLLECTED BY

Elizabeth Basset

JOHN KNOX PRESS
ATLANTA, GEORGIA

This arrangement © Elizabeth Basset 1973

First published in Great Britain in 1973 by
Darton, Longman and Todd Ltd
85 Gloucester Road
London SW7 4SU

*All royalties earned by the sale
of this book are being given to
Feed the Minds
2 Eaton Gate
London SW1*

Library of Congress Cataloging in Publication Data

Basset, Elizabeth, comp.
Love is my meaning.

1. Devotional literature. I. Title.
BV4801.B28 1974   242   74-3708
ISBN 0-8042-2300-9

American edition published by John Knox Press,
Atlanta, Georgia, 1974
Printed in the United States of America

Foreword by
Her Majesty Queen Elizabeth the Queen Mother

I am sure that many will be glad to read and use this anthology.

It brings to us, in its carefully arranged chapters, the insights and inspirations of many different writers.

We live in a world of unusually rapid change. It is no wonder, therefore, that thinking and sensitive people want to know what is fundamentally changeless.

It is my hope and belief that this book can help to assure us that we can, at one and the same time, be truly contemporary men and women *and* have our thoughts and lives rooted in truths that do not change.

Moreover for many of us it is difficult to convey at all clearly the faith and hope that is in us. I am sure, therefore, that those who read this anthology will find expressed in the pages what in our hearts we believe but find so hard to say.

ELIZABETH R.
Queen Mother

My God, I desire to love Thee perfectly,
    With all my heart which Thou madest for Thyself
With all my mind, which only Thou canst satisfy
    With all my soul, which feign would soar to Thee.
With all my strength, my feeble strength, which shrinks before
So great a task and yet can choose naught else but spend itself
In loving Thee.
    Claim Thou my heart,
    Fill Thou my mind,
    Uplift my soul and
    Reinforce my strength,
    That when I fail Thou mayest succeed in me
    And make me love Thee perfectly.

Preface

THIS COLLECTION of writings has grown over the years, from its beginning in a note-book kept to record passages I had heard or read or wanted to remember.

So many of the writings have helped me through the sad times and these I would like to share with my friends and any who chance to read the book.

As a title I would have liked 'He Who Is' – St Bernard's answer to the question 'Who Is God?'. However, other authors and other publishers have already used this title. Nevertheless throughout the writings the one theme common to them all is a belief in Someone other, and infinitely greater than ourselves. Expressed implicitly or explicitly this is the one idea which binds them all together and in this lies assurance and reassurance. 'Love is my meaning', the title I have finally chosen, is taken from the writings of Dame Julian of Norwich.

I have a very deep sense of gratitude to all the authors who having braved "the perils of human expression" have brought assurance, hope and renewed courage to their readers.

An anthology is usually looked upon as a bedside book to be dipped into at random but here the chapters have separate themes and I believe that each is perhaps best read consecutively. There is a thread which links each quotation to the one that follows and if the thread is broken, something is lost.

For me, almost without exception, the writings have found the answering "Yes, this is true" often with joy and thankfulness, sometimes with reluctance and even with regret.

There are so many people I would like to thank for their contributions to what can only be described as a combined effort. It is impossible to mention them all, but there are a few without whose encouragement and advice this book would never have been published. I think particularly of Her Majesty Queen Elizabeth the Queen Mother, Sir John Betjeman, Miss Constance Babbington-Smith, Dr Patricia Graeme, Miss Agatha Norman and Mr Robin Baird-Smith.

Elizabeth Basset
London, June 1973

To Ronny, my husband
And Peter, my son

Contents

I

Worship, Adoration and Thanksgiving

"Fill Thou my life, O Lord my God, in every part with praise"

I

From **Centuries** *by* Thomas Traherne

THE FIRST CENTURY

An empty book is like an infant's Soul, in which anything may be written. It is capable of all things, but containeth nothing.

I have a mind to fill this with profitable wonders. And since Love made you put it into my hands I will fill it with those Truths you love without knowing them: and with those things which, if it be possible, shall shew my Love, to you, in communicating most enriching Truths: to Truth in exalting her beauties in such a soul.

Do not wonder that I promise to fill it with those Truths you love, but know not; for though it be a maxim in the schools that there is no love of a thing unknown, yet have I found that things unknown have a secret influence on the soul, and like the centre of the earth unseen violently attract it. We love we know not what, and therefore everything allures us. As iron at a distance is drawn by the loadstone, there being some invisible communications between them, so is there in us a world of Love

2

to somewhat though we know not what in the world that should be. There are invisible ways of conveyance by which some great thing doth touch our souls, and by which we tend to it. Do you feel yourself drawn with the expectation and desire of some great thing?

From **Readings from St John's Gospel** *by* William Temple

> *To Worship is to Quicken the Conscience by the Holiness of God,*
> *To feed the mind with the Truth of God,*
> *To purge the imagination by the Beauty of God,*
> *To devote the will to the Purpose of God.*

Both for perplexity and for dulled conscience the remedy is the same; sincere spiritual worship. For worship is the submission of all nature to God. It is the quickening of conscience by His holiness; the nourishment of mind with His truth; the purifying of imagination by His beauty; the opening of the heart to His love; the surrender of will to His purpose – and all this gathered up in adoration, the most selfless emotion of which our nature is capable and therefore the chief remedy for that self-centredness which is our original sin and the source of all actual sin.

Yes – worship in spirit and truth is the way to the solution of perplexity and to the liberation from sin.

From **Our Daily Prayers** *by* W. J. Carey, D.D.

O my God, Thou art good; there is none good but Thee; all greatness Thou art, but all goodness first. Out of Thy goodness Thou madest us; by Thy goodness we know Thee; for Thy goodness we love Thee; after Thy goodness would we walk; to the goodness of Thy Kingdom, come. Thy goodness follows us all the days of our life, and most blessed of all is the promised end that we shall see Thee, come to Thee, live with Thee. Let us begin that heaven here through the Spirit Thy bounty gives us. Be the sense of Thy goodness ever in our souls, waking a goodness there to answer Thine. Let the Lord be praised daily, even the God who shews us His goodness plenteously and pours His benefits upon us. Praise Thou the Lord O my soul.

From **Worship** *by* Evelyn Underhill •

THE LORD'S PRAYER

Asked how men should pray, Jesus lifts them at once to the summit of the worshipping life, selfless adoration – the lauding and magnifying of the Holy Reality of God – and sets the mystery of His Being before them as the object of loving delight. All else is to be subordinated to this Fact of facts: the prevenient God in His unchanging splendour, standing so

3

decisively over against us, yet in closest and most cherishing contact with our fluctuating life.

> So shalt thou bring with thee
> A burning earnestness of Love,
> A fiery flame of devotion, leaping and ascending into the very goodness of God Himself;
> A loving longing of the soul to be with God in His Eternity;
> A turning from all things of self into the freedom of the Will of God. With all the forces of the soul gathered into the unity of the Spirit; Thanking and glorifying God, and loving and serving Him in everlasting reverence.

(Ruysbroeck)

Prayer:

GOD

> unto whom all hearts are open
> unto whom all wills do speak
> from whom no secret thing is hidden
> I beseech Thee
> so I cleanse the purpose of my heart
> with the unutterable gift of Thy grace
> that I may perfectly love Thee and worthily praise Thee.
> Amen.

From **The Bible and Meditation** *by* C. R. Bryant, S.S.J.E.

MAKING AN ACT OF FAITH

The act of faith is more than a bare statement of belief; it is turning to face the living God. Perhaps the simplest way to make it is to address God as present, telling Him what you believe about Him: "Lord God, you made us, you know us, you love us; you are in me, sustaining me, guiding me, correcting me." The prayer of adoration is an act of faith of a special kind, in which we declare the infinite greatness of God and our own nothingness by comparison. As there can be no genuine prayer without faith, the act of faith which begins prayer underlies all the prayer which follows.

From **My God My Glory** *by* E. Milner-White

BENEDICTUS DOMINE

> Blessed be thou, O Lord, in all things
> that have befallen me:
> Blessed be thou in my temptations, when I have continued
> with thee,

4

and in thy deliverances when I have wandered away:
Blessed be thou in thy wholesome reproofs,
  in all discipline and chastisement of my pride,
  and in thy lifting up, when I have sought thy face:
Blessed be thou in any advances and victories,
  the whole praise whereof I ascribe unto thee
    with a thankful heart:
Blessed be thou for guiding my steps, most wonderfully,
  when I knew not, understood not, nor even cared:
Blessed be thou for my holy calling,
  for the joy of oblation,
  for communion with thyself,
  for aught thou hast wrought through me:
Blessed be thou for all whom I have loved,
  and who have loved me:
And for thy love, from all eternity, beyond compare
  or compass: merciful, tender, unalterable,
    irremovable.

Blessed be thou in all things that befall me,
  and that shall befall me;
O grant me this last blessing, O God of my praise –
  to be true to thee, and close to thee,
    unto the end, without end.

From The Compassion of God and The Passion of Christ *by* Eric Abbott, Dean of Westminster

"To God be the glory." Think how Jesus lived, prayed, worked, and suffered, all to the greater glory of God. He sought always the Father's glory. His pure ambition was the glory of God and the Kingdom of God. Pre-eminently Jesus could have said: "To Thee O Father be the glory for ever and ever: Amen." "I seek not mine own glory, but the glory of Him that sent me." All was done to the Father's greater glory . . .

"To God be the glory for ever and ever: Amen." Let us live, speak, work and pray "to the greater glory of God", "ad majorem Dei gloriam". This will afford us the same motive as Christ our Lord had. This will direct all our work to an end beyond ourselves. This will afford us a worthy ambition – the glory of God and the Kingdom of God. It will also strengthen us when life seems to lack purpose, to lose cogency. "Ad majorem Dei gloriam" will also lift us out of our self-centredness, to look beyond our own glory to God's. It will give us a simple and salutary form

5

of self-examination – "whose is the glory I am seeking, in the things I do and say?" It will help us to see that we are instruments only in the hand of our Lord; to realise that we enjoy being used but "not unto us, not unto us, but unto Thy name give the praise".

... When we come to the end, therefore, let us commend our spirits to God our Creator and Redeemer in faith, believing that He who raised Jesus from the dead will be able to take what we have done for Him, whether explicitly or implicitly, and will gather it into His Kingdom, to be in that Kingdom that particular enrichment of the Kingdom's glory which our particular life has to contribute.

For there is something which only you can bring into the Kingdom.

From **A Manual for Interior Souls** *by* John Nicholas Grou, S.J.

St Paul says that "All things work together for good to them that love God ..." First of all, the Apostle says, "all things". He excepts nothing. All the events of Providence, whether fortunate or unfortunate, everything that has to do with health, or wealth, or reputation; every condition of life; all the different interior states through which we may have to pass – desolation, dryness, disgust, weariness, temptations, all this to be for the advantage of those who love God; and more than this, even our faults, even our sins. –We must be resolved never to offend God wilfully; but if unfortunately we do offend Him, our very offences, our very crimes may be made use of for our advantage, if we really love God. We have only to remember David, we have only to remember St Peter, whose sins only served to make them more holy afterwards, that is to say, more humble, more grateful to God, more full of love ... But all these Divine arrangements are only good for those who love God, that is to say, for those whose will is united and submissive to the will of God – those who in His service consider before all things the interests of God, the glory of God, and the accomplishment of His good pleasure – who are ready to sacrifice to Him everything without exception, and who are persuaded that there is nothing better for a creature than to be lost in God and for God, because it is the only means of finding one's self again in Him: for all this is loving God truly, and with one's whole heart.

Psalm 36: 5 and 6

> *Thy steadfast love, O Lord, extends to the heavens,*
> *thy faithfulness to the clouds.*
> *Thy righteousness is like the mountains of God*
> *thy judgements are like the great deep;*
> *man and beast thou savest, O Lord.*

From **Worship** *by* Evelyn Underhill

Each Christian life of prayer, however deeply hidden or apparently solitary in form, will affect the life of the whole Body. By the very fact of its entrance into the sphere of worship, its action is added to that total sacrifice of praise and thanksgiving in which the life of the Invisible Church consists . . .

Each distinct life of prayer, with its particular rhythm, timespan and capacity makes its essential contribution to that total response which is the essence of worship. Hurried advocates of corporate religion have sometimes tended to regard such hidden and personal lives of prayer as exclusive, other-worldly, lacking in social value and open to the charge of spiritual selfishness. But this superficial view does not bear examination. In obeying the first and great commandment, the life of personal worship obeys the second too. Its influence radiates, its devoted self-offering avails for the whole. Indeed the living quality of the great liturgic life of the community, its witness to the holy, depends in the last resort on the sacrificial lives of its members; and it is only from within such intensive lives that intercessory power – the application to particulars of the Eternal Love – seems to arise.

Hence it is that all great masters of worship insist on the importance of the secret personal life of adoration as the first essential for a Christian; "the only condition under which he can hope to become a channel of the Divine Charity, and co-operate in the sanctification of life". For it is the self-oblivious gaze, the patient and disciplined attention to God, which deepens understanding, nourishes humility and love; and by the gentle processes of growth, gradually brings the creature into that perfect dedication to His purpose which is the essence of the worshipping life.

"Set apart" says Bossuet to one of his penitents, "a certain amount of time morning and evening, whether the mind be filled with God or not, doing so with no other object than the adoration which is the duty of His creature. Adore Him with all the capacity you have, yet without anxiety as to the degree of your success or of your love, as to whether you are concentrated on God or on yourself, whether your time is profitable or wasted . . . There is no question here of stages of prayer. We are concerned only with adoring God without any motive save that we are bound in duty to do so, without any desire save to offer adoration, or if we fail in this, to accept failure with patience and humility . . . The value of our prayer depends on the degree to which we die to self in offering it. There is no place for calculations or precautions. Strive to adore and let that suffice."

If, then, on the one hand the Christian must always worship as a member of the Supernatural Society, mindful of its great interests and subordinated to its life; on the other hand he must also worship as the secret child of God, humbly aware of a direct and most sacred relationship with Him and utterly abandoned to His Will.

All that he does partakes of this double character. It is part of "a chain variously intertwisted with, variously affecting, and affected by, numerous other chains and other lives"; but it also involves "another, a far deeper, a most daring and inspiring relation . . . each single act; each single moment joined directly to God Himself not a chain, but one great Simultaneity" (Von Hugel).

Each of these aspects of the life of worship – the successive and the absolute – safeguards and completes the other; and a full and balanced Christianity needs and gives place for both. So a living corporate worship will only be found where this double movement is present: where there is a nucleus of praying souls, maintaining direct essential contact with the Transcendent, whilst not forgetful of their social vocations as servants of the living God, and this realistic correspondence of the individual soul, its adherence to the Holy is encouraged, stabilised and fed. The periods of Christian decadence have always been periods when this costly interior life of personal devotion has been dim. Revival has always come through persons for whom adoring and realistic attention to God and total self-giving to God's purposes have been the first interests of life. These persons it is true have become fully effective only when associated in groups: but the ultimate source of power has been the dedication of the individual heart. The Benedictines, the Franciscans, and the Friends of God; and within more recent times the Quakers, the Methodists and the Tractarians, all witness to this. Indeed Christian history is lit throughout its course by these "flames of living love". These facts cannot astonish us, when we consider that it is by worship alone that we have access to the Holy and the Real: and that where His prevenient revelation truly breaks in upon a soul, an unconditional personal devotion bringing all levels of life into subjection to His Will is the inevitable response.

From **Our Daily Prayers** *by* W. J. Carey, D.D.

O Jesus, my Lord and Master,
  I bless and praise Thee because I am in Thee;
I realise that my life is now included in Thine:
  I am part of Thee: bound to Thee by the Spirit.
It is no longer I that live to myself,
  My life is hid with Thee, and in Thee;
Do Thou speak through me, act through me,
  Work through me, suffer in me, die in me,

8

Rise again in me, and ascend to the Father in me:
  Because Thou art in me, and I in Thee.
I remember all Thou hast done for me:
  Thy birth, Thy work, Thy weariness:
Thy love, Thy scourging, Thy Cross and Death:
  Thy Resurrection, Thy glory and Thy salvation offered:
Thy gift of the Church as Thy mystical Body.
  For all this I humbly thank Thee and give to Thee
My worship, my loyalty, my love, my service.
  But above all, I pray Thee, bring me to the Father,
That in Thee – the Way – I may approach Him and worship Him
  In Spirit and in Truth,
For the Father seeketh such to worship Him.

From **Lent with William Temple**

SELF-CENTREDNESS

Life cannot be fully integrated about the self as centre; it can only be fully integrated when it becomes God-centred. For God is the real centre of the real world; His purpose is its controlling principle; only in Him therefore can all creatures find a centre which brings them all to harm only with one another and with themselves . . .

It is evidence of how mortally deep is our self-centredness that even our deliverance from it in respect of many sides of life may become itself an occasion for self-esteem. This is that demon of spiritual pride which most of us are not nearly good enough even to encounter, but which the saints assure us is waiting on the top rung of the ladder of perfection to catch us even there and throw us down. It is not mere self-satisfaction at our own goodness like that of the Pharisee in the parable, though this is often confused with it. It belongs to a far more advanced stage of spiritual progress. It occurs where the self, being by nature self-conscious, which is indeed the condition of all spiritual progress whatever, contemplates its own state of deliverance from self-centredness and finds in that a self-centred satisfaction. It is not merely pride in being good; it is pride in being delivered from pride; it is pride in being humble. It turns even self-sacrifice into a form of self-assertion. So the proper object of the self's surrender is the Spirit of the Whole which we call God; but if attention is diverted from God Himself to the self's satisfaction in being surrendered to Him, adoration itself is poisoned. The satisfaction is real, and there is no reason for refraining from attention to it so long as it is in the second place. Man's chief end is to glorify God and (incidentally) to enjoy Him for ever; but if a man were to say that his end was to enjoy God for ever and (with that aim) to glorify Him, he would be talking pernicious heresy.

The true aim of the soul is not its own salvation; to make that the chief aim is to ensure its perdition ("Whosoever would save his soul shall lose it" – Mt 16:25) for it is to fix the soul on itself as centre. The true aim of the soul is to glorify God; in pursuing that aim it will attain to salvation unawares. No one who is convinced of his own salvation is as yet even safe, let alone "saved". Salvation is the state of him who has ceased to be interested whether he is saved or not, provided that what takes the place of that supreme self-interest is not a lower form of self-interest but the Glory of God.

From **My God My Glory** *by* E. Milner-White

Lord, in the choices of every day,
grant me to choose aright
as in thy Presence and to thy glory:
to discriminate not only between the good and the evil,
but between the good and the better,
and to do the best.

Save me from treason to Thee,
O my Master and my King,
by disguising to myself Thy demands,
by any choice of ashes for bread,
by any surrender to popular standards,
by any accommodation of duty or faith
to my own ease,
by any the least betrayal of purity.

Rather grant me the Spirit of judgement
to choose with clear eyes
the ways of grace,
the eternal wisdom and the eternal will:
not only to choose but to pursue
all that is true, all that is of good report,
all that is lovely;
and in all to exalt thy praise and honour,
my Lord and my God.

From **Worship** *by* Evelyn Underhill

. . . Christian worship is never a solitary undertaking. Both on its visible and invisible sides, it has a thoroughly social and organic character. The worshipper, however lonely in appearance, comes before God as a member of a great family; part of the Communion of Saints, living and dead. His own small effort of adoration is offered "in and for all". The first words of the Lord's Prayer are always there to remind him of his corporate status and responsibility, in its double aspect. On one hand he shares the great life and action of the Church, the Divine Society, however he may define this difficult term, or wherever he conceives its frontiers to be drawn. He is immersed in that life, nourished by its traditions, taught, humbled, and upheld by its saints. His personal life of worship, unable for long to maintain itself alone, has behind it two thousand years of spiritual culture, and around it the self-offerings of all devoted souls. Further, his public worship, and commonly his secret devotion too are steeped in history and tradition; and, apart from them, cannot be understood.

There are few things more remarkable in Christian history than the continuity through many vicissitudes and under many disguises of the dominant strands in Christian worship. On the other hand the whole value of this personal life of worship abides in the completeness with which it is purified from all taint of egotism, and the selflessness and simplicity with which it is added to the common store. Here the individual must lose his life to find it; the longing for personal expression, personal experience, safety, joy, must more and more be swallowed up in Charity. For the goal alike of Christian sanctification and Christian worship is the ceaseless self-offering of the Church in and with Christ her head, to the increase of the glory of God.

"Blessed be God . . ."

> *Blessed be God, the only God, three Persons in one eternity of love.*
> *Blessed be God for all that he is.*
> *Blessed be God for all that he has done.*

From **What is common to all** *by* C. R. Bryant, S.S.J.E.: *an excerpt from an article written for* Faith and Unity

The principle affirmation I want to make about a spirituality for today is the priority of adoration, of the worship of the living God of Abraham, Isaac and Jacob, the God who spoke by the prophets, who revealed Himself to the man who died and rose and reigns. Worship is a response to what God has said and is saying to us.

God is addressing us now through everything that happens in the world; and the interpreting clue to what He is saying now is what He has said in the past and principally what He has said in Jesus Christ. The priority that belongs to worship is, I believe, something fundamentally human, something proper to man as man. William Temple, the former Archbishop of Canterbury, has said "It is not that conduct is the end of life and worship helps it; but that worship is the end of life and conduct tests it." Temple was giving a wide meaning to worship. He meant a response to God that ran through the whole of a man's life. A man declares his allegiance to God by the things he does and the way he does them, by his attitude to people, to work, to leisure. Worship in the narrower sense of the word focuses and directs the Godward orientation of the whole of life. The quality of worship is not to be measured by the amount of time spent in saying prayers or reciting psalms. It is possible that a man who does not normally go to Church except on Sundays may be more God-oriented in his life than a monk who spends two or three hours every day in the worship of God. However the time factor is one that cannot be ignored. And those who value the Godward orientation of their whole life will be ready to give time to focusing it and directing it.

Irish Hymn

> Be Thou my vision, O Lord of my heart;
> > Naught be all else to me, save that Thou art –
> Thou my best thought, by day or by night,
> > Waking or sleeping Thy presence my light.
>
> Be Thou my wisdom, Thou my true word;
> > I ever with Thee, Thou with me, Lord;
> Thou my great Father, I Thy true son;
> > Thou in me dwelling, and I with Thee one.
>
> Be Thou my battle-shield, sword for the fight;
> > Be Thou my dignity, Thou my delight,
> Thou my soul's shelter, Thou my high tower:
> > Raise Thou me heavenward, O Power of my power.
>
> Riches I heed not, nor man's empty praise,
> > Thou mine inheritance, now and always:
> Thou and Thou only, first in my heart,
> > High King of Heaven, my treasure Thou art.
>
> High King of heaven, after victory won,
> > May I reach heaven's joys, O bright heaven's Sun!
> Heart of my own heart, whatever befall,
> > Still be my vision, O Ruler of all.

Prayer:

O God, most glorious, make our life a vision of Thee to the praise of Thy Glory, that we all, as a mirror, may reflect it and be transformed into the same image from glory to glory, world without end. Amen.

From **The Call to the Religious Life** *by* Sister Edna Mary

"But religious have to live out this life in and for the world. So worship cannot be lived in isolation from the world – it is offered for and on behalf of the world, constantly against the background of the world and its needs."

Thus Dr Langmead Casserly writes in an article on Benjamin Britten's War Requiem:

"In the strange but penetrating visions the author of the last book of the New Testament was privileged to enjoy, we find ourselves confronted with the astounding truth that ultimately, in the Kingdom of God, that is, in the Church Triumphant, the context of life is liturgy. Nothing remains to me but the highest act of love, and so 'They rest not day or night' in the eternal adoration of the living God . . . But here on earth, in the Church Militant, the context of liturgy is life."

After speaking of the way in which the words and music of the requiem are constantly interrupted by the soloists singing of the horrors of war, he goes on:

"It is, after all, right that the liturgy should thus be continually accompanied by the tormented cries of baffled and defeated men. If we do not hear them at Mass, we may be sure that God does. We must not seek to pass to the one from the other, but to one with the other. Even in the joy and release of the Church's worship we must not forget the agony of the world's pain, for the agony of the world's pain is our agony also."

These last words were echoed almost verbatim by an enclosed nun whom the author heard recently describing what had led her to enter an enclosed community and stressing that to do so seemed the only way of meeting in any degree the suffering of the world. It is enclosed religious who here come nearest to the life of the Church Triumphant, where worship is the sole and ultimate way of meeting human need; but for most religious there is the need to do this in other ways also. So Walter Hilton tells the devout man to whom he writes that to think only of God and have no concern for others is like crowning a person's head but leaving his body ragged; and he bids the anchoress for whom he writes The Scale of Perfection to be so conscious of the needs of others, that although she cannot leave her enclosure she will attend to those who come to her, even if it means breaking off her prayers to do so.

Alcazar *from* **St Theresa of Jesus** *by* E. Allison Peers

TO JESUS

Jesus, Thy ever-holy name I bless;
Jesus, may all my will stretch out to Thee;

13

Jesus, my soul's desire for ever be;
Jesus, as God and Man I Thee confess;
    Jesus, my speech of Thee shall ere be praise;
Jesus, for Thee with living faith I'll fight;
Jesus, Thy law shall be my sole delight;
Jesus, I'll glory in Thee all my days.
    Jesus, Thy Being may I contemplate;
Jesus, my heart shall kindle with Thee near;
Jesus, on Thee my thought shall meditate;
Jesus, I'll love Thee, Thou to me so dear;
Jesus, within Thee be my soul's estate;
Jesus, when I call Thee, do Thou hear.

Prayer *by* Archbishop Hamilton, 1511–71

Glory be to God in the highest, the creator and Lord of heaven and earth, the preserver of all things, the Father of all mercies who so loved mankind as to send his only begotten Son into the world, to redeem us from sin and misery, and to obtain for us everlasting life. Accept, O gracious God, our praises and thanksgiving for thine infinite mercies towards us, and teach us O Lord to love Thee more and serve Thee better; through Jesus Christ our Lord.

From Readings from St John's Gospel *by* William Temple

It is probable that in most of us the spiritual life is impoverished and stunted because we give so little place to gratitude. It is more important to thank God for blessings received than to pray for them beforehand. For that forward-looking prayer, though right as an expression of dependence upon God, is still self-centred in part, at least, of its interest; there is something which we hope to gain by our prayer.

But the backward-looking act of thanksgiving is quite free from this. In itself it is quite selfless. Thus it is akin to love. All our love to God is in response to His love for us; it never starts on our side.

"We love because He first loved us" (1 Jn 4:19): and His love is most of all shown in His treatment of our sin. "God commendeth His own love toward us in that while we were yet sinners, Christ died for us" (Rm 5:8). That is the fact which constrains our gratitude and so inspires our love . . .

"Here is the meaning of my life and the hope of eternal life for me, the Son of God loved me and gave Himself up for me" (Ga 2:20).

He will draw to Himself all men – even Caiaphas and Pilate, even Judas – even me, at last, not only (as I already trust) to a genuine though intermittent devotion, a deliberate though half-hearted service, but to that fulness of adoring companionship which is foreshadowed in the

14

promise "where I am in the intimate fellowship of the Father's love, there also shall my servant be".

Prayer:

O Almighty God, who alone canst order the unruly wills and affections of sinful men; grant unto Thy people that they may love the thing which Thou commandest and desire that which Thou dost promise; that so among the sundry and manifold changes of the world our hearts may surely there be fixed where the true joys are to be found; through Jesus Christ our Lord.

Revelations of Divine Love *by* Dame Julian of Norwich: *taken from* A Book of Comfort *by* Elizabeth Goudge

And also to prayer belongeth thanking. Thanking is a true inward knowing, with great reverence and lovely dread turning ourselves with all our might unto the working that our good Lord stirreth us to, enjoying and thanking inwardly. And sometimes for plenteousness it breaketh out with voice, and saith: Good Lord, I thank Thee! Blessed mayst Thou be! And sometimes when the heart is dry and feeleth not, or else by temptation of our enemy – then it is driven by reason and by grace to cry upon our Lord with voice, rehearsing His Blessed Passion and His great Goodness; and the virtue of our Lord's word turneth into the soul and quickeneth the heart and entereth it by His grace into true working, and maketh it pray right blissfully. And truly to enjoy our Lord, it is a full blissful thanking in His sight.

Let Me be Mindful *by* Virginia Thesiger

Let me be mindful of God's splendour,
not only in those quiet half hours
plucked from the day between sleeping and rising,
from the silent room on peaceful evenings,
with books outspread.
But as I rush through the world,
race through that strident turbulence
of urgency and incidence,
let me so carry God's great glory
like a torch in my hand,
a sun in my face,
a flame in my heart,
that people may turn in their tracks,
feeling the warmth of it,
catching the light.

Oh let my pillar of fire be seen
burning clearly in the confusion,
and not only in those quiet half hours
with books outspread.

O Worship the Lord in the beauty of Holiness *by* J. S. B. Monsell, 1811–75

O Worship the Lord in the beauty of Holiness!
Bow down before Him, His glory proclaim;
With gold of obedience, and incense of lowliness,
Kneel and adore Him: the Lord is His name!

From The Bible and Meditation *by* C. R. Bryant, S.S.J.E.

THE PRAYER OF THANKSGIVING

The prayer in which I express my recognition of God as the author of the good both of creation and redemption is the prayer of thanksgiving. Thanksgiving both expresses gratitude and expands faith. Through thanksgiving we open ourselves to God's renewing action in Christ, and the potentialities of grace are made actual. The Eucharist is at the same time the greatest expression of thanksgiving and the greatest means of our renewal. Every paragraph of the New Testament could be a starting point for thanksgiving, for every paragraph bears directly or indirectly on the great act in which God visited and redeemed His people.

Meditation on the Bible can both enrich our participation in the Eucharist and lead us on to a deeper communion with the God of all grace, whose goodness touches our lives at every point.

From Edges of His Ways *by* Amy Carmichael

Shadow and coolness, Lord,
Art Thou to me;
Cloud of my soul, lead on,
I follow Thee.
What though the hot winds blow,
Fierce heat beats up below?
Fountains of water flow –
Praise, praise to Thee.

Clearness and glory, Lord,
Art Thou to me;
Light of my soul, lead on,
I follow Thee.
All through the moonless night,

Making its darkness bright,
Thou art my Heavenly Light –
Praise, praise to Thee.

Shadow and shine art Thou,
Dear Lord, to me;
Pillar of cloud and fire,
I follow Thee.
What though the way is long,
In Thee my heart is strong –
Thou art my joy, my song,
Praise, praise to Thee.

Prayer:

My God I love Thee and desire to love Thee more and more, and above all things, and all others for Thee; Quicken my love and make me wholly Thine. Amen.

From **Worship** *by* Evelyn Underhill

THE PRINCIPLES OF PERSONAL WORSHIP

Understood in the deepest sense personal worship is man's return-movement of charity to the inciting Charity of God; and therefore organic to his spiritual life. As it develops, it will be exercised in two directions; vertically in adoration, and horizontally in intercession, as the ancient sacrifice was at once an act of oblation and impetration, a gift made to the Unseen and a petition made on behalf of the seen. Thus it is intimately concerned with both aspects of our double-relatedness, the eternal and the successive. In both, not one alone, it reached out towards the Holy, as the final and sufficing object of worship and love; first in surrender to His pure Being, and secondly in loving co-operation with His creative activity. This loving co-operation is the essence of intercession; which is, when rightly understood, an act of worship directed to the Glory of God. Within the Eternal Charity all spirits are united. We each have our place in that order, and self-giving to its saving purposes is the substance of our worshipping life. The true intercessor offers the oblation of his imperfect love, that he may become a channel of the Absolute Love. Here he prays from the Cross. According to the degree of his self-offering is the power of his prayer; and a part of his self-offering will be an entire willingness to work and suffer in the dark, asking for no assurance of result. All that he does and endures, is done and endured as the adoring tool and servant of the Creative Love; and in the last result, his intercessory action is part of the movement of Its Will. "Even the prayer of demand", as Brémond

17

has said, "is not truly prayer except in so far as it is also adoration". It is those who best practise the loving adoration who will best practise the loving expansion; since dwelling in Charity they dwell in God, and become effective channels of His generosity. At their full development the two movements are merged in that one, all-inclusive act of self-giving and obedient love which Christians find revealed in the life of Jesus and supremely expressed in the Cross: the arms stretched out to embrace the world, and the eyes lifted up towards the Eternal God.

There is nothing in man's mixed experience which cannot be brought within the radius of this willing and all-inclusive response to the demand of Reality. Thus the subtle experience of his own inner life, witnessing more clearly with every advance in self-knowledge to the penetrating charity of His creature, restoring the soul, challenging the mind, ever delicately working within life, must evoke an answering movement of gratitude and awe; and in the demands of the world without, its call upon his pity and service, he will again hear the voice of charity inviting his devotedness by means of its creature's needs. Some ascetic effort, too, must enter into any individual worship worthy of the name; expressing the soul's deliberate choice of God, and loving renunciation of all that hinders total self-giving to God – the act of will which throws the human spirit with its preferences and desires at His feet. Even disciplines which in themselves are childish, acquire in this context a certain nobility; and humbling failures occasioned by the greatness of the aim and fragility of the creature become, when rightly accepted, a true part of that creature's self-oblation.

For the personal life of worship – that is to say the increasingly adoring relation to the Holy – is grounded in two qualities: humility and charity. Humility is or should be what man feels about himself over against God. Charity is or should be what that same creature feels about God standing over against himself, and ever more penetrating and possessing his life, till at last that life becomes "so far transformed and perfected in the Fire of Love that not only is it united with this Fire, but has become one living flame within it". These characters are inseparable; they rise and fall together in the soul, and are the only valid index of the worth of its worship. Their presence means that this worship has introduced it into the world of supernatural realities, however dimly, crudely or uncertainly these realities may be conceived. Humility in its beginning arises from negative contrast; man's sense of his own faults and imperfection, his nothingness over against God. But at its height it is caused by positive contrast: the supreme love, worth, and beauty of God in Himself, His perfection striking upon the soul. Charity in its beginning is the creature's response to the divine attraction; and in its fulfilment rises to that unconditioned act of Pure Love which is the very substance of the super-natural life.

Thus the personal life of worship involves on the human side an utter self-abandonment of the creature to God, as the Existent of all existents and doer of all that is done – a total Godward reference of will and act and desire, purging egotism and quickening Charity – and on the divine side, the ever-increasing action of the Creative Love, breaking in, possessing, and moulding the soul. Each worshipping movement of that soul, whether expressed under the formula of devotion or of service – each "act of the will wrought in charity"as St John of the Cross says – increases its capacity for God, and so contributes to that total transfiguration of life, that redemption of the world, which is the Christian goal.

Nor is this ideal intended only to apply to "advanced souls" or persons of mystical capacity. It is, on the contrary, the essence of the Christian spiritual life as plainly taught in the New Testament.

The living core of individual worship, then, is a loving dedication of the will; but a dedication which is itself the result of, and the response to, God's prevenient act and pressure. Thus we come to realise our true position, as units in a vast spiritual economy: each with a degree of freedom, and each with its own part to play, but all vivified and sustained by the Charity which is God. "Our prayer", says Von Hugel, "will certainly gain in depth and aliveness, if we thus continually think of God as the true inspirer of our most original-seeming thoughts and wishes, whensoever these are good and fruitful – as Him Who secretly initiated what He openly crowns".

Evening Prayer *by* Josephine Johnson

> *The air was palpable with gold*
> *Too brimming for the sky to hold*
> *As burnish'd oak leaves, one by one*
> *Held up a mirror to the sun.*
> *The birds above the fountain rim*
> *Were cherubim and seraphim,*
> *Lifting translucent wings in flight*
> *Against the radiance of the light.*
> *No smallest whisper seemed to stir*
> *The invisible threads of gossamer*
> *Laid on the lawn, yet rainbows ran*
> *Shimmering from span to span.*
> *Midges and gnats with rise and fall*
> *Moved to an ancient ritual*
> *In gauzy dance, O King of Kings*

19

It was the hour of humble things!
The small sweet clover magnified
Beheld the bridegroom, was the Bride
And every lowly plantain head
Was haloed by the glory spread!
Then lifting high each shining sword
The grass stood up and praised the Lord!

Praise to the Lord! *by* J. Neander, 1650–80: *translated by* C. Winkworth

Praise to the Lord! O let all that is in me adore Him!
All that has life and breath, come now with praises before Him!
Let the Amen
Sound from His people again:
Gladly for ay we adore Him.

Foreword to **A Book of School Worship** *by* William Temple

Worship is the most practical thing in all existence. It is a fundamental attitude of mind, and it consequently determines our approach to the whole of life. By it we recognise a standard to be accepted as absolute, as altogether good, and true, and beautiful, before which we must bow in respect and adoration. Those who have no such guide are left rudderless on an uncharted sea. Sooner or later they founder in their own abysmal ignorance, or they run aground in shallows and in miseries.

We might well be lost and terrified in the search for such an absolute to which we can attach our allegiance and find safety.

For the Christian, however, it has been revealed; and that, not as some austere and unattainable ideal, but as a loving Creator, Redeemer, and Friend, who is no mere figure in past history or remote influence from beyond the furthest star, but a Person who enters into most intimate union with us, "closer to us than breathing, nearer than hands and feet". There is our hope and strength, the source of our quietness and confidence in the grim but exhilarating battle of life.

1 Chronicles 29: 10-13, adapted

Blessed be Thou, Lord God our Father, for ever and ever. Thine, O Lord, is the greatness, and the power, and glory, and the victory, and the majesty: for all that is in the heaven and in the earth is Thine: Thine is the Kingdom, O Lord, and Thou art exalted as head above all. Both riches and honour come of Thee, and Thou reignest over all; and in Thy hand is the power and might; and in Thy hand it is to make great and to give strength unto all.

Now, therefore, our God, we thank Thee, and praise Thy glorious name.

From Life Together by Dietrich Bonhoeffer

In the Christian community thankfulness is just what it is anywhere else in the Christian life. Only he who gives thanks for little things receives the big things. We prevent God from giving us the great spiritual gifts He has in store for us, because we do not give thanks for daily gifts. We think we dare not be satisfied with the small measure of spiritual knowledge, experience, and love that has been given to us, and that we must constantly be looking forward eagerly for the highest good. Then we deplore the fact that we lack the deep certainty, the strong faith, and the rich experience that God has given to others, and we consider this lament to be pious. We pray for the big things and forget to give thanks for the ordinary, small (and yet really not small) gifts. How can God entrust great things to one who will not thankfully receive from Him the little things? If we do not give thanks daily for the Christian fellowship in which we have been placed, even where there is no great experience, no discoverable riches, but much weakness, small faith, and difficulty; if on the contrary, we only keep complaining to God that everything is so paltry and petty, so far from what we expected, then we hinder God from letting our fellowship grow according to the measure and riches which are there for us all in Jesus Christ.

Prayer by George Herbert (1593–1633)

Thou hast given so much to us, give one more thing, a grateful heart; for Christ's sake. Amen.

Prayer by Rufus Ellis, adapted

O Lord we lift our hearts to thee this day in great thankfulness humbly acknowledging thy mercy and thy truth, thy large and tender providence, thy nearness at all times. Grant us thy Spirit of wisdom and might and peace, that all we say and do and think may be to thy greater glory. Amen.

2

The Gift of the Holy Spirit

"Closer is He than breathing: Nearer than hands and feet"
"That we may evermore dwell in Him and He in us"

Ephesians 3:14-19

From **Readings from St John's Gospel** *by* William Temple

Heard at the final session of the Hatfield Lent course: **The People Next Door**

Prayer: O Lord Jesus pray in us

From **Readings from St John's Gospel** *by* William Temple

Poem *by* S. R. Lysaght. If Love should count you worthy

From **The Path to Glory** *by* J. R. H. Moorman. THE COST OF DISCIPLESHIP

Expectations Expected *by* Charles Sorley

From **The Fruits of the Spirit** *by* Evelyn Underhill. "The words . . . I speak . . . are Spirit"

St Theresa. He is so near that He will hear us

Spirit

Come Down, O Love Divine *by* Bianco da Siena: *translated by* R. F. Littledale

From **Address in Canterbury Cathedral** *by* Eric Abbott, Dean of Westminster

I Corinthians 2:13

Prayer: Look graciously upon us, O Holy Spirit

From **An Anthology of the Love of God** *by* Evelyn Underhill

Prayer: O Holy Spirit, giver of light and life

St Patrick's Breastplate, *ascribed to* St Patrick: *translated by* Mrs C. F. Alexander

Ephesians 6:10-20

Love bade me welcome *by* George Herbert: *taken from* **The Use of Praying** *by* J. Neville Ward

From **Our Daily Prayers** *by* W. J. Carey, D.D. O Holy Spirit of God

From **The Light of Christ** *by* Evelyn Underhill

From **Readings from St John's Gospel** *by* William Temple

Prayer *by* Erasmus (1466-1536). O Lord Jesus Christ, who art the Way
From **An Anthology of the Love of God** *by* Evelyn Underhill
"Narrow is the House of my soul . . ."
From **Living Prayer** *by* Metropolitan Anthony Bloom
Prayer: Grant unto us, O Lord, the royalty of inward happiness
Isaiah 61:1-4, 11. The Spirit of the Lord is upon me
From the **Mundaka Upanishad**, *taken from* **Mysticism** *by* F. C. Happold

---

Ephesians 3:14-19

This, then, is what I pray, kneeling before the Father, from whom every family whether spiritual or natural takes its name:

O, of his infinite glory, may he give you the power through his Spirit for your hidden self to grow strong, so that Christ may live in your hearts through faith, and then, planted in love and built on love, you will with all the saints have strength to grasp the breadth and length, the height and depth; until, knowing the love of Christ, which is beyond all knowledge, you are filled with the utter fullness of God.

From Readings from St John's Gospel *by* William Temple

O Lord Jesus Christ, Thou word and revelation of the Eternal Father, come we pray Thee, take possession of our hearts and reign where Thou hast right to reign. So fill our minds with the thought and our imaginations with the picture of Thy love that there may be in us no room rof any desire that is discordant with Thy Holy Will. Cleanse us, we pray Thee, from all that may make us deaf to Thy call, or slow to obey it, who with the Father and the Holy Spirit art one God blessed for ever. Amen.

Heard at the final session of the Hatfield Lent course: The People Next Door

When we begin to love with the love of Jesus, we are grasped by a love greater than our own love. When we begin praying in the name of the Lord Jesus we are consumed by a prayer more powerful than our own prayer. When we search together in love and prayer for the truth of Jesus, we are illuminated by a truth beyond our reach and grasp of truth. If we are open to one another and to Him the Holy Spirit makes us not only His dwelling-place but the channel through which He can flow to others. In so far as we learn to listen to one another we find that the truth of God is springing out of a company of friends. As we allow each one to contribute the truth he understands, every one of us is lifted up by the Holy Spirit into a fuller understanding.

Prayer:

O Lord Jesus pray in us. Dwell in us and we in Thee. Unite us with Thyself so that our prayers may become Thy prayers and Thy prayers our prayers. Make us to love Thee for Thine own sake and not for what we hope from Thee. Teach us to love as Thou lovest. Amen.

From **Readings from St John's Gospel** *by* William Temple

When we pray "Come Holy Ghost our souls inspire", we had better know what we are about. He will not carry us to easy triumphs and gratifying successes, more probably He will set us some task for God in full intention that we shall fail, so that others learning wisdom by our failure, may carry the good cause forward. He may take us through loneliness, desertion by friends, apparent desertion even by God; that was the way Christ went to the Father. He may drive us into the wilderness to be tempted by the devil. He may lead us from the Mount of Transfiguration (if ever He lets us climb it) to the hill that is called the place of the skull. For if we invoke Him, it must be to help us in doing God's will not ours. We cannot call upon the "Creator Spirit, by whose aid the world's foundations first were laid" in order to use omnipotence for the supply of our futile pleasures or the success of our futile plans. If we invoke Him, we must be ready for the glorious pain of being caught by His power out of the petty orbit into the eternal purposes of the Almighty, in whose onward sweep our lives are as a speck of dust. The soul that is filled with the Spirit must have been purged of all pride or love of ease, all self-complacence and self-reliance; but that soul has found the only real dignity, the only lasting joy. Come then great Spirit come. Convict the world and convict my timid soul.

Poem *by* S. R. Lysaght

> *If Love should count you worthy and should deign*
> *One day to seek your door and be your guest,*
> *Pause! ere you draw your bolt and bid Him rest*
> *If in your old content you would remain.*
> *For not alone He enters, in His train*
> *Are Angels of the mists, the lonely quest,*
> *Dreams of the unfulfilled and unpossessed,*
> *And sorrow and life's immemorial pain.*
> *He wakes desires you never may forget,*
> *He shows you stars you never saw before,*
> *He makes you share with him for evermore*
> *The burden of the world's divine regret.*

How wise you were to open not and yet,
How poor if you should turn Him from your door.

From **The Path to Glory** *by* J. R. H. Moorman

THE COST OF DISCIPLESHIP

The Christian who reads in these verses (Mk 14:25-35) of the price of discipleship will see that, if he is to take the divine words seriously, he must learn not to be too much "entangled in the affairs of this life", whether human affairs and relationships, or personal or material things. He must learn to think of these as things that he can do without, including life itself.

No one knows what he may be called upon one day to face or to do in loyalty to his profession as a Christian disciple – especially in a world as dangerous and uncertain as that in which our lives are cast. The man who is bogged down by worldly ties and considerations will find obedience much harder if God should call him one day to some sacrificial act. The price of discipleship, therefore, is to be willing to give up everything if occasion should demand it, and in the meanwhile to live as men "looking for their Lord", with loins girt and lamps burning, ready for action when the word is given. Discipleship is, or may be, a very costly thing. It may cost us all we have. In this passage, therefore, Jesus introduces a fourth condition, and that is that we should not go into it except with our eyes wide open. He does this in the form of three little parables, those of the tower builder who carefully surveys his material; the warrior-king who closely considers his chances of success; and the salt, which, if it cannot last out, goes bad.

Jesus bids us count the cost of discipleship. Can we face it? Is it going to be too much for us? Dare we risk failure and be cast out? "He that hath ears to hear," let him hear: let him ponder: let him decide.

Expectations Expected *by* Charles Sorley

> *This sanctuary of my soul*
> *Unwitting I keep white and whole,*
> *Unlatched and lit, if Thou shouldst care*
> *To enter or to tarry there.*

> *With parted lips and outstretched hands*
> *And listening ears Thy servant stands,*
> *Call Thou early, call Thou late,*
> *To Thy great service dedicate.*

From **The Fruits of the Spirit** *by* Evelyn Underhill

Jesus said, "It is the Spirit that quickeneth. The words that I speak unto you, they are Spirit and they are life."

25

With all our Spiritual powers: intelligence, heart, and will, we call upon God, we breathe Him into our souls, and immediately He comes down and dwells within us; and an active fruitful contact is established between Him and us. God is in us, God dwells in us. The Divine source whence flow rivers of living water for life everlasting.

> *Speak to Him Thou for He hears*
> *And Spirit with Spirit can meet,*
> *Closer is He than breathing:*
> *Nearer than hands and feet.*

(St Theresa)

Now consider what St Augustine said. He sought Him in many places and came to find Him within himself . . . However quietly we may speak, He is so near that He will hear us . . . a restless soul has no need of wings to go to seek Him, but only to place herself in solitude, to consider Him within her, and not to estrange herself from so kind a guest . . . If you speak try to remember that there is one within you to Whom you may speak; if you are listening, recollect that you have one to listen to, Who speaks more nearly . . . If you wish you need never be separated from such good company.

Spirit

Spirit alone can have fellowship with Spirit. God is Spirit, and fellowship with Him is fellowship in Spirit. The Breath of God in man which warranteth the inmost, utmost things of Faith.

Come Down, O Love Divine *by* Bianco da Siena: *translated by* R. F. Littledale

> *Come down, O Love Divine,*
> *Seek Thou this soul of mine,*
> > *And visit it with Thine own ardour glowing;*
> *O Comforter draw near,*
> *Within my heart appear*
> > *And kindle it, Thy holy flame bestowing.*
>
> *O let it freely burn*
> *Till earthly passions turn*
> > *To dust and ashes in its heat consuming;*
> *And let Thy glorious light*
> *Shine ever on my sight,*
> > *And clothe me round, the while my path illuming.*

Let holy charity
Mine outward vesture be,
    And lowliness become mine inner clothing;
True lowliness of heart
Which takes the humbler part
    And o'er its own shortcomings weeps with loathing.

And so the yearning strong,
With which my heart will long,
    Shall far outpass the power of human telling,
For none can guess its grace
Till he become the place
    Wherein the Holy Spirit makes His dwelling.

From **Address in Canterbury Cathedral** *by* Eric Abbott, Dean of Westminster

Our prayer is His prayer in us. The prayer of Christ the Son of God the Father in the love of the Holy Spirit is the prayer which now the Eternal Christ who took our humanity offers on earth through us who are the members of His Body.

1 Corinthians 2:13

But as it is written, eye hath not seen, nor ear heard, neither have entered into the heart of man, the things which God has prepared for them that love Him.

But God hath revealed them to us by His Holy Spirit; for the Spirit searcheth all things, yea the deep things of God.

For what man knoweth the things of man save the spirit of man which is in him? Even so the things of God knoweth no man, but the Spirit of God.

Which things also we speak not in the words which men's wisdom teacheth, but which the Holy Ghost teacheth; comparing spiritual things with spiritual.

Prayer:

Look graciously upon us, O Holy Spirit. Give us for our hallowing thoughts that pass into prayer, prayers that pass into love and love that passeth into life with Thee for ever. Amen.

From **An Anthology of the Love of God** *by* Evelyn Underhill

If sacrifice, total self-giving to God's mysterious purpose, is what is asked of us, His answer to that sacrifice is the gift of power. Easter and Whitsuntide complete the Christian mystery by showing us first our Lord

Himself and then His chosen Apostles possessed of a new power – the power of the Holy Spirit – which changed every situation in which they were placed. That supernatural power is still the inheritance of every Christian and our idea of Christianity is distorted and incomplete unless we rely on it. It is this power and only this which can bring in the new Christian society of which we hear so much. We ought to pray for it, expect it and trust it; and as we do this, we shall gradually become more and more sure of it.

Prayer:

O Holy Spirit, giver of light and life, impart to us thoughts higher than our own thoughts, and prayers better than our own prayers and powers beyond our own powers, that we may spend and be spent in the ways of love and goodness, after the perfect image of our Lord Jesus Christ. Amen.

St Patrick's Breastplate, *ascribed to* St Patrick: *translated by* Mrs C. F. Alexander

> *I bind unto myself today*
>   *The strong name of the Trinity,*
> *By invocation of the same,*
>   *The Three in One and One in Three.*
>
> *I bind this day to me for ever,*
>   *By power of faith, Christ's incarnation;*
> *His baptism in the Jordan river;*
>   *His Death on Cross for my salvation;*
> *His bursting from the spiced tomb;*
>   *His riding up the heavenly way;*
> *His coming at the day of doom;*
>   *I bind unto myself today.*
>
> *I bind unto myself the power*
>   *Of the great love of cherubim;*
> *The sweet "Well done!" in judgement hour;*
>   *The service of the seraphim.*
> *Confessor's faith, apostle's word,*
>   *The patriarch's prayers, the prophet's scrolls,*
> *All good deeds done unto the Lord,*
>   *And purity of virgin souls.*
>
> *I bind unto myself today*
>   *The virtues of the star-lit heaven,*
> *The glorious sun's life-giving ray,*
>   *The whiteness of the moon at even,*

The flashing of the lightning free,
  The whirling wind's tempestuous shocks,
The stable earth, the deep salt sea
  Around the old eternal rocks.

I bind unto myself today
  The power of God to hold and lead,
His eye to watch, His might to stay,
  His ear to hearken to my need,
The wisdom of my God to teach,
  His hand to guide, His shield to ward,
The word of God to give me speech,
  His heavenly host to be my guard.

Against the demon snares of sin,
  The vice that gives temptation force,
The natural lusts that war within,
  The hostile men that mar my course;
Or few or many, far or nigh,
  In every place, and in all hours,
Against their fierce hostility
  I bind to me these holy powers.

Against all Satan's spells and wiles,
  Against false words of heresy;
Against the knowledge that defiles,
  Against the heart's idolatry,
Against the wizard's evil craft,
  Against the death-wound and the burning.
The choking wave, the poisoned shaft,
  Protect me, Christ, till Thy returning.

Christ be with me, Christ within me
  Christ behind me, Christ before me,
Christ beside me, Christ to win me,
  Christ to comfort and restore me,
Christ beneath me, Christ above me,
  Christ in quiet, Christ in danger,
Christ in hearts of all that love me,
  Christ in mouth of friend and stranger.

I bind unto myself the name,
  The strong name of the Trinity,

29

By invocation of the same,
The Three in One, and One in Three,
Of whom all nature hath creation,
Eternal Father, Spirit, Word.
Praise to the Lord of my salvation:
Salvation is of Christ the Lord.

Ephesians 6:10-20

Finally, my brethren, be strong in the Lord, and in the power of his might. Put on the whole armour of God, that ye may be able to stand against the wiles of the devil. For we wrestle not against flesh and blood, but against principalities, against powers, against the rulers of the darkness of this world, against spiritual wickedness in high places. Wherefore take unto you the whole armour of God, that ye may be able to withstand in the evil day, and having done all, to stand. Stand therefore, having your loins girt about with truth, and having on the breastplate of righteousness: And your feet shod with the preparation of the gospel; Above all, taking the shield of faith, wherewith ye shall be able to quench all the fiery darts of the wicked.

And take the helmet of salvation, and the sword of the Spirit, which is the word of God: Praying always with all prayer and supplication in the Spirit, and watching thereunto with all perseverance and supplication for all saints; And for me, that utterance may be given unto me, that I may open my mouth boldly, to make known the mystery of the gospel. For which I am an ambassador in bonds: that therein I may speak boldly, as I ought to speak.

Love bade me welcome *by* George Herbert: *taken from* **The Use of Praying** *by* J. Neville Ward

Love bade me welcome: yet my soul drew back,
Guilty of dust and sin.
But quick-eyed Love, observing me grow slack
From my first entrance in,
Drew nearer to me, sweetly questioning
If I lacked anything.
"A guest," I answered, "worthy to be here."
Love said, "You shall be he."
"I the unkind, the ungrateful? Ah, my dear,
I cannot look on Thee."
Love took my hand, and smiling did reply,
"Who made the eyes but I?"

"Truth, Lord, but I have marred them: let my shame
Go where it doth deserve."
"And know you not," says Love, "who bore the blame?"
"My dear, then I will serve."
"You must sit down," says Love, "and taste my meat,"
So I did sit and eat.

From **Our Daily Prayers** *by* W. J. Carey, D.D.

O Holy Spirit of God,
Come into my heart and fill me:
I open the windows of my soul to let Thee in.
I surrender my whole life to Thee:
Come and possess me, fill me with light and truth.
I offer to Thee the one thing I really possess,
My capacity for being filled by Thee.
Of myself I am an unprofitable servant, an empty vessel.
Fill me so that I may live the life of the Spirit,
The life of Truth and Goodness, the life of beauty and love,
The life of Wisdom and Strength.
And guide me today in all things:
Guide me to the people I should meet or help:
To the circumstances in which I can best serve God,
Whether by my actions, or by my sufferings.
But above all make Christ to be formed in me,
And make Him King.
Bind and cement me to Christ by all Thy ways
Known and unknown:
By holy thoughts and unseen graces,
And sacramental ties:
So that He is in me, and I in Him,
Today, and for ever.

From **The Light of Christ** *by* Evelyn Underhill

An act of prayer at the heart of every act of service, a self-offering to His purpose so that the action may be His and not our own. That in its perfection is the secret of the Saints.

I live – yet not I! Christ is the boundless source of energy and love.

From **Readings from St John's Gospel** *by* William Temple

In the spiritual life it is of urgent importance that we remember from whom our strength comes – the Holy Spirit, the "Giver of Life". He is the Spirit of Christ, whom disciples receive through their companionship with Christ. Christ is therefore in that sense the source or sender of the Spirit. He withdraws His visible presence; but He does not leave us desolate; on the contrary, He makes our loss into a blessing. "If I go not away, the Comforter will not come to you, but if I depart I will send Him to you."

Prayer *by* Erasmus (1466–1536)

O Lord Jesus Christ, who art the Way, the Truth and the Life, we pray Thee suffer us not to stray from Thee who art the way: nor to distrust Thee, who art the Truth, nor to rest in any other thing than Thee, who art the Life. Teach us by the Holy Spirit what to believe, what to do, and where to take our rest. We ask it for Thy own name's sake.

From **An Anthology of the Love of God** *by* Evelyn Underhill

The outpouring of His Holy Spirit is really the outpouring of His love, surrounding and penetrating your little soul with a peaceful, joyful delight in His creature: tolerant, peaceful love full of longsuffering and gentleness, working quietly, able to wait for results, faithful, devoted, without variableness or shadow of turning. Such is the Charity of God.

Love breaks down the barrier that shuts most of us from heaven. That thought is too much for us really, yet it is the central truth of the spiritual life. And that loving self-yielding to the Eternal Love – that willingness that God shall possess, indwell, fertilise, bring forth the faith of His Spirit in us, instead of our own – is the secret of all Christian power and Christian peace.

"Narrow is the House of my soul . . ."

> *Narrow is the House of my soul:*
> *Do Thou enlarge it, that it may be able to receive Thee.*
> *It is ruinous:*
> *Do Thou restore it.*
> *That it has within it those things which most offend Thine eyes,*
> *I both confess and know.*
> *Who can cleanse it but Thou?*
> *Therefore do Thou cleanse it*
> *And abide therein for ever.*

From **Living Prayer** *by* Metropolitan Anthony Bloom

. . . As the Fathers say, the Holy Spirit is always there when there is prayer, and according to St Paul, "No man can say that Jesus is Lord but by the Holy Ghost" (1 Co 12:3).

It is the Holy Spirit who will in due time fill prayer, faithful and patient as it has been, with the meaning and depth of new life.

Prayer:

Grant unto us, O Lord, the royalty of inward happiness and the serenity which comes from living close to Thee. Daily renew in us the sense of joy and let Thy Eternal Spirit dwell in our souls and bodies, filling every corner of our hearts with light and gladness. So that bearing about with us the infection of a good courage, we may be diffusers of life, giving Thee thanks always for all things; through Jesus Christ our Lord. Amen.

Isaiah 61:1-4, 11

The Spirit of the Lord is upon me, because He has anointed me to preach the gospel to the poor. He has sent me to bind up the broken-hearted, to proclaim liberty to the captives, to proclaim the acceptable year of the Lord. To give unto them that mourn a garland for ashes, the oil of joy for mourning, the garment of praise for the spirit of heaviness; that they might be called trees of righteousness, the planting of the Lord, that He might be glorified. For as the earth bringeth forth her bud, and as the garden causeth the things that are sown in it to spring forth; so the Lord God will cause righteousness and praise to spring forth before all the nations. The Spirit of the Lord is upon me, because He has anointed me to preach the gospel.

From the **Mundaka Upanishad,** *taken from* **Mysticism** *by* F. C. Happold

My son! There is nothing in this world that is not God. He is action, purity, everlasting Spirit. Find Him in the cavern; gnaw the knot of ignorance.

Shining, yet hidden, Spirit lives in the cavern. Everything that sways, breathes, opens, closes, lives in Spirit; beyond learning, beyond everything, better than anything; living, unliving.

It is the undying blazing Spirit, that seed of all seeds, wherein lay hidden the world and all its creatures. It is life, speech, mind, reality, immortality . . .

He who has found Spirit, *is* Spirit.

3
On Prayer
"Lord, teach us how to pray"

From **Abba Father** *by* Evelyn Underhill

In those rare glimpses of Christ's own life and prayer which the Gospels vouchsafe us, we always notice the perpetual reference to the unseen Father, so much more vividly present to Him than anything that is seen.

Behind that daily life into which He entered so generously, filled as it was with constant appeals to His practical pity and help, there is ever the sense of that strong and tranquil Presence, ordering all things and bringing them to their appointed end: not with frigid and mechanical precision, but with the freedom of a living, creative, cherishing thought and love.

Throughout His life the secret utterly obedient conversation of Jesus with His Father goes on.

He always snatches opportunities for it, and at every crisis He returns to it as the unique source of confidence and strength: the right and reasonable relation between the soul and its source.

From **My God My Glory** by E. Milner-White

Lord, Thou hast given me this space for prayer:
  fill it with Thy gifts of grace:
  fill it with the showings of Thy truth,
    with holy counsels and inspirations;
    with the communion of peace.

Occupy it with the work of love,
    to beg Thy mercies upon them I love,
    upon all my acquaintance;
    upon all in need;
    upon all whom Thou lovest.

Overshadow me with Thy Spirit,
    with the light that is THOU;
Banish distraction, inattention, coldness;
Make mine eyes to see, mine ears to hear,
    my tongue to speak, my soul to be still;
And then be merciful to my prayer,
    and to me a sinner;
      for Christ's sake.
                    Amen.

From **Readings from St John's Gospel** by William Temple

THE LORD'S TEACHING ON PRAYER

First must be put the fundamental principle that God is perfect love and wisdom; He has no need that we should tell Him of our wants or desires; He knows what is for our good better than we do ourselves, and it is always His will to give it: "Your Father knoweth what things ye have need of before ye ask Him" (Mt 6:8). Consequently we must not in our prayer have any thought of suggesting to God what was not already in His mind – still less of changing His mind or purpose.

But what things are good for us may depend on our spiritual state. Food which is wholesome and nourishing for those who are in good health may be lethal poison to any in high fever.

The worst of all diseases of the soul is detachment from God, whether by ignorance or by neglect. If all our wants are supplied while we have no

35

thought of God, this may confirm us in our detachment from Him, and so the things which should have been for our wealth are unto us an occasion for falling (Psalm 69:22). Consequently the question whether what is normally a blessing such as deliverance from the enticement of some temptation, will be in actual fact a blessing to me may often depend on whether or not I recognise God as the source of all good things. So the first requirement in prayer is that we trust to God for all blessing.

Our Lord, according to His custom, states this in its place without qualification and without reserve. He goes to the greatest possible length in the demand that as we pray we shall believe that God will hear and answer, and in the promise that God will then grant our petitions. Many sayings might be quoted; one is sufficient: "All things whatsoever ye pray and ask for, believe that ye have received them and ye shall have them" (Mk 11:24).

The next requirement is apparently inconsistent with this; for this next requirement is that we should persevere in prayer in spite of disappointment. We are to be sure that God will grant our prayers; and when He does not, we are to go on praying. Our Lord gives His teaching about perseverance in two parables which belong to that well-marked group of parables whose point is that the comparison fails. For in these the Lord illustrates God's dealing with us, or our duty before God, by reference to human actions which are not morally admirable. Such are evidently the parable of the Unjust Steward (Lk 16:1-9) and, as I think, the parable of the Labourers in the Vineyard (Mt 20:1-16). The duty of perseverance in prayer is urged upon us in the parable of the Importunate Friend (Lk 11:5-10) and of the Unjust Judge (Lk 18:1-8).

We know that God does not grant petitions in order to rid Himself of the nuisance which we become by our persistence; His choice of parallel so completely inapposite is a challenge to us to seek the real reason why God may make long delay and then grant our request.

The first requirement was perfect confidence. Does God wish to test our confidence? Of course not; He knows perfectly well what it is worth. But He may very likely wish to deepen it. The faith which takes the form – almost necessary at first – of confidence that God will do what we ask, is, after all, faith in our own judgement as much as faith in God. We may not pray for anything except so far as we believe it to be God's will; that belief is very fallible.

The purpose of God's delay may well be to detach our faith in Him from all trust in our own judgement. Scarcely anything deepens and purifies faith in God for His own sake as surely as perseverance in prayer despite long disappointment.

So the purification of confidence by perseverance leads us to the third and deepest requirement. The other two were enjoined upon all His hearers; this was urged upon His more intimate disciples in these closing discourses recorded by St John. Here are the great sayings:

"Whatsoever ye shall ask in My name, this will I do, that the Father may be glorified in The Son. If ye shall ask anything in My name, I will do it" (14:13–14).

"If ye abide in Me and My sayings abide in you, ask whatsoever ye will, and it shall come to pass for you" (15:7).

"If ye ask anything of the Father, He will give it you, in My name; until now ye did not ask anything in My name; ask and ye will receive, that your joy may be fulfilled" (16:23–24).

When the condition mentioned is satisfied, our wills are identified with the will of God; we are praying for what He desires to give and waits to give until we recognise Him as its source so that our reception of it will strengthen our faith and not encourage our neglect of Him.

This means that the essential act of prayer is not the bending of God's will to ours – of course not – but the bending of our wills to His. The proper outline of a Christian's prayer is not "Please do for me what I want" but "Please do in me, with me, and through me what you want". The pattern prayer that our Lord taught us is based on this principle; "after this manner pray ye" (Mt 6:9). What is the manner?

When we come into our Father's presence, our Lord seems to say, we should be so filled with the thought of Him that we forget all about ourselves, our hopes, our needs, even our sins; what we want most of all, and therefore utter first is that all men may know how glorious God is and reverence Him accordingly – "Hallowed be Thy Name". (How often do we pray that? We say it every day; but do we pray it?) Our next desire is to be that everyone should obey Him, so that He is truly King of His own world – "Thy Kingdom come" – then that His whole purpose of love may be carried out, unspoilt by the selfishness in ourselves and others – "Thy will be done".

Only after this do we turn to ourselves, and when we do it is to ask for those things which are necessary if we are to serve God with all our hearts: freedom from harassing anxiety: "daily bread" or "the morrow's bread"; and restoration to the favour we have forfeited – "forgive us our trespasses"; and no moral adventures, for there is plenty on the straight path of duty to test character and develop grit without being "led" to the lairs of dragons – "lead us not into temptation"; and some evil grip upon us from which we cannot free ourselves – "deliver us from that" – and why? It is because we are all the time concerned with God's Kingdom, Power and Glory.

The two sons of Zebedee once approached our Lord with a prayer which perfectly illustrated the wrong way to pray: "Master we would that thou should'st do for us whatsoever we shall ask of Thee". After that we are not surprised that their request was selfish in the worst sense – it was for something by gaining which they would keep others out of it. To such a prayer for selfish advantage there is and can be only one answer; "Can you share My sacrifice?" (Mk 10:35–38).

The essence of prayer is to seek how we may share that sacrifice. It finds its fullest expression in the Eucharist where we offer ourselves to Christ that He may unite us with Himself in His perfect self-offering to the Father – that self-offering to which He dedicated Himself in the great prayer, which St John calls us to hear with adoring wonder (Jn 17).

From **My God My Glory** *by* E. Milner-White

WORK OF PRAYER

My God and Father,
help me to pray
as my first work,
mine unremitting work,
my highest, finest and dearest work;
as the work I do for thee, and by thee,
and with thee,
for Thy other children and for the whole world.

Infuse and influence it with Thy blessed Spirit,
that it be not unwilling, nor unworthy, nor in vain;
that it be not occupied with my own concerns,
nor dwell in the interests dear to myself,
but seek thy purposes, thy glory, only;
that it be holy and more holy unto the Holiest,
and ever and all through Thy Son,
my Saviour Jesus Christ.

The Necessity for Prayer *by* Evelyn Underhill *taken from* **Concerning the Inner Life**

Enrichment of the sense of God is surely the crying need of our current Christianity. A shallow religiousness, the tendency to be content with a bright ethical piety wrongly called practical Christianity . . . seems to me one of the defects of institutional religion at the present time. We are drifting towards a religion which consciously or unconsciously keeps its eye on humanity rather than on Deity – which lays all the stress on service and hardly any of the stress on awe: and that is a type of religion which in practice does not wear well. It does little for the soul in those awful moments when the pain and mystery of life are most deeply felt. It does not provide a place for that profound experience which Tauler calls "suffering in God". It does not lead us to sanctify: and sanctity after all is the religious goal. It does not fit those who accept it as adequate for the solemn privilege of guiding souls to God . . . In fact it turns its back on the most profound gifts made by Christianity to the human race. I do not think we can deny that there is . . . a definite trend in the direction of religion of this shallow type . . .

It will only be checked in so far as the clergy are themselves real men of prayer. Therefore to become and continue a real man of prayer seems to me the first duty of a parish priest.

What is a real man of prayer? He is one who deliberately wills and steadily desires that his intercourse with God and other souls shall be controlled and actuated at every point by God Himself; one who has so far developed and educated his spiritual sense that his supernatural environment is more real and solid than his natural environment. A man of prayer is not necessarily a person who says a number of offices or abounds in detailed intercessions; but he is a child of God who is and knows himself to be in the deeps of his soul attached to God and is wholly and entirely guided by the Creative Spirit in his prayer and his work. This is not merely a bit of pious language. It is a description . . . of the real apostolic life. Every Christian starts with a chance of it; but few develop it.

The laity distinguish in a moment the clergy who have it from the clergy who have it not: there is nothing you can do for God or for the souls of men which exceeds in importance the achievement of that spiritual temper and attitude.

The Commerce of Love *by* Evelyn Underhill *taken from* **Theophanies**

> *In the Triumph of prayer,*
> *Twofold is the spell:*
> *With the folding of hands*
> *There's a spreading of wings*
> *And the soul's lifted up to invisible lands*
> *And ineffable peace. Yet it knows being there*
> *That it's close to the heart of all pitiful things;*
> *And it loses and finds and it gives and demands;*
> *For its life is divine, it must love, it must share*
> *In the triumph of prayer.*
>
> *In the Anguish of prayer*
> *It is well, it is well!*
> *Then only the victory of love is complete,*

When the soul on the cross
Dies to all save its loss.
When in utmost defeat
The light that was fair
And the friend who was sweet
Flee away, then the truth of its love is laid bare
In the anguish of prayer.

From **This World and Prayer** *by* Sister Edna Mary

Prayer does not depend upon the human effort because it is not a question of establishing a relationship with God; the relationship already exists, and prayer is the opportunity to recognise this.

The Christian knows (or should know) that he is surrounded by God, by His love and care, His power, His sheer being, every moment of the day and night. It is what God does that is infinitely more important than what man does. Jeremiah has a quaint phrase in which he speaks of the Lord rising early and sending prophets to His people; this vivid little picture of God awake and active while man still lies abed, of God concerned and caring for man before man has given Him a thought, is a picture which applies to prayer.

It is the vision of God – His might or His holiness or His love – which awakes the human response of adoration; it is the same vision which by contrast awakes also the response of penitence, and when the sinner turns in penitence to God he finds God already there waiting to welcome him, as the prodigal son found his Father waiting with arms outstretched; He knows before we ask the things of which we have need; and when we make the slightest turn towards Him, however small and inarticulate, He Himself formulates our prayers.

Thus the part of the Christian in prayer is very largely the recognition of the presence of God, a resting in Him and attention to Him, an active desire to do His will. When he sees it in this perspective the Christian will still make an effort, because he will want to respond to love with love – and even that response he will recognise as made possible by God's presence in him and not by his own efforts. The effort in prayer will be the consequence of the relationship into which God calls a man, and not the ground of that relationship, and therefore it will be joyful and confident, and not anxious lest the effort be insufficient.

He will rejoice with St Theresa in the assurance that "provided the intention remains firm, my God is not the least meticulous".

Another reason why a person's prayers do not depend on his own efforts is that he is never alone in his prayers. Christian prayer is never "the flight of the alone to the Alone", it is joining in the perfect worship of the

God who is not alone but in the perfect society of the Three in One. This is most obvious in liturgical worship, but is equally true of what is miscalled "private prayer".

One side of this truth is that all prayer is intercession, for the Christian in speaking with God speaks with and for all other Christians and all other men. The other side of it is that all prayer is joining in something much greater than the individual, joining in the great stream of prayer and praise which never for a moment ceases, in which Christians on earth join as they are able in the ceaseless praise of those in Heaven, led by Christ Himself "who ever lives to make intercession for us" and to praise the Father on our behalf.

St Augustine

Without God we cannot. Without us God will not.

From **Letters:** William Law, *taken from* **A Book of Comfort** *by* Elizabeth Goudge

Reading is good, hearing is good, conversation and meditation are good; but then they are only good at times and occasions, in a certain degree, and must be used and governed with such caution as we eat and drink and refresh ourselves, or they will bring forth in us the fruits of intemperance. But the spirit of prayer is for all times and all occasions, it is a lamp that is to be always burning, a light to be ever shining; everything calls for it, everything is to be done in it and governed by it, because it is and means and wills nothing else but the whole totality of the soul, not doing this or that, but wholly incessantly given up to God to be where and what and how He pleases.

From **Spirituality for Today,** *edited by* John B. Coburn
THE HONEST TO GOD DEBATE

When Bishop Robinson was asked how he prayed to "the ground of your being" he replied: "I do not pray to the ground of my being. I pray to God as Father. Prayer for the Christian, is the opening of oneself to that utterly gracious personal reality which Jesus could only address as 'Abba, Father!' I have no interest in a God conceived in some vaguely impersonal pantheistic terms. The only God who meets my needs as a Christian is 'the God of Abraham, Isaac and Jacob', the God and Father of our Lord Jesus Christ."

From **Markings** *by* Dag Hammarskjöld

Prayer, crystallised in words, assigns a permanent wavelength on which the dialogue has to be continued, even when our mind is occupied with other matters.

On Praying *by* Alan Ecclestone, *taken from* Spirituality for Today

BEGINNING TO PRAY

There are three commonly-experienced moments in everyday living which can be used as the beginning of praying: three moments which seem by their very nature to prompt us to pray.

(1) When we feel glad, grateful, pleased, relieved, exhilarated, joyful, etc.

(2) When we feel the need for help: when we are frightened, anxious, distressed, in pain, perplexed, etc.

(3) When we are tired to the point of exhaustion, flat out, beaten, etc.

(1) The Moment of Gladness

The simplest thing that we can do when we come to this moment is to say "Thank you". We should say this straightforwardly to someone who has given us something or done something for us. The glad moment is the recognition of something given or done, and the right response on our part is gratitude. The praying is simply saying "Thank you for that".

It is so obvious that many people do this spontaneously, saying "Thank God for that", and they vary a good deal in the implications they give to using the word God. If you are used to saying "God", go on doing so, but if not simply say "Thank you" and leave the "you" to be pondered upon later. The important thing is to let the gratitude take hold of you and to surround your experience with gratitude . . .

What is here prompted by a spontaneous recognition of the good thing encountered now needs to be used as the willed basis for praying when we come to sit down or kneel down to reflect upon a day's experience.

It may well be that at no time during the day have we felt glad, or has occasion for gratitude been clearly grasped. What we are to do now in our praying is to review that experience and pick out what we can say "Thank you" for. We are to give gratitude a chance to germinate in the events that have already become our experience.

We shall not learn to do this quickly nor shall we put ourselves to the trouble of attempting it unless we see how important it is. To have lived through a day and yet not be able to be thankful for one moment of it is to be living a death-in-life. It means our senses and our faculties are being deadened so that instead of providing us with a rich store of valued experience they are simply enabling us to exist. This was a condition in which a great many human beings were placed in concentration camps by the deliberate act of their persecutors. But what more do we do for ourselves

42

if we fail to make possible the growth of pleasure in and gratitude for some part of our daily experience? To learn to sift that experience in a way that picks out more and more what engenders gratitude is what praying is about, and it should be clear from this that such praying is a deep necessity in human life.

Without such growth in sensitive awareness of, and thankful response to, the events of potential enrichment, we do in fact die spiritually.

So much then turns upon our will to say "Thank you". It prompts this simplest act which can be extended in reflective rumination over the whole fabric of our day's experience, growing ever more keen in discrimination and far-sighted in making connections so that what begins with moments is extended into actual tracts of experience. It is the "practised eye" which begins to discern what the fabric itself is really like. The old counsel "Count your blessings" was right enough so far: what is needed is this growing capability of seeing in things that don't look like blessings at all still deeper occasions for gratitude.

All this has a further frame of reference with regard to other people. We are set to learn to say "Thank you" not only for our experience but for theirs too. Our praying must take account of other people's lives and enmesh them in this network of gratitude. It can begin on the simple level of our observation of their moments of gladness and be deliberately pursued in reflective prayer that uses such knowledge as we gain of them, then surround them with thankfulness. The kind of prayer called intercession must have its roots in this. One other point deserves to be noticed here. It is more useful in learning to take these first steps in prayer to leave such questions as "To whom do we pray" than to try to sort out our theology of prayer.

Walt Whitman addressed his poems to "You whoever you are" and Leslie Fiedler comments: "Is there an Other to whom one can speak, a real audience, a real God?" In our praying we speak to "You whoever you are" and mean the Other who is more real than anything else in the Universe. To conceive of the Other in terms of personality is the best we can do, and the gratitude we address to the Other is likewise the best we can offer. It is in the willed deliberate extension of this that we learn more of the Other, and it is far better that we should avoid trying to enclose in fixed terms what we are in process of learning. Much that is most valuable in the arts and in literature is chock full of ambiguities: much that is most important in learning to pray is laid hold of under the same conditions of ambiguity.

(2) The Moment of Need

Just as people say "Thank God for that", so too they exclaim "God help

43

me", meaning much or little in both cases. It is the felt need that is the starting point here and this has a reality for us which we are not in doubt about. If I am frightened, I need to be reassured; if I am anxious I need to be relieved; if I am perplexed, I need redirection. I may be hazy or even wrong about the causes of my troubles, but the kind of praying we are concerned with here simply expresses my need for help and my belief, hope and expectations that I can be helped. The Syro-Phoenician woman's very straightforward plea, "Lord help me" is the model of praying in this kind. Again, as with the prayer of thankfulness, it hardly matters whether you repeat "Help me" in words or whether you silently shape your whole frame of mind to an attitude of supplication for help. The important thing is to grasp and prolong the attitude of the moment and to permit it to become deepened so that the immediate felt need that prompted it is extended to still greater need. The quality of this may be more clearly grasped if we see the difference between this extended plea for help and the condition of worrying. Our very intention which is to oust anxiety and worry prompts the assertion of something like recognised and accepted dependence on "You whoever you are". This kind of praying, indeed like the prayer of gratitude, is a process affair in which we are to learn to pass from the suddenly-felt dependence to an adult-minded recognition of dependence as a continuing condition of our life. "Dependence", wrote Dr Harry Guntrip, "is in fact, an ineradicable element in human nature, and the whole development of love and affection arises out of our need for one another." From this point of view religion is concerned with the basic fact of personal relationship and man's quest for a radical solution to the problems that arise out of this dependent nature. We have in this process to grow into the kind of dependence that is an essential part of maturity and a good deal will depend upon our progress in praying along this road.

We shall have to learn to pass, for example, from the ejaculatory stage – real and important as that is – to the deliberately acknowledged fact of the need for help in the tracts of experience which we learn to scrutinise in quietness. Just as gladness should prompt gratitude, need should evoke confidence.

It will not do this unless by our very persistence and importunity we shape our whole attitude to be of the kind that refuses to be put off. It is of course reinforced by recognition of the occasions when we have been helped already, and part of the prayer in need can quite usefully pick up recollection of these occasions and use it to reinforce the intensity with which we now pray for help. Importunity does not mean clamour; on the contrary, in all that is suggested here we aim at a deliberate reduction of what is said to be the simplest, barest words that can express our approach.

There is no need to say more than "Lord help me" but in the quiet prolongation of this utterance we begin to stretch it over the whole of life to bind ourselves, our need for help, and the Lord, together in an unbreakable relationship.

To pray in this way for others is an essential part of this relationship and it can be done as simply as we propose to do it for ourselves. In the course of a single day we meet, hear about, receive letters from, remember a great number of people. We can in the moment of remembering them, in the moments after meeting them, pray, "Lord help them", and learn to recall them with greater deliberation at some other time of the day or night. They have needs like our own; peculiar needs of their own, secret needs no other person knows, but the prolonged holding of their needy condition in the attention we give is what really matters. A recognition of their need has been lodged in the fabric of experience.

(3) The Moment of Exhaustion

The simplest thing to be done at this moment is to "let go" deliberately. In traditional language it was expressed in words like "Into Thy hands I commend my spirit." If words like these help you to pray at such moments use them as fully as you can.

If you are not accustomed to them or helped by them, find the shortest phrase that expresses for you the entire act of putting yourself into the keeping of the Other. It may be done with such words as "I/We are in your hands", "We are yours" or simply reflecting "let go" while you permit your body to relax. It is probable that we should learn to do this regularly and not just leave it to the times of exhaustion, but if we are going to learn to do it at all, we can begin with those desperate moments. What we are doing in this kind of praying is of quite immense importance and is the necessary counterpart to all our striving, all our pleas for help, all our enjoyment, all our conscious addressing of ourselves to the demands of living. "The night cometh" and it matters a great deal whether its inevitable coming fills us with a sense of "panic and emptiness" or becomes an occasion for utter relief in letting go ourselves trustfully like a child dropping off to sleep.

But it is not easily learned: all of us carry to the point of exhaustion the accumulations of problems and difficulties. Yet we have argued throughout that praying is a necessary part of truly living, and nowhere is this more true than in respect of the tired, beaten condition which active people find themselves in again and again. To be able to pray "let go" is so important a part of our life that it deserves all the practice that it requires to become part of our maturing way of living, and its connection with the final letting go should not be forgotten.

What Prayer Is *by* Jeremy Taylor

Prayer is the peace of our spirit, the stillness of our thoughts, the evenness of our recollection, the seat of meditation, the rest of our cares and the calm of our tempests: prayer is the issue of a quiet mind, of untroubled thoughts. It is the daughter of charity and the sister of meekness.

4

Contrition, Forgiveness

"Through my own fault, my own most grievous fault"

From **Morning Prayer** *in the* **Book of Common Prayer**
From **Palm Sunday to Easter** *by* William Temple. OUR PENITENCE
The Jesus Prayer
From **The Treasury of Devotions** *compiled by* T. T. Carter. ACT OF LOVE
From **Honest to God** *by* J. A. T. Robinson
From **Living Prayer** *by* Metropolitan Anthony Bloom
From **The Treasury of Devotions** *compiled by* T. T. Carter
Dear Lord and Father of mankind *by* J. G. Whittier, 1807–92
From **Our Daily Prayers** *by* W. J. Carey, D.D. In Christ I worship Thee
From **Lent with Evelyn Underhill.** FORGIVENESS
Prayer: Help me O God to see all my own sins
From **My God My Glory** *by* E. Milner-White. CONTRA MUNDUM PRO
    MUNDO
From **The Cloud of Unknowing.** When thoughts of sin press on thee
From **An Anthology of the Love of God** *by* Evelyn Underhill. CHRIST
    THE RESCUER
From **The Times,** *an article by* Dr F. R. Barry, former Bishop of Southwell.
    TOWARDS THE RECOVERY OF BELIEF IN GOD
Negro Spiritual. Were you there when they crucified my Lord?
From **The Times,** *a sermon preached in Westminster Abbey by* the Rt Rev.
    Hugh Montefiore. LIVING IN A MORE AND MORE GODLESS AGE
My Song is love unknown *by* S. Crossman

From **Morning Prayer** *in the* **Book of Common Prayer**

If we say that we have no sin we deceive ourselves, and the truth is not in us; but if we confess our sins, He is faithful and just to forgive us our sins, and to cleanse us from all unrighteousness.

47

From **Palm Sunday to Easter** *by* William Temple

OUR PENITENCE

It is penitence which creates intimacy with our Lord. No one can know Him intimately who has not realised the sickness of his own soul and obtained healing from the physician of souls. Our virtues do not bring us near to Christ – the gulf between them and His holiness remains unbridgeable. Our science does not bring us near to Him, nor our art. Our pain may give us a taste of fellowship with Him, but it is only a taste unless the great creator of intimacy – penitence – is also there.

For in my virtue, my art, my knowledge, there is sure to be some pride. But I cannot be proud of sin which is really admitted to be sin. I can be proud of my daredevilry; oh yes, and of anything I do to shock respectability. But then I am not admitting to myself that it is sin – only that other people think it so. When I find something in myself of which I really am ashamed, I cannot at the time be proud of that – though alas! I may be proud of my shame at it, and so make this, too, worthless.

In straightforward shame at my own meanness there is no pride and no expectation of forgiveness except through trust in the love of Him who forgives. So it is penitence which brings me in all simplicity to appeal to the sheer goodness and love of God. And we can turn our very sins into blessings if we will let them empty us of pride and cast ourselves upon the generosity of God. "We receive the due reward of our sins: Jesus, remember me." "Today shalt thou be with me in Paradise." Today. We do not have to wait for some far off divine event. When true penitence opens our hearts to the love of God, forthwith. He enters there to reign. Because His Kingdom is spiritual, the sovereignty of His love over hearts that are open to its claim and appeal, we do not have to wait for Him to come in His Kingdom. No doubt its perfection when all hearts are open and respond, is in the future. But the power of His Kingdom is focused in His Cross. He reigns from the Tree. Let us come with our hearts ready to respond to that shining forth of the Love of God. Let us see how we look in that presence. Then let us acknowledge our unfitness to be near Him, and hear Him say in answer: "Today shalt thou be with Me."

The Jesus Prayer

O Lord Jesus Christ, Son of the living God, have mercy upon me a sinner.

From **The Treasury of Devotions** *compiled by* T. T. Carter

ACT OF LOVE

I love Thee, O my God, above all things, because Thou hast been so good, so patient, so loving to me, notwithstanding all the sins by which I have so grievously offended Thee. I love Thee O Blessed Jesus, my Saviour, because Thou didst suffer so much for love of me an ungrateful sinner, and didst die on the Cross for my salvation. O make me love Thee more and more, and show my love to Thee by faithfully keeping Thy commandments all the days of my life. Amen.

From **Honest to God** *by* J. A. T. Robinson

Let us begin by listening once again to Tillich, as he speaks of the state of our human condition. For I believe his words have the power to speak universally, even to those with no sense of religion or of any God "out there" who might be called upon to intervene.

"The state of our whole life is estrangement from others and ourselves, because we are estranged from the Ground of our being, because we are estranged from the origin and aim of our life. And we do not know where we have come from, or where we are going. We are separated from the mystery, the depth, and the greatness of our existence. We hear the voice of that depth: but our ears are closed. We feel that something radical, total, and unconditioned is demanded of us; but we rebel against it, try to escape its urgency and will not accept its promise.

We cannot escape, however. If that something is the Ground of our being, we are bound to it for all eternity, just as we are bound to ourselves and to all other life. We always remain in the power of that from which we are estranged. The fact brings us to the ultimate depth of sin; separated and yet bound, estranged and yet belonging, destroyed and yet preserved, the state which is called despair. Despair means that there is no escape. Despair is "the sickness unto death". But the terrible thing about the sickness of despair is that we cannot be released, not even through open or hidden suicide. For we all know that we are bound eternally and inescapably to the Ground of our being. The abyss of separation is not always visible. But it has become more visible to our generation than to the preceding generations, because of our feeling of meaninglessness, emptiness, doubt, and cynicism – all expressions of despair, of our separation from the roots and the meaning of life. Sin in its most profound sense, sin as despair, abounds among us.

It is this union-in-estrangement with the Ground of our being – what Paul Althaus once described as "inescapable godlessness in inescapable relationship to God" – that we mean by hell. But equally it is the union-in-love with the Ground of our being, such as we see in Jesus Christ, that is the meaning of Heaven. And it is the offer of that life, in all its divine depth, to overcome the estrangement and alienation of existence as we know it that the New Testament speaks of as the "new creation". This new reality is transcendent, it is beyond us, in the sense that it is not ours to command. Yet we experience it, like the Prodigal, as we "come to ourselves". For it is a coming home, or rather a being received home, to everything we are created to be. It is what the New Testament can only call grace. And in the same sermon Tillich speaks of it in a way that shows how little it can be contained within any purely naturalistic categories, and yet how it is "nearer to us than we are ourselves": "for it is our new being". Yet we cannot will it.

It happens; or it does not happen. And certainly does not happen if we try to force it upon ourselves, just as it will not happen so long as we think, in our self-complacency, that we have no need of it. Grace strikes us when we are in great pain and restlessness. It strikes us when we walk through the dark valley of a meaningless and empty life. It strikes us when we feel that our separation is deeper than usual, because we have violated another life, which we loved or from which we were estranged. It strikes us when our distrust for our own being, our indifference, our weakness, our hostility, and our lack of direction and composure have become intolerable to us. It strikes us when year after year, the longed for perfection of life does not appear, when the old compulsions reign within us as they have for decades, when despair destroys all joy and courage. Sometimes at that moment a wave of light breaks into our darkness and it is as though a voice were saying: "You are accepted. You are accepted, accepted by that which is greater than you, and the name of which you do not know. Do not ask for the name now; perhaps you will find it later. Do not try to do anything now; perhaps later you will do much. Do not seek for anything, do not perform anything, do not intend anything. Simply accept the fact that you are accepted!" If that happens to us, we experience grace. After such an experience we may not be better than before, and we may not believe more than before. But everything is transformed. In that moment, grace conquered sin, and reconciliation bridges the gulf of estrangement. And nothing is demanded of this experience, no religious or moral or intellectual presupposition, nothing but acceptance.

In the light of this grace we perceive the power of grace in our relation to others and to ourselves. We experience the grace of being able to look frankly into the eyes of another, the miraculous grace of reunion of life with life. We experience the grace of understanding each other's words. We understand not merely the literal meaning of the words, but also that which lies behind them, even when they are harsh or angry. For even then there is a longing to break through the walls of separation. We experience the grace of being able to accept the life of another, even if it be hostile and harmful to us, for, through grace we know that it belongs to the same Ground to which we belong, and by which we have been accepted. We experience the grace which is able to overcome the tragic separation of the sexes, of the generations, of the nations, of the races, and even the utter strangeness between man and nature. Sometimes grace appears in all these separations to reunite us with those to whom we belong. For life belongs to life.

From **Living Prayer** *by* Metropolitan Anthony Bloom

Coming nearer to God is always a discovery both of the beauty of God and of the distance there is between Him and us. "Distance" is an inadequate word, because it is not determined by the fact that God is holy and that we are sinful. Distance is determined by the attitude of the sinner to God. We can approach God only if we do so with a sense of coming to judgement. If we come having condemned ourselves; if we come because we love Him, in spite of the fact that we are unfaithful; if we come to Him, loving Him more than a godless security, then we are open to Him and He is open to us, and there is no distance; the Lord comes close to us in an act of compassionate love. But if we stand before God wrapped in our pride, in our assertiveness; if we stand before Him as if we had a right to stand there, if we stand and question Him, the distance that separates the creature and the creator becomes infinite.

There is a passage in *The Screwtape Letters* in which C. S. Lewis suggests that distance, in this sense, is a relative thing: when the great archangel came before God to question Him, the moment he asked his question, not in order to understand in humility but in order to compel God to give account, he found himself at an infinite distance from God. God had not moved, nor had Satan, and yet without any motion, they were infinitely far apart. (Letter XIX.)

Whenever we approach God the contrast that exists between what He is and what we are becomes dreadfully clear. We may not be aware of this as long as we live at a distance from God, so to speak, as long as His presence or His image is dimmed in our thoughts and in our perceptions; but the nearer we come to God, the sharper the contrast appears. It is not the constant thought of their sins but the vision of the holiness of God, that makes the Saints aware of their own sinfulness. When we consider ourselves without the fragrant background of God's presence, sins and virtues become small and somewhat irrelevant matters; it is against the background of the divine presence that they stand out in full relief and acquire their depth and tragedy.

The world shall never know peace while one man will look at another and pass judgement on him, for this is the seed of war.

But I say to you; when a man can look at another and understand why he is so, and being totally unaffected by what he sees can guide his need, then self will be overcome and peace on earth shall be fulfilled through the heart of Jesus Christ our Lord.

From **The Treasury of Devotions** *compiled by* T. T. Carter

O Lord God who lightenest every man that cometh into the world, enlighten my heart, I pray Thee, with the light of Thy grace, that I may fully know my sins, shortcomings and negligencies, and may confess them with that true sorrow and contrition of heart which befits me. I desire to make full amends for my sins and live more holily for the future and for the salvation of my soul, through Jesus Christ our Lord.

Dear Lord and Father of mankind *by* J. G. Whittier, 1807–92

> *Dear Lord and Father of mankind,*
> *Forgive our foolish ways!*
> *Reclothe us in our rightful mind,*
> *In purer lives thy service find,*
> *In deeper reverence praise.*
>
> *In simple trust like theirs who heard*
> *Beside the Syrian sea,*
> *The gracious calling of the Lord,*
> *Let us, like them without a word*
> *Rise up and follow Thee.*
>
> *O Sabbath rest by Galilee!*
> *O calm of hills above,*
> *Where Jesus knelt to share with Thee*
> *The silence of eternity,*
> *Interpreted by love!*
>
> *Drop thy still dews of quietness,*
> *Till all our strivings cease;*
> *Take from our souls the strain and stress,*
> *And let our ordered lives confess*
> *The beauty of Thy peace.*
>
> *Breathe through the heat of our desire*
> *Thy coolness and Thy balm;*
> *Let sense be dumb, let flesh retire;*
> *Speak through the earthquake, wind and fire,*
> *O still small voice of calm!*

From **Our Daily Prayers** *by* W. J. Carey, D.D.

In Christ I worship Thee. Together with the whole Church, His mystical Body, I praise, adore and worship Thee, in Him. Holy, Holy, Holy, is the Lord God of Hosts. Heaven and earth are full of the Majesty of Thy glory.

In the worship, the love, the obedience, which Thy dear Son (in the name and nature of Man) offered and offers to Thee, I would have my part. Because by the power of the Spirit, I am in Him. By the sacrifice of His Cross I ask for my forgiveness and for the forgiveness of the world. And for all that Thou hast done for Thy Creation I thank thee: and for Thy blessings to me and to all mankind. And I pray Thee to bless us and use us day by day; to bless me and Thy Church and all men, and all I love. And for Christ's sake forgive us all: our treacheries and weaknesses, our apathy and neglect, our lusts and hardness, our coldness to others. All we remember of evil done, all we cannot remember, forgive for Christ's sake. Amen.

From **Lent with Evelyn Underhill**

FORGIVENESS

There is no lesson Christ loves better to drive home than this disconcerting fact of our common human fragility, which when we have truly grasped it, kills resentment and puts indulgent pity in its place. Let the man, the group, the nation that is without sin cast the first stone. God's forgiveness means the compassionate recognition of the weakness and instability of man; how often we cannot help it, how truly there is in us a "root and ground of sin", an implicit rebellion against the Holy, a tendency away from love and peace. And this requires of us the constant compassionate recognition of our fellow-creatures' instability and weakness; of the fact that they too cannot help it. If the Christian penitent dares to ask that his many departures from the Christian norm, his impatience, gloom, self-occupation, unloving prejudices, reckless tongue, feverish desires, with all the damage they have caused to Christ's Body, are indeed to be set aside, because – in spite of all – he longs for God and Eternal Life, then he too must set aside and forgive all that impatience, selfishness, bitter and foolish speech, sudden yieldings to base impulse in others have caused him to endure. Hardness is the one impossible thing. Harshness to others in those who ask and need the mercy of God sets up a conflict at the very heart of personality and shuts the door upon grace.

And that which is true of the individual soul, is also true of the community; the penitent nation seeking the path of life must also conform to the law of charity.

This principle applied in its fullness makes a demand on our generosity which only a purified and self-oblivious love can hope to meet. For every soul that appeals to God's forgiveness is required to move over to His side, and share the compassionate understanding, the unmeasured pity, with which He looks on human frailty and sin. So difficult is this to the proud and assertive creature, that it comes very near the end of our education in prayer. Indeed the Christian doctrine of forgiveness is so drastic and so difficult, where there is a deep injury to forgive, that only those living in the Spirit, in union with the Cross, can dare to base their claim on it.

Prayer:

Help me O God to see all my own sins, never to judge my neighbour, and may the glory all be Thine. Into Thy hand I commend my spirit. Thy will be done.

From **My God My Glory** *by* E. Milner-White

CONTRA MUNDUM PRO MUNDO

O Lord Christ,
for the world's sake
thou didst stand against the world;
thou didst empty thyself,
that thou mightest fill all things;
thou wert made a curse,
to bless all creation.

O Lord forgive our ignorance, blindness, stupidity;
our vain glory and cruelty;
all sin we do in our darkness;
all our additions to the suffering of man.

O Lord let me stand alongside thee
for cleanness of hand and pureness of heart;
stand after thine example,
against the small, the shallow, the spiteful and cruel;
stand for the world,
against the world;
stand for thee and thy righteousness and love;
who livest and reignest with the Father and
the Holy Ghost, God for ever and ever.

From **The Cloud of Unknowing**

When thoughts of sin press on thee "look over their shoulders seeking another thing, the which thing is God".

From **An Anthology of the Love of God** *by* Evelyn Underhill

CHRIST THE RESCUER

God enters human life not only to help, teach and complete it but to over-rule, transform, rescue and control circumstances – a saving energy intervening with an entire and noble freedom, constrained only by love. Kyrie Eleison! Christe Eleison! Lord have mercy! Christ have mercy!

It was like that when He went up to the disciples in the ship and the wind ceased . . . and there was a calm. Then the situation was transformed by His presence. One way or another, life brings every awakening Christian soul this experience. When we recognise and reflect on it – for it may come in a way that seems very simple – it fills us with awe and grateful love. God in Christ intervenes between us and the storm that threatens to overwhelm us. His power is brought into action just where our action fails; He comes to the rescue of those caught in the toil of circumstance . . . Sometimes it is on our soul that He lays His tranquillising touch and stills the storm; sometimes on the hurly-burly of our emotional life, sometimes on events that we think must destroy us or the people or causes we love . . . We do feel sometimes as if we are left to ourselves to struggle with it all. He is away praying on the mountain, or He is asleep in the boat; the waves seem to be getting higher, the night is dark . . . we begin to lose our nerve for life and no-one seems to mind. Certainly life is not made soft for Christians; but it *is*, in the last resort, safe. The Universe is safe for souls. The disciples were frightened, exhausted, soaked to the skin but not destroyed. At the critical moment He went up into the ship and restored safety, sanity, peace . . .

So Christ stands over against history and in its darkest and most dangerous moments we receive a new revelation of His power.

From **The Times,** *an article by* Dr F. R. Barry, former Bishop of Southwell

TOWARDS THE RECOVERY OF BELIEF IN GOD

Are we really meant to spend 40 days "lamenting our sins and acknowledging our wretchedness", intensifying our guilt and self-hatred? Guilt is not a state of mind to foster. True penitence follows on the vision of God, guilt is a barrier between man and God, from which the Gospel offers us deliverance. And Lent is preparation for Easter – the triumph of invincible love and goodness over all that threatens destruction to personal life.

There must be something amiss with their religion if it makes people unduly introspective; most of us are too much in-turned already. Living in a closed, naturalistic world in which there seems to be no window open into any supra-temporal reality, we tend to be driven in upon ourselves and pre-occupied with our own subjective states. But that way there is no moral growth.

The way of growth is by moving out from the self in response to the life-giving factors in our environment, the source and fountain of which is the living God. If Christ is risen, our closed world is opened by the breaking in of the life from beyond it. Lent is the time for growth towards God, as in spring the plants are growing towards the sun.

It is not more guilt we need but more conviction. What is paralysing men's wills today and driving them into the apathy of despair is the sheer lack of anything to believe in. Men and women are seeking, the world over, in ways that are sometimes false and sometimes dangerous, to vindicate man's freedom and human dignity, and that is an essentially "Christian" quest.

But we do not know what it is to be truly human if we leave out man's relationship to God – which is what the Christian religion is about. The deepest need of the human world today is the recovery of faith in God.

The primary question before the Churches is not how to organise their institutions, but whether Christianity is true; and if their spokesmen appear to be uncertain, what hope is there for the untheological layman? There is a powerful pressure group working to extirpate Christianity from the school and the public philosophy. What is worrying is that the Christian case is too often being allowed to go by default. If the church gives the impression of regarding the Gospel itself as an open question and the being of God as an interesting hypothesis, has it anything very important left to say? After all it is meant to stand for something.

Surely the time has come, in all the churches, for a resolute move from the circumference to the centre, to the fundamentals of Christian belief in God and in man through Jesus Christ. This is no plea for a take it or leave it dogmatism, which violates God's will for our free response, or for uncritical traditionalism. But it is a plea for a confident and convincing reaffirmation of positive Christian faith, in a context of free thinking and honest criticism. The foundation of that faith is not "ideas" which must change with the changing movements of secular thought, it is the historical and living person, yesterday and today the same and for ever. Other foundations no man can lay; and apart from Easter the church has no existence.

We can overdo "religionless Christianity". We have allowed ourselves to be mesmerised by Bonhoeffer's enigmatic phrase. Are we likely to find God in the world if we do not keep ourselves in the Presence by what Bonhoeffer called the "secret discipline", the well-tried rules of Christian spirituality? What religion most needs today is not to be talked about but to be nourished. "Fasting" means spiritual concentration. "Spending and getting, we lay waste our powers", and Lent is the time for interior conservation. Jesus needed whole nights of prayer to repair the exhaustion of his active ministry.

We must try to extend the frontiers of awareness into that transcendent dimension to which the present age has become blind. That may be through study of the Bible, exposing ourselves to the impact of the Gospels as though we were now seeing them for the first time; or through other receptive "spiritual reading", not only or necessarily "religious" – great poetry, for example; or through music; or by the methods of formal retreat; or innumerable other ways. Religion starts from God, not from man; our part is to train ourselves in receptivity. Private prayer is not liturgical worship. With due regard to the corporate tradition – for we cannot understand Christianity except from within the believing community – everyone is free to devise his own approaches according to temperament and opportunity, and the fresher they are, the more likely to be rewarded. Individuality is to be encouraged. One thing at least is within reach of all of us – to create oases of solitude and silence. For we cannot hear if we must be always chattering. "Be still, and know that I am God."

Negro Spiritual

> *Were you there when they crucified my Lord?*
> *Were you there when they nailed Him to the Tree?*
> *Sometimes it makes me tremble, tremble, tremble –*
> *Were you there when they crucified my Lord?*

From **The Times,** *a sermon preached in Westminster Abbey by* the Rt Rev. Hugh Montefiore

LIVING IN A MORE AND MORE GODLESS AGE

... What was it that distinguished the death of Jesus from the martyrdom of so many others down the centuries? What distinguished his death from that of so many others of his era who suffered what the historian Tacitus called a most cruel death, through crucifixion? This question must be answered at three levels; first, from the purely human level, secondly from the divine perspective, and thirdly what difference does it make to us now?

Let us be clear that it is not our sins that were the cause of his passion, any more than the Jews today can in any way be responsible for his death: But the weaknesses which we inherit are precisely those which effectively caused his death; and they were not particularly uncommon or terrible weaknesses. One of his own friends betrayed him for money – something that occurs daily in the world of business and commerce. The rest of his friends let him down by running away in fear of their lives: and not many of us possess large reserves of moral and physical courage.

The Roman Governor, although he knew Jesus to be innocent, condemned him because he feared that otherwise he would be informed against and relieved of his office – the kind of action that one finds again and again in imperial history. The High Priest thought that one man's death was worth while if it could keep the Jews in with the Romans – and in a sense he was right, it did prevent punitive measures being taken against the Jews, and history is strewn with similar judicial murders for political reasons.

Some of the leading religious figures of his time felt threatened by Jesus, because he upset their deepfelt religious convictions: they persuaded themselves that he was best out of the way – and tragically in the history of Christendom, similar kinds of threats have resulted in similar persecutions. The Sadducees on the other hand felt that Jesus threatened their religious status in the established religion of the day: one of the tragedies of established religion is that it can so easily lead to the persecution of Prophets. Herod laughed at him. The Roman soldiers mocked him. The Zealots had no use for him as he would not use force. The crowds were led as crowds are still led today by their cheerleaders. And so Jesus was killed on a cross.

The Cross of Christ shows up the potentialities of our own ordinary weaknesses and frailties. It shows them up even more startlingly when we reflect that he who died was not merely Jesus of Nazareth, a Jewish prophet of the time of the Emperor Tiberius. He was also as Christians believe, God's personal self-disclosure within human personality in so far as human personality can disclose God.

Here then is a glimpse of what the Passion of Jesus shows us about ourselves and about God. What does it mean for us now? How is it relevant to us today? In the first place Christians are called to follow the blessed steps of Christ's most holy life. Christians must not expect to conquer by power or by force: they must use the same means as Jesus, steadfastness to the truth, acceptance of being misunderstood and being rejected, victory through suffering. This is a dreadfully difficult lesson for us to learn. We want to have it the way of the world. We want the Church to be triumphalist and triumphant.

Today there is, as ever, much natural goodness in the world, goodness which at times puts the Church to shame. But we are living in a more and more godless age, an age which has not so much rejected the Christian Faith as lacks almost any knowledge of what its message really is. It is not therefore surprising that in many fields the values of society are totally

opposed to Christian convictions. For example the ruination of environment and the rape of irreplaceable natural resources is totally opposed to
any Christian notion of stewardship and obligation to posterity.

The withdrawal of censorship and sexual permissiveness is resulting in
a state of affairs where children are being brought up to a cheapened view
of sexuality totally opposed to the genuine eroticism of Christian tradition.
Some powerful trades' unions are making demands for their own members which they know are bound to make the poor and needy even poorer
– demands totally opposed to Christ's demand to care for those in need.

We are no longer a Christian country, and we have nothing by which
to live instead. Let us face it: as a country, morally and spiritually we have
lost our way. Even the Church itself is being strangled by the safeguards of
democracy and forced to operate with a structure which imprisons it
terribly when compared with the freedom with which Jesus walked and
talked in Galilee and Jerusalem. Many ministers find themselves trapped
within a system when they want to be free to preach a Gospel.

In this situation there is much suffering and passion, personal and
corporate. The Church and the individuals who comprise it would do well
to remember that the way out of passion and suffering is not through force,
nor by hatred nor by dominating the world. What we can do, we should
do, to put things right. But Jesus the Son of God won through to victory
through his obedience, his witness to truth, his faithfulness: in a word by,
acceptance of his Passion.

My Song is love unknown *by* S. Crossman

My song is love unknown,
> *My Saviour's love for me,*
Love to the loveless shown,
> *That they might lovely be.*
>> *O who am I,*
>>> *That for my sake*
>>> *My Lord should take*
Frail flesh, and die?

He came from his blest throne,
> *Salvation to bestow;*
But men made strange, and none
The longed-for Christ would know.
>> *But O, my Friend,*
>>> *My Friend indeed,*
>>> *Who at my need*
His life did spend!

Why, what hath my Lord done?
What makes this rage and spite?
He made the lame to run,
He gave the blind their sight.
Sweet injuries!
Yet they at these
Themselves displease
And 'gainst him rise.

They rise, and needs will have
My dear Lord made away;
A murderer they save,
The Prince of Life they slay.
Yet cheerful he
To suffering goes.
That he his foes
From thence might free.

Here might I stay and sing.
No story so divine;
Never was love, dear King,
Never was grief like thine!
This is my Friend,
In whose sweet praise
I all my days
Could gladly spend.

5

Intercession and Petition

"Lord, teach us to be channels of Thy Love"

Dame Julian of Norwich, *taken from* **The School of Prayer** *by* Olive Wyon

From **The School of Prayer** *by* Olive Wyon. PRAYER AND THE PURPOSE OF GOD

Prayer: Set free, O Lord, our souls

St Theresa (sixteenth century)

From **The Watchword,** *an address by* Kenneth Mathews. ON INTERCESSION

From **The Mystery of Suffering** *by* Hugh Evan Hopkins. A FACTORY OF PEACE

From **The Use of Praying** *by* J. Neville Ward. DESIRING OTHER PEOPLE'S GOOD

From **Life as Prayer** *by* Evelyn Underhill

From **Jesus, a Dialogue with the Saviour** *by* Father Lev

From **The Use of Praying** *by* J. Neville Ward

In **The Nestorian Evening Office** *from* **Worship** *by* Evelyn Underhill

At Christmas, *from the writings of* Fra Giovanni, AD 1513

Prayer *by* Lady Jane Grey, *taken from* **A Book of School Worship** *by* William Temple

From **A Book of School Worship** *by* William Temple

Dame Julian of Norwich, *taken from* **The School of Prayer** *by* Olive Wyon

I am the ground of thy beseeching: first, it is My will that thou have it; and after, I make thee to will it; and after I make thee to beseech it. How should it then be that thou shouldst not have thy beseeching?

From **The School of Prayer** *by* Olive Wyon

The first step in intercession is to make a definite "act" of union with this stream of God's love and power, which is flowing ceaselessly out of His Heart and back to Him again . . . Making a conscious effort to unite our wills and hearts with the ever flowing river of the love of God will give us a restful energy.

As we realise that the love of God is flowing through us and using us as it passes all merely natural strain will disappear. If suffering comes to us in our time of intercession, we must accept it, and still remain tranquilly surrendered to God for His purpose.

If we experience difficulty in "getting going" it would be well to search our hearts to see whether, after all, we are praying that God will bless our efforts for His glory, rather than seeking to be united with His will.

The greatest works wrought by prayer have been accomplished not by human effort but by human trust in God's effort.

In prayer of this kind we are united with the very life of God, sharing His work.

It is the unseen, unknown part of intercession which makes our part both possible and important. It is the wind of the Holy Ghost blowing through us, it is the tide of God's providence, it is the current of the divine desire, which really accomplish the work of intercession; and yet the human agent is essential for the accomplishment of the activity. Intercession is the expression of God's love and desire which He has deigned to share with man, and in which He uses man . . . The essence and heat of intercession is self-offering.

The deeper our surrender to God, the more true and powerful will be our intercession. Intercession is indeed a basic principle of human living: it expresses that corporate sense of community which is the real nature of human living: it expresses that instinct to give to the point of sacrifice which is one of the deepest elements in our nature, fulfilled once for all by Christ on the Cross.

Thus intercession covers the whole world; all the sins and cruelties and miseries of men; all the horrors of war, the sighing of prisoners and captives, the sufferings of the oppressed and the outcast; the despair of those who are far from God. Christian intercession is the completion and expression of self-giving.

We offer poor imperfect love to God to be a channel of His perfect and redeeming love.

We offer ourselves to be a way through which God will reach, and save, and bless the whole world.

Prayer:

Set free, O Lord, our souls from all restlessness and anxiety; give us that peace and power which flow from Thee; keep us in all perplexities and distresses, in all fears and faithlessness; that so upheld by Thy power and stayed in the rock of Thy faithfulness we may always abide in Thee.

St Theresa (sixteenth century)

> *Christ has*
> *No body now on earth but yours;*
> *No hands but yours;*
> *No feet but yours;*
> *Yours are the eyes*
> *Through which is to look out*
> *Christ's compassion to the world;*
> *Yours are the feet*
> *With which He is to go about*
> *Doing good;*
> *Yours are the hands*
> *With which He is to bless men now.*

From **The Watchword,** *an address* by Kenneth Mathews

ON INTERCESSION

"That invalids may use their suffering for the work of the Church, and the service of others, by prayer and intercession." These words are printed on the cover of every *Watchword*. And of this intercession I want to say something today. "For why?" as the metrical psalms of Scotland ask. By which I mean, if God is almighty and all loving what possible difference can our prayers for other people make? Will He not act for the greatest good of those for whom we pray, irrespective of anything we may or may not do? These are great questions; questions that greatly bother some people especially, I think, when vitality is low and faith is weakened.

Let me say first that in any reading of God's dealing with men it is clear that God will not do things regardless of us; He will not ride roughshod over anyone. For, wonderfully, and humbly, He has chosen the role of partnership. We see the principle stated in these words Jesus spoke on the eve of the Passion: "henceforth I call you no longer servants, for the servant knoweth not what his Master doeth: but I have called you friends". And it is this principle that we see worked out in the realm of intercession. As an old French Priest had it: "Just as we require a point of contact to move the bar of a lever, so God wills that all the action of heaven and earth should have a point of contact here on earth, and this point of contact is the disciple of Jesus who is still pursuing his pilgrimage in this life."

That first, then second: our Lord left us in no doubt at all that not only were we to pray for people but that this was something which He did Himself. "Simon, Simon," He said, "I have prayed for thee that thy faith fail not". So He prayed for His disciples and for those who would believe in Him because of their words. And so, as He came to His Cross, did He pray for those who had brought Him there. And if He did what I have described, as indeed He did, the Christian will have no hesitation in doing likewise if he is to share in the Church's royal priesthood standing, as any priest should do on man's Godward side and becoming the point of contact, the channel through which God's love and healing, forgiving power is communicated to the other.

And if this is what we are to be, then the kind of prayer we are to make will surely follow. They will be confident, these prayers of ours, for Jesus said: "whatsoever ye shall ask in My name, that will I do", again "what things soever ye desire, when ye pray, believe that ye shall receive them, and ye shall have them". "In My name" – that is the determining condition, implying some likeness to Himself. Some realisation of the character of God as revealed by Him, some understanding of His eternal purposes of love. What is luminously clear about the greatest of all intercessory prayers as we see it in the 17th chapter of St John is His singleminded absorption in His Father's will and glory. "I glorified Thee, I manifested Thy Name, I consecrated Myself." And that this absorption in the Father's will and glory is paramount is evident in the fact that when He then goes on to pray that they may be one it is because He and His Father are one. Then when He proves this by asking that the Father would keep them from evil, and yet not take them out of the world, it is that His obedience to the Father's will may be reflected in them and in us, for which He prays.

So absorbed then in the Father's will (and that's what praying in His name must always mean) do we come to have the mind of Christ. "So", as one said who knew much of these things, "are we swept into the stream of Christ's redeeming life. So must we bring those for whom we pray into that stream to be cleansed and strengthened and carried up to God". That must always be the pattern the character of the intercession we seek to make.

That does not mean that we may not pray for material things; that we may not bring particular anxieties for people into the Presence. Yet (and this is the point I am concerned to make) they must not, as they can, distract our attention from God, His love, His plan. Indeed the great experts are clear that, as time goes on such specific prayers tend to become fewer and fewer, and that what grows most is simply the desire that God will enfold with His love those for whom we pray, that His name may be increasingly hallowed in their lives.

One final thought – on paper the fact that one is bedridden or house-bound suggests that one has all the time in the world to pray, to intercede. Nevertheless the fact that one is weak or downright ill may make one powerfully disinclined to pray at all. "I cannot pray; I cannot say a single prayer", said that wonderfully good man Maurice Baring, when he was near to death. Whenever you feel like that, remember those words from *The Cloud of Unknowing*: "this work asketh no long time or it be once truly done, as some men ween, for it is the shortest work of all that men may imagine."

So though it may be the act of an instant, and therefore within the compass of everyone, however weak, the result may be incalculable and people, like the woman who wrote to me the other day, find themselves carried along through the darkest day or night in ways beyond their imagining. And as they discover, in words that I owe to another, that it is not the duration of time but the totality of self-giving to God which is the criterion.

From **The Mystery of Suffering** *by* Hugh Evan Hopkins

Mary Webb beautifully describes the comfort and cheer that a broken heart can bring to others in trouble in her poem

A FACTORY OF PEACE

> *I watched her in the loud and shadowy lanes*
> *Of life; and every face that passed her by*
> *Grew calmly restful, smiling quietly,*
> *As though she gave, for all their griefs and pains,*
> *Largesse of comfort, soft as summer rains,*
> *And balsam tinctured with tranquillity,*
> *Yet in her own eyes dwelt an agony.*
> *'Oh, halcyon soul!' I cried, 'what sorrow reigns*
> *In that calm heart which knows such ways to heal?'*
> *She said – 'Where balms are made for human uses,*
> *Great furnace fires, and wheel on grinding wheel*
> *Must crush and purify the crude herb juices,*
> *And in some hearts the conflict cease;*
> *They are the sick world's factories of peace.'*

From **The Use of Praying** *by* J. Neville Ward

DESIRING OTHER PEOPLE'S GOOD

If prayer is regarded simply, without qualification, as a request to God to do certain things he would not do if we did not ask him and will do simply because we ask him, we are wasting our time.

If we are simply wanting something done in a certain situation we ought ourselves, no doubt in faith, to be doing something to support the creative agencies relevant to the subject of our concern. There is no reason to think that God will do "on his own" what he purposes to do "with man". If man will not end war, then, though we pray for ever, God will not end it for man.

Accordingly when we pray for the peace of the world, we do not pray in order to inform God about some area where war is threatened or raging, nor to give him information about our own anxieties. He knows both better than we. Nor do we pray in order to persuade him to take the nobility and agony of human freedom and responsibility from us and intervene in some set of circumstances to alter them. We pray in order to express, in a context of Christian faith and worship, our compassion for humanity and our anxiety about its present and future fortunes together with our continuing trust in God. We hold together, in the presence of God, the situation that dismays us and our nevertheless still trusting minds. We do this because this is the way Christian love functions, whether the individual praying Christian understands it theologically or not. We do it because we believe this relationship of candour and trust in relation to God is what he desires and is strengthened by this kind of expression, and because we believe that God instructs minds so disposed and acts through them for the fulfilling of his purpose . . .

When someone we deeply love is in special need which we are apparently unable to help, the more we realise that prayer is the only channel of activity left us, and the more earnestly we want to help this person, the more doubts begin to nag at the mind.

What claim have I on God's great storehouse of power? What right have I to assume that God wishes to use his power in the way suggested by the prayer that is even now forming in my mind? And suppose there is some relation between God's available power and the obedience of his children? There is a tradition that the prayer of a righteous man availeth much, but I have obeyed so little, blasphemed so much, drifted along with God a merely marginal consideration in this or that passage of fear through which I have at intervals lived. What if only those who have put something into the Bank of Grace can assume that their cheques drawn on it will be honoured.

The more one thinks on these lines the more gloom descends. But it is not useless gloom, because it suggests that this way of thinking about prayer cannot be right because it must necessarily lead either to pride or to despair. I must conclude that God will certainly hear my prayer, or that he will certainly not.

The mistake is the familiar one of thinking of God as someone to be persuaded to help, a source of power to be brought into a situation from which he has been excluded until he is brought in by prayer. This is a form of attempting to use God, and is no part of the Christian use of praying.

The Christian idea of intercession is that it is not a means we employ to persuade God to act in a situation he has presumably overlooked or into which he needs to be summoned, but a means God employs to summon our help through our membership in the Body of Christ.

"If you abide in me, and my words in you, ask whatever you will and it shall be done for you" (Jn 15:7). The guarantee of the effectiveness of the asking resides in the fact that he who asks is "in Christ" and will therefore not ask the nonsense and infantile dream of uninstructed human asking, but only "in His name". Truly Christian prayer is part of the eternal prayer and sacrifice of the great High Priest. Our prayer is Christian prayer as we enter into the self-offering of Christ, as we want to be part of God's purpose and channels through which his love can act.

Accordingly, when we pray for someone in great trouble, it is quite legitimate to ask for him to be delivered from the evil in his situation. We are expressing our natural desire that he should be given "a happy issue out of all his afflictions", but we are not trying to persuade God to do anything about the situation other than bring in his kingdom there (and this he does not need to be persuaded to do). We are expressing the natural desires of natural human love within the context of our faith in God. Faith means that we are prepared for things to go any way, better or worse as we understand these terms, and that in either case we wish that this person will continue to serve God and that we ourselves shall too, and that we believe that all of us whether we live or die are the Lord's.

God is not a human being who gets up from place A and goes to place B and does something because he has been asked. He just is present and as love, through people who are in right relationship with him; and through them he does more than we ask or think . . .

Every Christian prayer for others involves the realisation that he who prays is inextricably bound up with the answer. His prayer is not a mere message sent to God, voicing a request. It carries him with it deep into all that costly action which is the purpose of God in the life of the world. If it is not this it is simply the crying of a child.

Each time you take a human soul with you into your prayer, you accept from God a piece of spiritual work with all its implications and with all its costs – a cost which may mean for you spiritual exhaustion and darkness, and may even include vicarious suffering, the Cross. In offering yourselves on such levels of prayer for the sake of others, you are offering to take your part in the mysterious activities of the spiritual world; to share the saving work of Christ... Real intercession is not merely a petition but a piece of work, involving perfect, costly self-surrender to God for the work he wants done on other souls.

From **Life as Prayer** *by* Evelyn Underhill

And so, when we pray for someone in the name of Christ, we are standing within God's redemptive purpose and asking that that purpose may reach out to that person and enfold him, and at the same time we are affirming our desire that we, if possible, may be used to bear God's mercy to him. We may well be used directly. Among the costliest prayers that can ever be said are the prayers of a husband for his wife, of parents for their children.

But the situation may be one in which we cannot be used in some act of direct service. God will then not be able to use more of us than the love which has driven us to pray, but this love while being used by him in ways beyond our understanding, can also pass into action in other spheres of life nearer to us (where what we do is important) and therefore affect for good that whole in which we and the person we feel we cannot directly serve have our sensitive being.

Even so, one cannot forget this haunting sense of belonging to one another which Christ seemed to want his disciples to feel very deeply. God wills to give himself in answer to our requests for each other, as well as our requests for ourselves, so that we may belong more closely to one another, in being in some degree responsible for one another. And so we can only surmise, we can never know (until he tells us at the end) how much of the pure air of his kingdom we now breathe because of other people's prayers.

To the Christian believer, the question: What should we pray for when we pray for others? is just another form of the question: What is most worth having in life?

If we are in touch with the source and substance of all good we shall be fools to ask for anything less than this, for anything less than the best.

The best thing in life is the kingdom of God. The best that can happen to anyone or the world, is to be filled with all the fullness of God. One cannot stand within the purpose, ready to pray in his name, and ask for anything less, or anything else.

The worst that can happen to anyone is to be separated from God, which must indeed be Hell, whether it feels like what people call "hell" or not. Anxiety is justified when it seems that people are falling into hell or are in danger of doing this. Rejoicing is justified when it appears that they are moving toward God or are in his presence and in some degree aware of this, even though they may never attach the word "God" to that upholding or gladness through which they are passing.

Christians pray for others because this is part of the Christian way of living and loving. We are attempting to live in what we understand is Christ's way; we desire to be wholly involved in this, and therefore all that, as taught by Christ, we consider important, we want to bring into this Christian attitude to life. We bring the person we love or the cause about which we are concerned into all that Christ has taught us about God and life, into our dependence on God and our desire to serve Him. Such love, such concern is consecrated by being so related to the thought of God (and we long for the consecration of life as in winter one longs for the spring). But consecration always modifies. By consecration the bread and wine in the Eucharist assume an entirely different meaning from that which they normally have. And the consecration of any wish with its being offered to God will most certainly change its substance.

We begin praying by thinking "this is what I hope for in this situation and I trust God not to let me down"; we end by thinking "this is how this situation looks in the light of God's purpose, this is what I must now do to serve God in it, and this is what I really want". And in some situations what we then do will obviously be very important, obviously materially helpful. But in some other situations, in our helplessness before the intractability and frustration of life, our prayer simply becomes one with that agony that, as Pascal said, "Christ will be in to the end of the world".

From Jesus, a Dialogue with the Saviour *by* Father Lev

My child, you are anxious about many people and many things.

You are anxious about your very life, about what you have undertaken, but I have asked you for only one thing, a thing so simple: to follow Me.

From The Use of Praying *by* J. Neville Ward

The presence or absence of Christian prayer in any situation is one of the many factors through which God's will is manifested. The elements of mystery and complexity which any doctrine of providence must recognise do not make intercessory prayer less necessary, but they do mean that we shall be less inclined to specify the divine action we desire. We shall find ourselves increasingly content to do as our Lord has taught us and simply ask that God's kingdom may come and his will be done in the situation about which we are praying. St John of the Cross points out that we are on surer ground when we simply lift up to God our needy condition than when we ask in detail for the things we need.

Some people are dismayed by the thought of the number of people and causes who should have place in their prayers. The great host of those for whom they have failed to find room in their devout attention stretches out into the imagined distance, each one an accusation. This is an unnecessary perplexity which disperses as we see our intercession as our participation in the saving action of the Body of Christ. Obviously we cannot embrace the whole world in our thought; but God can. If our prayer is part of the intercession of the great High Priest, whose love spans the universe we can play our part in it with gladness and seriousness and without agitation.

It is clearly God's will that we bring into our prayers those whose lives he has closely interlocked with ours in the three worlds which constitute most of our life, the worlds of our family, our friendships and our work. We shall also join in the wider intercessions of the liturgical life of the Church.

For the rest, though we do not forbid any name a mention in prayers, we need not be anxious about the natural limits of the mind's range. The power of prayer is not confined within such limits. If we abide in Christ and our prayer is in His name, all our prayers, actions, sufferings, are taken up into the infinite scope of his activity whose sovereign grace extends to all.

It is good to bring into our intercessions the thought of the infinity of the divine care. It is beautifully expressed in the liturgy of Basil the Great:

"And those whom we, through ignorance or forgetfulness or the number of names, have not remembered, do thou O God remember them, who knowest the age and the name of each one, who knowest each from his mother's womb. For thou, O God, art the help of the helpless, the hope of the hopeless, the saviour of the tempest-tossed, the harbour of mariners, the physician of the sick. Be thou thyself all things to all men, who knowest each and his petition and his dwelling and his need."

But we come back, as we must repeatedly do, to our belief that love is the only power through which God's kingdom will come. Accordingly, each individual's unique world of love is the holiest and most responsible area of his life. No doubt it is not wide enough; and one of the most demonstrable results of genuine faith is that our world of love will be widened. But at any time whether the person who prays is a young convert or a mature Christian, the people he likes and loves are particularly given to him to be lifted up to God in intercessory affection.

In **The Nestorian Evening Office** *from* **Worship** *by* Evelyn Underhill

PETITION

With request and beseeching we ask for the Angel of peace and mercy,
      From Thee O Lord.

Night and day throughout our life, we ask for continued peace
for Thy Church,
> *From Thee O Lord.*
We ask continual love, which is the bond of perfectness, with
the confirmation of the Holy Spirit,
> *From Thee O Lord.*
We ask for forgiveness of sins and those things which help our
lives and please Thy Godhead,
> *From Thee O Lord.*
We ask the mercy and compassion of the Lord continually and
at all times,
> *From Thee O Lord.*

At Christmas, *from the writings of* Fra Giovanni, AD 1513

I salute you. There is nothing I can give you which you have not;
but there is much that, while I cannot give you, you can take.
No Heaven can come to us unless our hearts find rest in it today:
> *Take Heaven.*
No peace lies in the future which is not hidden in the present:
> *Take Peace.*
The gloom of the world is but a shadow; behind it, yet within our
reach is joy:
> *Take joy.*
And so at this Christmas time I greet you, with the prayer that for you,
now and forever, the day breaks and the shadows flee away.

Prayer *by* Lady Jane Grey, *taken from* **A Book of School Worship** *by* William Temple

O merciful God, be Thou now unto us a strong tower of defence, we humbly entreat Thee. Give us grace to await Thy leisure, and patiently to bear what Thou doest unto us, nothing doubting thy goodness towards us; for Thou knowest what is good for us better than we do. Therefore do with us in all things what Thou wilt; only arm us, we beseech Thee, with Thine armour, that we may stand fast, above all things, taking to us the shield of faith, praying always that we may refer ourselves wholly to Thy will, being assuredly persuaded that all Thou doest cannot but be well; and unto Thee be all honour and glory, both now and ever. Amen.

From **A Book of School Worship** *by* William Temple

O God of Love, we pray Thee to give us love:
Love in our thinking, love in our speaking,
Love in our doing,

71

And love in the hidden places of our souls;
Love of our neighbours near and far;
Love of our friends, old and new;
Love of those with whom we find it hard to bear,
And love of those who find it hard to bear with us;
Love of those with whom we work,
And love of those with whom we take our ease;
Love in joy, love in sorrow;
Love in life and love in death;
That so at length we may be worthy to dwell with Thee,
Who art eternal Love.
                    Amen.

6

The Prayer of Loving Attention

"Be still and know that I am God"

From **Living Prayer** by Metropolitan Anthony Bloom

From **In the Silence** by Father Andrew

From **In Time of Temptation** by Ladislaus Boros

From **The Burrswood Herald** by John Sayers

From **Spirituality for Today,** an article by Archbishop Michael Ramsey. THE IDEA OF THE HOLY AND THE WORLD TODAY

From **Introversion** by Evelyn Underhill. "What do you find within, O Soul ...?"

From **The Cloud of Unknowing**

From **Parting at Morning** by Robert Browning

From **What worship means to me,** an address to the 1969 European Friends' Conference by Pierre Lacout

From **Selected Letters** by St Francis de Sales: Letter 43, to Baronne de Chantal

From **The School of Prayer** by Olive Wyon. The Prayer of Loving Attention

From **The School of Prayer** by Olive Wyon. True Prayer

From **Living Prayer** by Metropolitan Anthony Bloom

From **Jesus, a Dialogue with the Saviour** by Father Lev. Lord Jesus pray in me

From **The Life of the Spirit** by Herbert Waddams. The deep stream from which comes life

From **The Prayer Life** by Andrew Murray, adapted

Prayer by G. Tersteegen. God is in His Holy Temple

John Woolman taken from **The School of Prayer** by Olive Wyon. The place of prayer

From **The Journey Inwards** by F. C. Happold. The radiation of love

From **Vision, 1969,** a Retreat address by Trevor Huddleston

Isaiah 30:15

Prayer: The expression of a growing faith from **The Psychology of Prayer** by C. R. Bryant, S.S.J.E.

From **Living Prayer** *by* Metropolitan Anthony Bloom

As long as the soul is not still there can be no vision, but when stillness has brought us into the presence of God, then another sort of silence, much more absolute, intervenes: the silence of a soul that is not only still and recollected but which is overawed in an act of worship by God's presence; a silence in which as Julian of Norwich puts it, "Prayer oneth the soul to God."

A person who has become real and true can stand before God and offer prayer with absolute attention, unity of intellect, heart and will, in a body

74

that responds completely to the promptings of the soul. But until we have attained such perfection we can still stand in the presence of God, aware that we are partly real and partly unreal, and bring to Him all that we can, but in repentance, confessing that we are still so unreal and so incapable of unity. At no moment of our life, whether we are still completely divided or in a process of unification, are we deprived of the possibility of standing before God. But instead of standing in the complete unity that gives drive and power to our prayer we can stand in weakness, recognising it and ready to bear its consequences.

Ambrose of Optina, one of the last Russian Staretz, said once that two categories of men will attain salvation: those who sin and are strong enough to repent, and those who are too weak even to repent truly but are prepared, patiently, humbly and gratefully, to bear all the weight of the consequences of their sins; in their humility they are acceptable to God.

From **In the Silence** *by* Father Andrew

When the soul collects all its interior powers within, and when the body collects all its external senses and unites them to the soul, the Holy Spirit approaches and breathes into this union quietude and peace, and then it is that Jesus is present in the midst . . .

This heavenly rest is very peaceful. It alters nothing and yet it makes all things new. The cup of sorrow is seen to be the cup which is held by the Father's hand. The sorrow of life becomes a sacrament and in it is found the presence of the Man of Sorrows. This rest unites us to God and His rest because it makes us share His eternal tranquility.

From **In Time of Temptation** *by* Ladislaus Boros

Christ's existence was ruled by a great silence. His soul was listening. It was given over to the needs of others. In His innermost being He was silent, not asserting Himself, detached. He did not grasp at anything in the world. Thus He overcame in His life the power of habit and daily routine, of dullness and fatigue, and created within Himself a carefree tranquility, a place for every encounter. He was unreservedly receptive.

From **The Burrswood Herald** *by* John Sayers

It came to me as an arresting thought "What God wants of you is not your ability but your availability." It is not primarily what one man can do for God in any particular situation that counts, but what God can do through one man or woman who is fully available and responsive to Him. Paul's words to the Ephesian Christians remind us still that "By His power within us" He is able to do infinitely more than we ever dare to ask or imagine. Experience proves, often dramatically, that it is not our ability or the lack of it, but our availability to God that is the clue to all effective Christian action whether by individuals or by groups of Christians.

From **Spirituality for Today,** *an article by* Archbishop Michael Ramsey
THE IDEA OF THE HOLY AND THE WORLD TODAY

It is within human life, and indeed within the non-religious aspects of human life, that many of the phenomena which we call transcendence occur.

Transcendence is seen in human actions which are terrifying – perhaps terrifying in generosity, in forgiveness, in self-giving, in selfless identification with human misery. Here is seen *mysterium tremendum et fascinans,* a beyondness which tells of another world.

It would be wrong, however, to conclude from this that because we are to find true godwardness in our obedience within the world, therefore the apartness or particularity of prayer, contemplation and liturgy, should be abandoned. Such an idea runs counter to the example of Jesus who was found praying a great while before day, apart, in a desert place. This typical scene reveals what was a primary part of his mission. Those who tell us that our prayers should be contained within our encounter with people or that we can best pray while we are talking to people, are telling us a half-truth or perhaps a quarter-truth. We can pray only in the world, through the world, as ourselves part of the world, and there is no love for God within which the world is not included. We are in a sense never apart from the world. But we need to go apart from its preoccupation, its pressure and its noise in order to be open to our freedom as sons and creatures of God eternal.

The contemplation of God and contemplative prayer is, I believe, not necessarily an advanced state but something accessible to us very backward Christians – the waiting upon God in quietness can be our greatest service to the world if in our apartness the love for people is on our heart. As Aaron went into the holy of holies wearing a breastplate with jewels representing the twelve tribes upon it, so the Christian puts himself deliberately into the presence of God with the needs and sorrows of humanity upon his heart. And he does this best not by the vocal skill with which he informs the Deity about the world's needs, but by the simplicity of his own exposure to God's greatness and the world's needs. "As the soul is in the body," wrote the unknown author of the letter to Diognetus, "so are the Christians in the world".

From **Introversion** *by* Evelyn Underhill
"What do you find within, O Soul my Brother?
What do you find within?"

I find great quiet where no noises come.
Without the world's din:
Silence is my home.

"Whom do I find within, O Soul my Brother?
Whom do I find within?"
I find a friend that in secret came:
His scarred hands within,
He shields a faint flame.

From The Cloud of Unknowing

All rational beings, angels and men, possess two faculties, the power of knowing and the power of loving. To the first, to the intellect, God who made them is forever unknowable, but to the second, to love, he is completely knowable, and that by every separate individual. So much so that one loving soul by itself, through its love, may know for itself him who is incomparably more than sufficient to fill all souls that exist. This is the everlasting miracle of love, for God always works in this fashion and always will. Consider this, if by God's grace you are able to. To know it for oneself is endless bliss; its contrary is endless pain.

How right you are to say "for the love of Jesus". For it is in the love of Jesus that you have your help. The nature of love is such that it shares everything. Love Jesus, and everything he has is yours. Because he is God, he is maker and giver of time. Because he is Man, he has given true heed to time. Because he is both God and Man he is the best judge of the spending of time. Unite yourself to him by love and trust, and by that union you will be joined both to him and to all who like yourself are united by love to him . . .

So when you feel by the grace of God that he is calling you to this work, and you intend to respond, lift your heart to God with humble love. And really mean God himself who created you, and bought you, and graciously called you to this state of life. And think no other thought of him. It all depends on your desire. A naked intention directed to God himself alone is wholly sufficient. If you want this intention summed up in a word, to retain it more easily, take a short word, preferably of one syllable, to do so. The shorter the word the better, being more like the working of the Spirit! A word like God or Love. Choose which you like, or perhaps some other, so long as it is of one syllable, and fix this word fast to your heart, so that it is always there, come what may. It will be your shield and spear in peace and war alike. With this word you will hammer the cloud and the darkness above you. With this word you will suppress all thought under the cloud of forgetting. So much so that if ever you are tempted to think what it is that you are seeking, this one word will be sufficient answer . . .

Why does it penetrate heaven, this short little prayer of one syllable? Surely because it is prayed with a full heart, in the height and depth and length and breadth of the spirit of him that prays it. In the height, for it is with all the might of his spirit; in the depth, for in this little syllable is contained all that the spirit knows; in the length, for should it always feel as it does now, it would always cry to God as it now cries; in the breadth, for it would extend to all men what it wills for itself.

From **Parting at Morning** *by* Robert Browning

> *If I should stoop*
> *Into a dark tremendous sea of cloud,*
> *It is but for a time; I press God's lamp*
> *Close to my breast; its splendour soon or late*
> *Will pierce the gloom; I shall emerge one day.*

From **What worship means to me,** *an address to the* 1969 European Friends' Conference *by* Pierre Lacout

Silence purifies. Those who are dedicated to silence must preserve in our over-busy world zones of purified air. We must struggle against the asphyxiation, which threatens the cities of our consumer society. Might not the revolt of youth in its diverse forms be a reaction against asphyxiation, a cry for air? We live in a world mentally polluted by verbal intoxication. If dedication to silence did not exist, it would be necessary to invent it. But it does exist. Like the contemplation of the Carmelites, our Quaker worship is a dedication to silence.

From **Selected Letters** *by* St Francis de Sales: Letter 43, to Baronne de Chantal

Whatever time we decide to give God in prayer let us give it to Him with our thoughts free and disentangled from everything else, resolving never to take this time away from Him again, whatsoever toil comes our way.

Let us treat this time as something which no longer belongs to us; and even if you just spend the time actually aware of your insufficiency, do not let it upset you, even rejoice in it, thinking that you are a very good subject for God's mercy.

Often ask yourself whether you can really say "My beloved is mine and I am His." See whether there is not some part or faculty of your soul or some sense in your body which does not belong wholly to God; and having discovered it, take it, wherever it may be, and give it back to Him, for you are all His, and everything that is in you is His . . . Our Lord does not want you to think either about your progress or about your improvement in any way whatever; but to receive and use faithfully the occasion of serving Him and of practising the virtues at every moment, without any reflection either on the past or on the future.

Each present moment should bring its task, and the only thing we have to do as we turn towards God is to abandon ourselves utterly to Him and long for Him to destroy everything in us that opposes His plans . . .

Meditate; lift up your mind and let it rise up to God, that is to say, draw God into your mind: those are strong things. But with all that do not forget your distaff and your spindle: spin the thread of little virtues, do humble works of charity.

Anyone who tells you differently is making a mistake and is himself deceived.

From **The School of Prayer** *by* Olive Wyon

The writings and letters of St Francis de Sales, and of his friend and disciple, St Jeanne de Chantal, abound in allusions to the Prayer of Loving Attention; for example:

"There is a prayer of calm attention of the soul to God, which reduces too great an activity of the faculties, and establishes it in interior silence and in rest of its powers. Oh how good it is to listen more often to God in our hearts than to speak to Him!"

"Look on God and leave Him to act. That is all you have to do, and the only exercise God requires of you, to which alone He has drawn you. Keep your mind very simply and steadily, without effort or act, in that simple sight and single attention to God, completely abandoned to His holy will, without wanting to see, feel or make acts about it, and remain there, peaceful and at rest, trustful and patient, without considering to see how you are there, or what you are doing, feeling or suffering there, what the soul is doing, what it has done, or will do, or what will happen to it in any occurrence or any event. You must not move from there, for that single attention to God includes everything, particularly in suffering . . . As soon as you see your mind outside that, gently bring it back without any act, glance or reflection about anything or in anything: one thing only is necessary, and that is to have God."

"In prayer there is more listening than speaking to be done: it is for us to listen to the Son of God, and not to speak; we are not worthy to speak before Him."

"For prayer, the great secret is to follow in it the attraction that is given us. How many souls there are who trouble themselves at times about their prayer in order to be able to make it well, and yet there is nothing to do but

79

to follow the attraction; and the purer, simpler, and more denuded of object prayer is, the more excellent and perfect it is, for God is Spirit and a very simple essence. That is why the more tenderly and simply the soul deals with Him, the more capable it is of being united with Him."

From **The School of Prayer** *by* Olive Wyon

True prayer, the prayer of adoration and communion, is also co-operation with God. Not only do we forget ourselves in the worship of God; not only do we rest in the presence of our Lord and receive strength for daily life; but we are called to take part in the work of God, and this co-operation always begins in the secret place of communion with God, though it issues in fruitful action, in external life. The first impulses are born in the presence of God Himself; as we look at Him, we long that others should see His Glory, and we pray "Hallowed be Thy name". We find the joy of obedience, and we pray "Thy will be done" in the lives of others. Then as we move about amongst our fellows we notice needs we never saw before, and we are moved to intercession. Intercession is a great mystery; no intellectual argument ever fully explains it to the mind. But to the heart that loves, it is a necessity; to the Christian it is enough to know that Jesus prayed for His friends, for those who hated Him, and for the world.

From **Living Prayer** *by* Metropolitan Anthony Bloom

One of the reasons communal worship or private prayer seem so dead or so conventional is that the act of worship, which takes place in the heart communing with God, is too often missing.

Every expression either verbal or in action may help, but they are only expressions of what is essential, namely a deep silence of communion . . .

If we want to worship God we must first of all learn to feel happy being silent together with Him.

From **Jesus, a Dialogue with the Saviour** *by* Father Lev

You, Lord Jesus pray in me. Let me be silent so that your voice alone may be heard.

If your prayer becomes mine, if I let You pray in me then all events and all creatures in the world will enter into my prayer and will be influenced by it.

From **The Life of the Spirit** *by* Herbert Waddams

The mysteries of life, of love, of truth, run like a deep stream within our own natures and beneath all the outward surface appearances which we see. It is a deep stream from which comes life, and as we open ourselves to its reality, we sense the mystery of our own being, and know ourselves to be part of a mysterious immensity, a tiny but great part of it.

In this awareness of mysterious reality, of ourselves and of the world, we touch the fringes of the garment of Holy Being which we call God, the source of life of all that is. It is the Spirit of God to whom countless men and women have borne witness by their writings, but above all by their lives, and it is the origin and life force of our lives . . .

So the life of the Spirit is seen to be our life lived in accord with the Spirit of God which is our true end and happiness.

From **The Prayer Life** by Andrew Murray, *adapted*

O Lord Jesus teach us to understand that it is the indwelling Spirit streaming from Thee, uniting to Thee, who is the Spirit of prayer. Teach us to honour and trust Him as a living Person to lead our lives and our prayer. Teach us to wait in holy silence and give Him place to breathe within us His unutterable intercession. Teach us that through Him it is possible to pray without ceasing, without failing, because He makes us partakers of His never ceasing and never failing intercession.

Prayer *by* G. Tersteegen

God is in His Holy Temple, let all that is in thee be still before His Face: be still in thy tongue, in thy will, in all thy desires and thoughts; cease from thine own activity: O how precious in the sight of God is a gentle and quiet spirit, silent in His presence.

John Woolman *taken from* **The School of Prayer** *by* Olive Wyon

The place of prayer is a precious habitation; for I now saw the prayers of the saints were precious incense; and a trumpet was given to me that I might send forth this language; that the children might hear it and be invited together to this precious habitation, where the prayers of the saints, as sweet incense, arise before the throne of God and the Lamb. I saw this habitation to be safe – to be inwardly quiet when there were great stirrings and commotions in the world.

. . . The trumpet is sounded; the call goes forth to the Church that she gather to the place of pure inward prayer.

From **The Journey Inwards** by F. C. Happold

The spiritual exercise of the radiation of love is perhaps the most important prayer of transformation which anyone can make. In some form it should, if possible, be used every day, when it may be done silently, without words at all, or through such simple prayer as: "Divine love, so fill me with Yourself that I may become all love; and let me, in the power

81

of Your love within me, suffuse all beings with the thought of love, compassion, joy and peace!

I have already written of the transforming effect of this Prayer of Love on the one making it. Can it, however, affect more than the one who makes it? There is a short story by E. F. Benson called *In a Convent Chapel*. It pictures a saintly nun, in the eyes of the world unimportant and unknown, praying in a convent chapel. Yet from that obscure chapel are radiating currents of spiritual power which have influence far beyond the chapel walls.

"This black figure knelt at the centre of reality and force and with the movements of her will and lips controlled spiritual destinies for eternity. There ran out from this peaceful chapel lines of spiritual power that lost themselves in the distance, bewildering in their profusion and terrible in the intensity of their hidden power."

Is that a fantastic idea? When I consider all the interrelationships and interlockings which characterise the material universe, I wonder. May not the same sort of interrelationships and interlockings exist also in the psycho-spiritual world? Perhaps Francis Thompson was stating a profound truth when he wrote:

> *When to the new heart of thee,*
> *All things by immortal power*
> > *Hiddenly*
> *To each other linked are,*
> *That thou canst not stir a flower*
> *Without troubling of a star . . .*

From **Vision**, 1969, *a Retreat address by* Trevor Huddleston

It is in retreat that we realise the meaning of community. It is in retreat that we are brought face to face with our failures in human relationships. We are members of the one body wherever we are and whatever we do. The deeper the silence, the deeper do we reach down to this truth.

Finally we discover that the meaning and purpose of life for us depends upon our being true to the Lord of all life in prayer and worship. In our noisy, complex society, one sometimes gets terrified at the difficulties many people experience when it comes to finding the opportunity for silence, for worship and for prayer. Africa spoils one in this respect by its very vastness. It speaks about the immensities of God and by its silence it speaks about the silence of God and his creativity. But in these concrete jungles, we firmly believe that we are here to fulfil God's plan and purpose for us as completely and perfectly in the secular city as anywhere else.

But we are not likely to do this unless we are prepared to give ourselves and our time to the direct activity of worship and prayer in silence. In the end there is only one question directed to us by the Lord Jesus, the same question He directed to Simon Peter: "Lovest thou me more than all this," more than all these persons, more than all the attractive things with which you are surrounded?

It is in retreat that we are given the opportunity of making our answer.

Isaiah 30:15

> For thus said the Lord God, the Holy one of Israel:
> In returning and rest you shall be saved;
> In quietness and in trust shall be your strength.

Prayer: The expression of a growing faith *from* **The Psychology of Prayer** *by* **C. R. Bryant, S.S.J.E.**

The Christian mystical tradition teaches men to find God's presence within . . . The metaphor which is for me the most satisfying of all is that of the soul's centre as the focus of the divine action. The centre of a circle is equidistant from all the points on the circumference; and to say that God acts upon the soul from the centre suggests that the sweep of his action takes in the whole personality and not merely the narrow area of consciousness. The metaphor also suggests that the experience of God within is an experience of being integrated, centred, made one. But I believe the centre is best understood as a potentiality that needs to be actualised if we are to grow to full maturity. Men tend to be pulled first one way then another by opposite tendencies; there is the urge to dominate and the urge to submit, to turn outwards to other people and to withdraw into your shell; there is the aspiration for the spiritual and there is the equally strong counter-pull of the flesh. As the centre becomes actualised the opposed tendencies are held in a creative tension and harnessed in the service of the personality as a whole. I regard this centre, once actualised, as both a point of focus to help concentration on God's action within and also through which God guides us. The symbol of the centre can help a man in practice to co-operate with God. God rules us through the whole of what we are, through our conscious thinking and deciding and through the unconscious that balances and corrects our conscious attitudes . . . As I learn to find God in the centre, this oscillation, this pendulum swing, is slowed down. In perplexity I turn to the centre for guidance; in weakness I turn to the centre for strength. I don't mean that God does not guide and strengthen me from outside. He addresses me through my brother, through the community of faith to which I belong, through every soul I meet. He speaks to me through the Scriptures, through the wisdom of the past, through prophets and wise men today. But the wisdom and help that comes from outside is only truly assimilated and made my own when I have referred it to the centre within. It is through the centre, I believe, that the Holy Spirit enlightens the mind, fires the heart, makes firm the will. It is the focus of God's action, the sanctuary where he dwells.

From **Something Beautiful for God** *by* Malcolm Muggeridge

The more we receive in silent prayer, the more we can give in our active life. We need silence in order to be able to touch souls. The essential thing is not what we say, but what God says to us and through us. All our words will be useless unless they come from within – words which do not give the light of Christ increase the darkness.

From **Quaker Worship**

A Quaker Meeting is the opportunity for a real encounter between persons in depth, for we seek to be open to one another at the most profound level of our existence. It is at this deep, still centre of our being that we know ourselves as real persons. From it arise our most valid insights into the motives and meaning of our lives. It is here also that we are most aware of our relationship to others.

All real life consists in such meetings, and all personal encounters at this depth point to a mystery which transcends human experience, yet is never divorced from it. We discover and are discovered by an awareness of love which gives meaning and purpose to living.

In deliberately setting aside a time in which we give conscious recognition to the deepest values by which we try to live, and in which we are drawn into a profound and meaningful communion with our friends, we find a sense of awe growing in us at the wonder of this rich experience.

In our deepest being we know that through the awareness of our real selves, and through our relationship with others, we have touched the kind of experience that saints and mystics have known, and that Jesus called God.

. . . A Quaker Meeting does not end when the period of worship closes, for those who have shared in it will continue to live in its strength. It is as they seek to interpret its deep meaning into action in their lives that the validity of this approach to worship is finally vindicated.

From **O Friend I Know Not** *by* William Wordsworth

Thy soul was like a star, and dwelt apart;
Thou hadst a voice whose sound was like the sea:
Pure as the naked heavens, majestic, free.

So didst thou travel on life's common way
In cheerful godliness, yet thy heart
The lowliest duties on herself did lay.

Theophan the Recluse *from* **The Art of Prayer:** An Orthodox Anthology

GOD'S NEARNESS AND PRESENCE IN THE HEART

Seek and ye shall find. But what is one to seek? A conscious and living communion with the Lord. This is given by the grace of God, but it is also essential that we ourselves should work, that we ourselves should come to meet Him. How? By always remembering God, who is near the heart and even present within it. To succeed in this remembrance it is advisable to accustom oneself to the continual repetition of the Jesus Prayer, "Lord Jesus Christ, Son of God, have mercy upon me", holding in mind the thought of God's nearness, His presence in the heart. But it must also be understood that in itself the Jesus Prayer is only an outer oral prayer; inner prayer is to stand before the Lord, continually crying out to Him without words.

By this means remembrance of God will be established in the mind, and the countenance of God will be in your soul like the sun. If you put something cold in the sun it begins to grow warm, and in the same way your soul will be warmed by the remembrance of God, who is the spiritual sun. What follows on from this will presently appear.

Your first task is to acquire the habit of repeating the Jesus Prayer unceasingly. So begin and continually repeat and repeat, but all the time keep before you the thought of our Lord.

And herein lies everything.

From **Spirituality for Today,** *an article by* Basil Moss

Not only Christianity, but all the great religions are clear that God is not someone or something that you could see or experience through your senses if only He were near enough. And if we can't directly experience God through our senses it follows that we can't literally imagine Him either, for all our powers of imagination spring from our senses. No doubt it is natural to form pictures of God when we are children, and Christian art and literature are full of colourful descriptions of the furniture of heaven and the temperature of hell. But the meaning these pictures have must always be an indirect and limited meaning like expressing "red" by the blast of a trumpet to a man born blind.

The Bible puts it this way: "No man has seen God at any time." "He dwells in unapproachable light and no man has ever seen or can ever see Him."

I am not saying that we have no clues about God. Every glimpse of the mystery of things – from the atom to the star – is a clue to God, and Christians find a supreme clue in Jesus, but God himself is invisible, unimaginable, "hid from our eyes". That's the way it is.

Listen now to an unknown English writer of the fourteenth century: "A cloud of unknowing is between thee and thy God, for all other creatures and their works, yes and the works of God himself can a man through grace have fullness of knowing and well can he think of them. But of God himself can no man think. For why, he may well be loved but not thought. By love may he be gotten and holden, but by thought never . . . and therefore thou shalt smite upon the thick cloud of unknowing with a sharp dart of longing love."

The word "love" is the heart of the matter. "He may well be loved but not thought; by love may he be gotten and holden but by thought never", for thought objectifies and that we cannot do for God. So praying is more like loving than anything else, and believing is more like loving than anything else. Why? Because the nearest we can get to God is to say that his nature and his name is love and we love him because he loved us first.

You can't see love. You can only see the clues to it and respond yourself. Every minute, every day someone says, Does she love me, Does he love me? You'll only find out by responding, by risking yourself in trust and hope. It's like that with God. It's no use wanting a certainty, wanting a vision. You must take seriously the claim that he is love and turn to him in love and "smite upon the cloud of unknowing with a dart of longing love." So prayer is the action-word for believing and the heart of prayer is courageously reaching out. In the words of Psalm 139: "Lord, thou hast searched me out, and known me . . . Such knowledge is too wonderful and excellent for me: I cannot attain unto it . . ." The fact that loving, not thinking, is the key to prayer helps us in dealing with dryness and unreality in prayer.

Of course, because God is God, our imagination is bound to let us down. But there's more to it than that. Our feelings, our emotions let us down as well.

Thank God when you have religious feelings, a sense of the reality and the presence. But never confuse feelings with faith and prayer. Is the sort of love that operates only when we feel like it real love? Since praying is responding to love with love, true prayer must stick at it courageously whether we pray with or against the grain of our feelings.

The unborn child in the womb might say, "I am in the dark – where is my mother?" But his mother totally sustains him – and one day he will enter new possibilities of vision. So, says faith, it will be with us.

86

From **The Path to Glory** *by* J. R. H. Moorman

FAITH THROUGH OBEDIENCE

So many people need to learn that Obedience must often come before faith; that is by going on patiently obeying the commandments of God and the teaching of Christ that faith will come to them; that faith is neither something to which they are entitled nor something which is either given or withheld, but something which has to be earned by a life of discipline and obedience. It is really no good saying: "I find it so difficult to believe" when we are doing little or nothing to build up faith by using the means of grace which God has provided for us and by bringing our lives under the control of his will. And if we are to practise obedience we can scarcely do better than begin with the three commands which Jesus gave to Peter in the boat. "Thrust out a little from the land": do not allow yourself to become earthbound, your life dominated by the things of this world; withdraw a little from the pleasures and interests and anxieties of what happens in this life and devote a little more of your time to the things of eternity. And then "launch out into the deep" and explore the depths of God's love; consider his nature, his goodness, his strength, let the thought of his majesty and of his tender mercy and compassion flow into your heart; learn to be alone with him in the deep. And then "Let down your nets for a draught"; learn to accept what God gives of his grace, his peace, his strength; spread the nets wide for that miraculous draught of all that your soul can need.

From **Retreat Notes** *by* Mark Meynell

Silence. One of the golden words of Prayer. A contrast to the clamours of the world, which is all words, speaking, talk.

We carry it over to the presence of God. It is therefore disastrous, we cease to be conscious of Him. We are passionate and busy about human concerns. God is infinitely more concerned. Let us give Him credit for concern. Attend to Him who is at the heart of humanity, Jesus Christ. Think of the things that silence you, yourself. Beauty, Joy, Grandeur. The creative part of silence, looking, listening, loving God.

In His presence is fullness of joy. Silence before the majesty and beauty. In intercession it is better to look at God. It is more effective for others than to present a string of needs, which inevitably takes attention off Him.

He sees in our hearts and attends without anything being said. Silence is effective prayer because all honour is given to God.

By R. S. Thomas

> *When I speak something is lost:*
> *The meaning is in the waiting.*

From **In Time of Temptation** *by* Ladislaus Boros

THE ABILITY TO KEEP SILENT

Revelation, the "object" of Christian conviction, is not a foolproof system of divine answers to human questions. It is not a system at all, but a destiny – the destiny of men with God and of God among men. So we have to take into account that God has revealed to us only as much as we need in order to dare the next step towards Him through the darkness, trusting that for us His light will not be extinguished for ever. God has revealed to us everything that will help us to get to heaven – all of it but no more. There are many questions to which Revelation gives no answer at all. God quite simply proves His love for us right to the end, to the Cross . . .

In the face of this act of God all questioning stops, even though there is no answer. This falling silent is one of the creative experiences of Christian prayer. The most beautiful words, those that give the most genuine help, are often born in a silence filled with suffering. Silence is the glowing furnace of the word, the forge of true speech and sensitivity. The people who have won the right to speak to us at the worst moments in our lives are those who have suffered in silence, before God, with God, and for his sake. God speaks to us through men whom – like his Son – he has led into the desert, into the loneliness of suffering, of inner hunger and unquenchable yearning, and who have become quite silent there. For them their suffering has become an election and a mission, they feel inwardly linked to all sufferers; God lets them suffer human need in order that they may be able to sit down alongside a stranger, on the dreary bed of his inner prison and say, "You are not alone". Such people have the right to bear another's pain and to seek out God in their hesitant prayer. Their words are more than "true". They are words of solidarity.

From **The Use of Praying** *by* J. Neville Ward

Thanking is the characteristic Christian state. It leads naturally to adoration, to the desire to praise the cause of our joy, not for having caused our joy (the self and its satisfactions have been by now left behind) but for what he is and must be in himself. This can become so persistent and excited that we begin to want a union with God and knowledge of him which it is not legitimate to expect in this life, and, as far as we can see, is not going to be given us. "My soul thirsteth for God, for the living God. When shall I come and behold the face of God?" (Psalm 42:2)

But there is a point at which the mind finds it possible simply to rest in contentment with one or other of the forms of God's presence that are in fact given us in this world . . . This affectionate looking at and resting in appreciated good is contemplation. Much of the experience cannot be put into words; indeed it seems to be part of the experience that verbalisation is effectively stopped; but it contains the conviction that this segment of reality in front of me has an infinite value, that beside it I myself do not matter at all, yet in being in its presence and loving it I seem to be at home, more myself, more alive than I am elsewhere; I know that it is good to be here and that it is a pity that life is not always like this; it is a kind of accusation against life that this must end and I return to what with devastating precision is called "ordinary life".

This experience is far more common than is commonly acknowledged. It is certainly not the preserve of those who care called mystics. Some of it is part of the regular experience of human beings, whatever their faith, degree of Christian faith, inability consciously to adhere to any faith.

"Wherever a man's mind has been uplifted, his temptations thwarted, his sorrows comforted, his resolutions strengthened, his aberrations controlled by the sight of purity, innocence, love or beauty – indeed wherever he has, even for a moment, recognised and responded to the distinction between good and evil, between better and worse – such a man has had in part the mystical experience. Dim though his mirror may have been, he has yet seen God. Where he has seen God once there he may see him again ... So far then from being rare, the mystical experience is at once the commonest and greatest of human accidents. There is not one of us to whom it does not come daily. It is only carelessness or custom that prevents our realising how divine it is in essence; only timidity which checks us from proclaiming that we too at such moments have seen God, even as if in a glass darkly ... What Christianity offers, with its fellowship and sacraments, its life of prayer and service, its preaching of the Incarnate Son of God, is the same vision in ever-increasing plenitude ..." (K. E. Kirk, *The Vision of God*).

This does not mean that the Christian thinks that practically everyone is "working with some kind of concept of God under another name and therefore already stands in a much more positive relation to the God of Christian faith than he himself is aware" (H. Gollwitzer, *The Existence of God*). But it does mean that there are, as Simone Weil puts it, implicit forms of the love of God in most lives and these can act as sympathetic leads to the Christian's more articulate and dynamic love of God. She says, for example, that the sense of beauty is present in all the preoccupations of secular life. If it were made true and pure it would sweep all secular life in a body to the feet of God (Simone Weil, *Waiting on God*). She points out that there is an incompleteness and pain about aesthetic love because its object is things which are incapable of answering to man's love, incapable of saying "yes", of surrendering. Ultimately we long to love the beauty of the world in the form of a living, responding being; and this is essentially the longing for the Incarnation. St Augustine, in his confessions, makes the similar point that all are seeking God but settle unsatisfactorily and unsatisfyingly for that which is less than God; and in the *De Trinitate* he says "Souls in their very sins seek but a sort of likeness of God".

But in these experiences of heightened awareness of life it is possible to rest in contentment. Normally the mind functions by means of sense-impressions, images (that is to say thoughts of a pictorial nature) and ideas (thoughts of an abstract conceptual nature). But the mind can function in another way. In the experience of the arts (listening to music, looking at a picture) or when enjoying the view of a wide and various landscape, or certain moments of tranquillity and happiness in the infinitely diverse experience of human love, the mind seems not to be doing anything at all; it is certainly not pursuing a series of verbal thoughts, it is simply attending in quietness and joy to what is in front of it. It is this faculty of the mind to attend, without one thought giving way to another, simply to be held, that is the characteristic feature of contemplation. Practically everyone is familiar with it. It is the commonest, wisest, safest way into God. The mystics of the great religions were people who were specially gifted with this mental aptitude and cultivated it according to their understanding of God.

What this type of experience means can, of course, be variously interpreted, but Christian spirituality has usually wanted to refer it to God.

"During the contemplation of a work of art, or while listening to a melody, the effort to understand relaxes, and the soul simply delights itself in the beauty which it divines . . . or merely a memory, a word, a line of Dante or Racine, shooting up from the obscure depths of our soul, seizes hold of us recollects and penetrates us. After this experience we know no more than we did, but we have the impression of understanding a little something that before we hardly knew, of tasting fruit at the rind of which we have scarcely nibbled" (De Grandmaison, quoted in H. Brémond, *Prayer and Poetry*).

A more recent writer argues more tentatively for this experience but eventually comes to make a similar claim for it:

"The conclusion to which I came at this point is that this peculiarly intense activity of mind . . . is of the greatest value because it makes us aware of ourselves as we never are in other circumstances . . . We really 'come alive', as we might put it. It is not merely that we are enjoying ourselves enormously . . .

We find ourselves transported into a mysterious region of value, and at the same time it is a sort of home-coming or an intimation of a peculiarly dynamic or (it may be) even of an overwhelming kind, that there is a goal which seems to recede even as we approach it" (Dom Illtyd Trethowan, *Theology and the University*).

But it is an earlier writer, oddly enough, the poet Baudelaire, who speaks most confidently for the religious interpretation of this experience:

"It is at once by poetry and by penetrating beyond it, by music and by penetrating beyond it, that the soul catches a glimpse of the splendour on the other side of the grave; and when an exquisite poem brings tears to the eyes, these tears are no proof of excessive pleasure. They are, rather, the witness of an irritated sensibility, a demand of the nerves, of a nature exiled in the imperfect, which longs to seize immediately on this very earth the paradise revealed to it" (Charles Baudelaire, *Les Fleurs du Mal*).

These experiences may not always be interpreted in such visionary terms, but it is our faith that they are the presence of God, from the momentary thrills of joy of life and love of it that comes to us all, to the sustained stillness of tranquil love attained by the disciplined contemplative. No one doubts that they are times of infinitely important living and that we are fools not to explore them more – to understand them better and to prepare the mind for their more frequent visitation. It is clear that they are always given. We do not make them ourselves. They come gratuitously and often unexpectedly. But it seems that a loving openness to experience and the ability to wait in silence make us more susceptible to them.

It is possible to prolong their presence by resting in such experience thankfully while it is there, letting the beauty of the moment work its work on us instead of rushing on to the next bit of ambiguous experience of twentieth century life. And this may well increase our responsiveness to the approach of these moments. And there is much evidence that, if cultivated, their influence spreads an enlightenment over the rest of life. Indeed action is inseparably connected with contemplation in the Christian use of praying; it is not an interruption of it but an addition to it, as Aquinas said, making a perfect whole of two elements which, singly, are incomplete and need each other.

From **Life Together** *by* Dietrich Bonhoeffer

SOLITUDE AND SILENCE

Let him who cannot be alone beware of community. He will only do harm to himself and to the community. Alone you stood before God when He called you; alone you had to answer that call; alone you had to struggle and pray; and alone you will die and give an account to God. You cannot escape from yourself; for God has singled you out. If you refuse to be alone you are rejecting Christ's call to you, and you can have no part in the community of those who are called. "The challenge of death comes to us all, and no one can die for another. Everyone must fight his own battle with death by himself, alone . . . I will not be with you then, nor you with me" (Luther).

But the reverse is also true: Let him who is not in community beware of being alone. Into the community you were called, the call was not meant for you alone; in the community of the called you bear your cross, you struggle, you pray. You are not alone, even in death, and on the Last Day you will be only one member of the great congregation of Jesus Christ. If you scorn the fellowship of the brethren, you reject the call of Jesus Christ, and thus your solitude can only be hurtful to you. "If I die, then I am not alone in death; if I suffer they [the fellowship] suffer with me" (Luther).

We recognise, then, that only as we are within the fellowship can we be alone, and only he that is alone can live in the fellowship. Only in the fellowship do we learn to be rightly alone and only in aloneness do we learn to live rightly in the fellowship. It is not as though the one preceded the other; both begin at the same time, namely with the call of Jesus Christ . . .

The mark of solitude is silence, as speech is the mark of community. Silence and speech have the same inner correspondence and difference as do solitude and community. One does not exist without the other. Right speech comes out of silence, and right silence comes out of speech . . .

"There is a time to keep silence and a time to speak" (Ecclesiastes 3:7). Silence is nothing else but waiting for God's Word and coming from God's Word with a blessing. But everybody knows that this is something that needs to be practised and learned, in these days when talkativeness prevails. Real silence, real stillness, really holding one's tongue comes only as the sober consequence of spiritual stillness.

But this stillness before the Word will exert its influence upon the whole day. If we have learned to be silent before the Word, we shall also learn to manage our silence and our speech during the day. There is such a thing as forbidden self-indulgent silence, a proud, offensive silence. And this means that it can never be merely silence as such. The silence of the Christian is listening silence, humble stillness, that may be interrupted at any time for the sake of humility. It is silence in conjunction with the Word. This is what Thomas à Kempis meant when he said: "None speaketh surely but he would gladly keep silence if he might."

There is a wonderful power of clarification, purification and concentration upon the essential thing in being quiet. This is true as a purely secular fact. But silence before the Word leads to right hearing and thus also to right speaking of the Word of God at the right time. Much that is unnecessary remains unsaid. But the essential and the helpful thing can be said in a few words.

We shall not discuss here all the wonderful benefits that can accrue to the Christian in solitude and silence. It is all too easy to go astray at this point. We could probably cite many a bad experience that has come from silence.

Silence can be a dreadful ordeal with all its desolation and terrors. It can also be a false paradise of self-deception, the latter is no better than the former. Be that as it may, let none expect from silence anything but a direct encounter with the Word of God, for the sake of which he has entered into silence. But this encounter will be given to him. The Christian will not lay down any conditions as to what he expects or hopes to get from this encounter. If he will simply accept it, his silence will be richly rewarded.

Prayer *from* **A Book of School Worship** *compiled by* William Temple

All through this day O Lord, may we touch as many lives as Thou wouldst have us touch for Thee; and those whom we touch do Thou with Thy Holy Spirit quicken, whether by the word we speak, the letter we write, the prayer we breathe, or the life we live. Amen.

From **In the Silence** *by* Father Andrew

> *We can only come to Him in humility.*
> *We who are very ignorant must come to Him for light;*
> *We who are very weak must come humbly to Him for strength;*
> *We who are very sinful must come humbly to Him for forgiveness.*
> *As we come to Him weak, His strong arm is about us to lift us up.*
> *As we come to Him stained and broken, His wise love is about us to*
> *heal and forgive.*

From **The Listening Heart** *by* Sister Jeanne D'Arc, O.P.

FACE TO FACE WITH GOD

The phrase taught by old Eli to the boy Samuel, "Speak, Lord, for thy servant hears" (1 Sam 3:9), expresses a fundamental attitude of the soul which knows by faith that its God wants to communicate with it direct. Thus the soul is constantly listening out for every appeal from God, on the watch for breath of the Spirit, "Blessed . . . are those who hear the word of God and keep it" (Lk 11:28). But the word speaks to us only when all things are wrapped in a profound silence. Give me, O Lord, a heart that listens for the Word does not use many words (Mt 6:7). When the Lord, who is uncreated Wisdom, takes possession of a soul, he does not cry or lift up his voice (Is 42:2), but rather he is silent in his love (Zp 3:17). He who listens to him dwells secure (Pr 1:33). All we have to do is to listen in our heart to the silence of God until our heart is purified in this silence and the Lord can give it wisdom (Pr 2:6), that gift of Wisdom which transforms silence into savour and enables us to delight in the uncreated savour which is the Spirit.

Encountering our fellow men

However, this heart that listens is not something that is relevant only at the deep level of our life with God. It is equally necessary in other fields and, first and foremost, in that of our human relationships ... In some obscure way, it is this kind of listening heart that all our fellow men look for in us.

In very many cases, the sick and the poor have a greater need for a heart that listens than for medicine or food. But do we not somehow sense this mute appeal even among those who are closest to us? Each one has his own cross to carry and burden to bear. At times, the heaviest burden of all may well be the demands of etiquette, the need to keep up appearances, to present to the world what we may describe as a "social I" quite distinct from the real "me" from whom no one can escape. Even when the "inner man is being renewed every day through the Spirit" (2 Co 4:16; Ep 3:16), all the rind of the "outer man" still clings to him like a shell or prison. And he cries out without managing to make himself heard, though all he really needs is to have near him a heart that listens ... this alone would probably enable him to open his own heart. If we once release our real selves, we are in a position to fulfil them in a true sense and make them really exist.

Carrying one another's burdens

Every one of our fellow men is in search of a heart ready to listen to him in such a way that he will no longer be *another* human being. Let us then try to give this kind of welcome, to pay him that depth of attention which comes from the bottom of the heart so that he will be at ease with us as he is with himself. So often the eyes of those who surround him and even of those closest to him are like so many distorting mirrors; instead, let him find in us a heart so clear and transparent that the refraction index, so to speak, is nil. "Bear one another's burdens" (Ga 6:2). We are so very weak that we are often unable to bear anyone else's burden. However, we can always at least relieve him of his load by letting him pour it out into us. All we have to do is to listen with our heart. It is not simply a question of exchanging confidences, though this may well come into it. It is a question of an interior welcome at a deep level, of a heart so full of fellow-feeling as to be on the alert for all that is best, and frequently most hidden and unexpressed, in all those with whom we come into contact. A silence impregnated with love, which listens in charity to the groans of the sufferer, is often far more effective than words of comfort...

The apostolate

When it comes to the active apostolate, how very damaging a certain desire to proclaim the truth and spread the light can prove to be. Very often we are merely projecting ourselves, proclaiming our own truth, spreading our own light, our own little store of knowledge and, in doing so, we make our victim a present of an intolerable burden. What is he to do with it? He has his own problems, his own perplexities, his own experiences which are not ours; he simply does not know what to do with all the surplus we heap onto him. A reply is only called for when a question has been asked and even then only when the question has matured and the questioner is ready to listen to what we have to say. We must approach our neighbour with reverence, in a sense kneeling before him, with that listening heart which love alone can give. Only by means of this silence and transparency in us will he be able to find the light. By thus opening out our arms to him in the depths of our heart, we shall ensure that our own response offers him precisely that truth which he can assimilate.

There is no richer teaching on this subject than the words of Christ: "I have yet many things to say to you, but you cannot bear them now" (Jn 16:12). The end is near. He is just about to leave his apostles for ever. He, the Word of God, who has come to cast fire upon the earth and whose one wish is that it were already kindled (cf. Lk 12:49), sees that in spite of all the love and care that he has put into their training, the apostles are not ready to receive what he has yet to give. He does not insist. He entrusts it all to the Holy Spirit. What a lesson for our impatience, for that projection of ourselves which we keep on directing at others instead of just listening in a constant attitude of openness and ready welcome.

Prayer *by* E.B.

O Lord Jesus give us hearts that listen. Hearts that listen to Thee in silence and love. Hearts that listen to those we meet, to those in trouble, in the silence of true compassion. Thy compassion and understanding. Help us to remember that there is a time for silence and a time for speaking and give us the wisdom to know when to speak and when to hold our peace.

Forgive us for all the times we have failed to listen and so missed the chance to help, leaving our friend uncomforted.
Silence us O Lord, for Thy Name's sake.

Amen.

From **Life Together** *by* Dietrich Bonhoeffer

THE MINISTRY OF LISTENING

The first service that one owes to others in the fellowship consists in listening to them. Just as love to God begins with listening to His Word, so the beginning of love for the brethren is learning to listen to them. It is God's love for us that He not only gives us His Word but also lends His ear. So it is His work that we do for our brother when we learn to listen to him. Christians, especially ministers, so often think they must always contribute something when they are in the company of others, that this is the one service they have to render. They forget that listening can be a greater service than speaking.

Many people are looking for an ear that will listen. They do not find it among Christians, because these Christians are talking where they should be listening. But he who can no longer listen to his brother will soon be no longer listening to God either; he will be doing nothing but prattle in the presence of God too. This is the beginning of the death of the spiritual life, and in the end there is nothing left but spiritual chatter and clerical condescension arrayed in pious words. One who cannot listen long and patiently will presently be talking beside the point and be never really speaking to others, albeit he be not conscious of it. Anyone who thinks that his time is too valuable to spend keeping quiet will eventually have no time for God and his brother, but only for himself and his own follies . . .

There is a kind of listening with half an ear that presumes already to know what the other person has to say. It is an impatient, inattentive listening, that despises the brother and is only waiting for a chance to speak and thus get rid of the other person. This is no fulfilment of our obligation, and it is certain that here too our attitude toward our brother only reflects our relationship to God. It is little wonder that we are no longer capable of the greatest service of listening that God has committed to us, that of hearing our brother's confession, if we refuse to give ear to our brother on lesser subjects. Secular education today is aware that often a person can be helped merely by having someone who will listen to him seriously, and upon this insight it has constructed its own soul therapy, which has attracted great numbers of people, including Christians. But Christians have forgotten that the ministry of listening has been committed to them by Him who is Himself the great listener and whose work they should share. We should listen with the ears of God that we may speak the Word of God.

From **Prayers of Life** *by* Michel Quoist

THE TELEPHONE

I have just hung up, why did he telephone?
I don't know ... Oh! I get it ...
I talked a lot and listened very little.

Forgive me, Lord, it was a monologue and not a dialogue.
I explained my idea and did not get his;
Since I didn't listen, I learned nothing,
Since I didn't listen, I didn't help,
Since I didn't listen, we didn't communicate.

Forgive me, Lord, for we were connected,
And now we are cut off.

From a programme in the **Ten to Eight** *radio series*

Slow me down, Lord!
Ease the pounding of my heart by the quieting of my mind.
Steady my hurried pace with a vision of the Eternal reach of time.
Give me, amidst the confusion of my day, the calmness of the
Everlasting hills.
Break the tensions of my nerves and muscles with the soothing music
of singing streams that live in my memory.
Help me to know the magical restoring power of sleep.
Teach me the art of taking minute vacations ... of slowing down to
look at a flower, to chat with a friend, to pat a dog, to read a few
lines from a good book.
Remind me each day of the fable of the hare and the tortoise that I
may know that the race is not always to the swift; that there is
more to life than measuring its speed.
Let me look upwards into the branches of the towering oak, and know
that it grew great and strong because it grew slowly and well.
Slow me down, Lord, and inspire me to send my roots deep into the
soil of life's enduring values that I may grow toward the stars of
my enduring destiny.

From **The School of Prayer** *by* Olive Wyon

OTHER WAYS OF PRAYING

It would be a grave error to imagine that the way of contemplative prayer is full of rest, light and sweetness. The opposite is very often the case. The new way often leads through very dark passages and tunnels, in which the only light is that "obscure faith" which is the only safe guide ...

Some of us may be called to pass through experiences when all that we thought we believed seems blotted out. When the darkness comes down upon our spirit, like a thick white mist on the lonely moor, then we may know for certain that God is in the cloud. Behind it is His Light and meanwhile He is training us to love and desire Him for Himself alone and not for any self-centred feelings of ours. Even if we feel that we are "doing nothing" and that we are "useless" in the service of God, we can take heart from the fact that thousands have been this way before us, and many have left us their witness, that in the midst of this trial God is not only purifying and training us, He is often using us in His service in a fuller way than ever before. So we may keep a stout heart, and show a cheerful front to the world knowing that the mist will lift and the sun will shine again. And we are in the hands of God, being guided and supported at every turn of the road, though we can neither feel nor see Him.

The chief temptation to people in this state of mind is to feel that prayer for the moment is useless and that it would be better to give it up, or at least to reduce it until the "better times" come. This is a serious temptation; the trial of faith may be severe, but it will only be surmounted if it is borne with courage and patience and self-forgetfulness. It is possible to worship, to intercede for others, and to give oneself continually to God during such periods as much as at other times when "the going is good". When this seems very hard we can take heart by the remembrance of the sufferings of Christ on the Cross, when for a brief but terrible moment, He felt the thick darkness sweep over His soul. One who suffered much in this way wrote: "When God takes the sweetness of His presence from us, and seems to have forsaken us like His divine Son on the Cross, so that we feel no longer any strength or help, then is the time not to lose courage, but to continue steadfast in our desolation and rely on the words of Jesus Christ in which all strength is hidden: 'Thy will be done!' How pleasing is this word to God! Happy is the soul that can say it heartily in that state."

At other times, there will be flashes of light, glimpses of glory, hints and intuitions of the love in which the universe is bathed; above all, a quiet awareness of God, which will be a solid support and inspiration in all the duties and trials of our lives.

But we must beware of the tendency to think that we can "learn" this way out of a book – that it is simply a "method" which we can acquire by a certain amount of perseverance, once we have "got the hang of it". What I have been trying to describe is really the entrance into our inheritance. Once we have plunged into the "Sea Pacific" and find it bearing us up, that is all that matters. We have found our native element. What we do once we are in the sea matters much less than the fact that we are there. All that matters is the Ocean: we are able to let our worries and problems go once we have found our true Home. Confidence and abandonment into the hands of God bring with them certain peace and joy, a peace which persists through all trials of darkness and suffering. We see now that until we plunge into this Ocean we are only half alive. For this we were made; this is already the beginning of Eternal Life.

The one test of the reality of such prayer is the fact that it leads us to want, in a way we never knew before, to do and bear the will of God. We have one desire only, and only one devotion, and that is the will of God. By whatever path of prayer we are led, all paths converge at this point: the sovereignty of the will of God. All who seek God only, find themselves drawn to this one practice, this one devotion, and this means that we seek above all else: the Glory of God.

St Catherine of Siena, *quoted in* **The School of Prayer** *by* Olive Wyon

"O Eternal Trinity! O Godhead! Thou art a deep Sea, into which the deeper I enter the more I find, and the more I find the more I seek . . . Thou art the Fire which burns without being consumed; Thou consumest in Thy heat all the soul's self-love; Thou art the Fire which takes away all cold; with Thy Light Thou dost illuminate me so that I may know all Thy truth . . . In the light of faith I am strong, constant and persevering. In the light of faith I hope, suffer me not to faint by the way. Of a truth this light is a sea; for the soul revels in Thee, Eternal Trinity, the Sea Pacific. Clothe me, O Eternal Truth, that I may run my mortal course with true obedience and the light of holy faith."

From **Living Prayer** *by* Metropolitan Anthony Bloom

DIFFICULTIES IN PRAYER

When we stand before God in these moments of dejection, we must pray from conviction if not from feeling, out of the faith we are aware of possessing intellectually if not with a burning heart.

At such moments the prayers sound quite different to us, but not to God; as Julian of Norwich says "Pray inwardly though thou thinkest it savour thee not, for it is profitable though thou feel not, though thou see naught, yea though thou think thou canst not. For in dryness and in barrenness, in sickness and in feebleness, then is thy prayer well pleasant to Me, though thou thinkest it savour thee naught but little and so is all thy believing prayer in My sight" (*The Cloud of Unknowing*).

In these periods of dryness when prayer becomes an effort, our main support is faithfulness and determination; it is by an act of will including them both that we compel ourselves without considering our feelings to take our stand before God and speak to Him, simply because God is God and we are His creatures. Whatever we feel at a given moment our position remains the same. God remains our creator, our saviour, our Lord and the one towards whom we move, who is the object of our longing and the only one who can give fulfilment.

Sometimes we think we are unworthy of praying and that we have no right to pray; again this is a temptation. Every drop of water, from wherever it comes, pool or ocean, is purified in the process of evaporation: and so is every prayer ascending to God.

When we make use of prayers which have been written by saints, by men of prayer, and are the results of their experience we can be sure that if we are attentive enough, the words will become our own: we shall grow into their underlying feeling and they will remould us by the Grace of God who responds to our efforts.

From **Vision,** Anon.

ON PRAYER

We must not repine and get out of heart when prayer is very difficult, when it seems as though we could not keep our minds fixed on God, when we cannot even feel sure that He is there; when no answer to our prayers can be discerned. We must not expect that people like us, whose wills have constantly been weakened by selfishness and sin can attain to close union with our Lord, so that we become His instruments for manifesting His life in the world, till we have passed victoriously through the greatest difficulties and temptations we are capable of enduring.

Some day in the next world, if not in this, we shall pour out our hearts in thanksgiving to Him because He did not let us have an easy life, because He went on trusting us to persevere in His own way, the narrow way, the way of the Cross, the way of habitual prayer, in spite of all its difficulties; because He called upon us to attain to a life of communion with Himself through the greatest efforts we were capable of making.

7

Prayer in Life

"An Act of Prayer at the heart of every action"
"The Love of God and the love of man can never be divorced"

The Two Loves *by* Evelyn Underhill *from* **Concerning the Inner Life**
Prayer: Almighty God, who Thyself art love
From **Lent with William Temple.** THE FATHER OF ALL
An excerpt from a sermon from **Lent with William Temple**
From **This World and Prayer** *by* Sister Edna Mary. CITIZENS OF TWO
   WORLDS
Fellow Workers With God *from* **The Art of Prayer:** An Orthodox
   Anthology
From **Jesus and the Word** *by* Rudolph Bultmann. THE CONJUNCTION OF
   THE COMMAND OF LOVE FOR NEIGHBOUR WITH THE COMMAND OF LOVE
   FOR GOD
From **Abba Father** *by* Evelyn Underhill
From **The Life of the Spirit** *by* Herbert Waddams
From **This World and Prayer** *by* Sister Edna Mary
From **Vision, Jan-Jun 1968:** *the sixth article in the series on* The Spiritual
   Life *by* D. E. Shapland. CONTEMPLATION, MISSION AND VOCATION
John Burns. They never sought in vain
From **The Call to the Religious Life** *by* Sister Edna Mary. The religious
   life
From **The Call to the Religious Life** *by* Sister Edna Mary. The life of
   the religious
Advent Letter to members of the Watchers' and Workers' Society
   from Mark Meynell
It Takes Two To Make Prayer *by* Eva Pinthus (Quaker Publication)
From **Readings from St John's Gospel** *by* William Temple
From the **Bhagavad Gita,** *quoted in* **Mysticism** *by* F. C. Happold
From **The Sufi Path of Love,** *quoted in* **Mysticism** *by* F. C. Happold.
   THE VISION OF GOD IN EVERYTHING
From **The Prophet** *by* Kahlil Gibran

The Two Loves *by* Evelyn Underhill *from* **Concerning the Inner Life**

Our deepest life consists in a willed correspondence with the world of Spirit, and this willed correspondence, which is prayer, is destined to fulfil itself along two main channels; in love towards God and in love towards humanity: two loves which at last and at their highest become one love. Sooner or later, in varying degrees, the power and redeeming energy of God will be manifested through those who thus reach out in desire, first towards Him, and then towards other souls.

Our Lord's life in ministry supported by much lonely prayer gives us the classic pattern of human correspondence with this our two-fold environment. The Saints tried to imitate that pattern more and more closely; and as they did so, their personality expanded and shone with love and power. They show us in history a growth and transformation of character which we are not able to grasp; yet which surely ought to be the Christian norm.

In many cases they were such ordinary even unpromising people when they began; for the real Saint is neither a special creature nor a special freak. He is just a human being in whom has been fulfilled the great aspirations of St Augustine "My life shall be a real life, being wholly full of Thee".

And as that real life, that interior union with God grows, so too does the Saint's self-identification with humanity grow. They do not stand aside wrapped in delightful prayers and feeling pure and agreeable to God. They go right down into the mess and there right down in the mess they are able to radiate God because they possess Him.

Prayer:

Almighty God, who Thyself art love, fill us with the spirit of Thy Holy Love, that our hearts being kindled by Thee, we may for ever and ever love Thee, and each other for Thee; through Jesus Christ our Lord. Amen.

From **Lent with William Temple**

THE FATHER OF ALL

Man's chief aim is to glorify God, the true aim of the soul is to glorify God ... But worship cannot be the whole of our activity here, because it is, in its own nature, a concentration upon the God who appoints us our duty in life, and part of our very duty to Him is that from time to time, and indeed for the greater part of our time, we should not be explicitly directing attention towards Him but devoting it with all our energy to the duty which He has given us to perform. The principle of the fourth commandment is an eternal principle. There must be some of our time set apart for God, in detachment from all other interests whatsoever, because unless we have that time for concentrated contemplation of Him there is no hope that we shall do our work in the world as a duty to Him and out of loyalty to Him. But it is also true that for the greater part of our time, represented in six days of the week, we have our duty to do in the power and under the direction of that spirit to whom at our moments of worship we specially open our hearts.

An excerpt from a sermon from Lent with William Temple

The fundamental fact about human life is that God in His love, has entered into fellowship with us; the loftiest hope for human life is that we may, in answering love, enter into fellowship with Him. This is not to be found in the devotional life alone, nor in the practical life alone, but only in the perfect blend of both.

From This World and Prayer by Sister Edna Mary

CITIZENS OF TWO WORLDS

The unity of prayer and action, communion with other people and communion with God, is what underlies Brother Lawrence's recognition "That our sanctification did not depend upon changing our works, but in doing that for God's sake which we commonly do for our own . . . That the most excellent method he had found of going to God, was that of doing our common business without any view of pleasing men and (as far as we are capable) purely for the love of God. That it was a great delusion to think that times of prayer ought to differ from other times; that we are strictly obliged to adhere to God by action in time of action as by prayer in its season."

Reference has been made to Teilhard de Chardin's balance in seeing God shining through the World. Though this adoration may begin in the contemplation of creation, it reaches its climax in prostration before the risen Lord; and it is when Christ who both overcame the world and loved it perfectly, is seen as coming "clothed in the glory of the world" that the Christian can both overcome the world and serve the world. And the "glory of the world" applies both to the natural creation and to human society, both of which can be, and for many people must be, primary means of the recognition of the presence of God.

This can be seen in the lives of many saintly Christians. The most often cited is Brother Lawrence, who has expressed in famous words probably the best known statement of this principle: "The time of business does not with me differ from the time of prayer; and in the noise and clatter of my kitchen, while several persons are at the same time calling for different things, I possess God in a great tranquillity as if I were upon my knees at the Blessed Sacrament." Another less-known but more dramatic exemplar of this principle is Margaret Godolphin, as Evelyn has immortalised her for us. A young girl, longing for peace and retirement, yet bound to live in attendance at the court of Charles II, moving in that dissipated company in deep recollection, yet gay and charming, never neglecting her duties, and sought after by all for her company or her assistance at balls and masques, "seasoning even her diversions with something of religion," as Evelyn writes, "so as nothing was more agreeable than her company wherever she came . . . she made virtue and holiness a cheerful thing, lovely as herself."

Christian peace and purity (two characteristics of those in close communion with God) are neither of them negative. The peace is something which can be at the centre of intense activity and be the mainspring of that activity . . . The purity is that of the white patches in a coloured television picture, where the white is not the absence of colour but the result of the perfect blending in perfect proportion of all the colours which go to make the picture.

Fellow Workers With God *from* **The Art of Prayer:** An Orthodox Anthology

The Lord sees your need and your efforts, and will give you a helping hand. He will support and establish you as a soldier, fully armed and ready to go into battle. No support can be better than His. The greatest danger lies in the soul thinking that it can find this help within itself; then it will lose everything. Evil will dominate it again, eclipsing the light that as yet flickers but weakly in the soul, and it will extinguish the small flame which is still scarcely burning. The soul should realise how powerless it is alone; therefore, expecting nothing of itself, let it fall down in humility before God, and in its own heart recognise itself to be nothing. Then grace – which is all powerful – will, out of this nothing, create in it everything. He who in total humility puts himself in the hand of the merciful God, attracts the Lord to himself, and becomes strong in His strength.

Although expecting everything from God and nothing from ourselves, we must nevertheless force ourselves to action, exerting all our strength, so as to create something to which the divine help may come, and which the divine power may encompass. Grace is always present within us, but it will only act after man himself has acted, filling his powerlessness with its own power. Establish yourself, therefore, firmly in the humble sacrifice of your will to God, and then take action without any irresolution or half-heartedness.

The Spirit of Grace and the spirit of the Pharisee
When you undertake some special endeavour, do not concentrate your

attention and heart on it, but look upon it as something secondary; and by entire surrender to God open yourself up to God's grace, like a vessel laid out to receive it. Whoever finds grace finds it by means of faith and zeal, says St Gregory of Sinai, and not by zeal alone. However painstaking our work, so long as we omit to surrender ourselves to God while performing it, we fail to attract God's grace, and our efforts build up within us not so much a true spirit of grace but the spirit of a Pharisee. Grace is the soul of the struggle. Our efforts will be rightly directed so long as we preserve self-abasement, contrition, fear of God, devotion to Him, and the realisation of our dependence on divine help. If we are self-satisfied and contented with our efforts, it is a sign that they are not performed in the right way, or that we lack wisdom.

From **Jesus and the Word** *by* Rudolf Bultmann

THE CONJUNCTION OF THE COMMAND OF LOVE FOR NEIGHBOUR WITH THE COMMAND OF LOVE FOR GOD

A scribe came, who had heard them (Jesus and the Sadducees) arguing and noticed that Jesus had answered them well. He asked Him, What command is the first of all?

"Jesus answered, the first is this: Hear, O Israel, the Lord our God is Lord alone, and you shall love the Lord your God with all your heart and with all your soul and with all your strength. The second is this: Love your neighbour as yourself. There is no commandment greater than these."

Then the scribe said to Him, "Master, you have spoken truly; there is One, and none beside Him. And to love Him with all the heart and with all the understanding and with all the strength, and to love one's neighbour as oneself, is worth more than all burnt-offerings and other sacrifices."

And Jesus saw that he had answered intelligently, and said to him, "You are not far from the Kingdom of God."

It can and must be said that this double command wins its full significance only when it appears in connection with the preaching of Jesus. Its meaning then is this: the two commands, to love God and to love one's neighbour are not identical, so that love of neighbour would be, without anything further, love for God. This misunderstanding can arise only when neighbour-love is taken in the philanthropic sense, when an intrinsic worth, something divine, is ascribed to man. Then truly the relation to God has been lost and for it a relation to man has been substituted.

You cannot love God; very well then, love men, for in them you love God . . . No; on the contrary, the chief command is this: love God, bow your own will in obedience to God's. And this first command defines the meaning of the second – the attitude which I take towards my neighbour is determined by the attitude which I take before God; as obedience to God, setting aside my selfish will, renouncing my own claims, I stand before my neighbours as for God.

And conversely the second command determines the meaning of the first: in loving my neighbour I prove my obedience to God. There is no obedience to God in a vacuum, so to speak, no obedience separate from the concrete situation in which I stand as a man among men, no obedience which is directed immediately toward God. Whatever of kindness, pity, mercy, I show my neighbour is not something which I do for God, but something which I really do for my neighbour; the neighbour is not a sort of tool by means of which I practise the love of God, and love of neighbour cannot be practised with a look aside toward God. Rather, as I can love my neighbour only when I surrender my will completely to God's will, so I can love God only while I will what He wills, while I really love my neighbour.

From **Abba Father** *by* Evelyn Underhill

Christ whose earthly life was both a correction and a completion of human life, taught above all else, by example as well as precept, this supreme art and privilege of the borderland creature.

For Him, man was a being set in the world of succession and subject to its griefs and limitations, yet able in his prayer to move out to the very frontiers of that world, to lay hold on the Eternal and experience another level of life.

How different such a doctrine and practice were from those of His own or any other time, is shown by the demand of His Disciples who had witnessed His nights of solitary prayer in the hills: "Teach us *how* to pray". Those who asked this were good and pious Jews, who already accepted the worship of the name and practice of daily prayer as a normal part of life.

But now they realised how far beyond these orderly acts of worship and petition was that living intercourse with the living Father, which conditioned every moment of Christ's life; His link with the Unseen Reality from which He came and the source of His power in the world to which He was sent.

Here for the first time they saw prayer, not as an ordered action or a religious duty, not even as an experience; but as a vital relation between man and his wholeness and the Being of God.

Here was one who knew in the full and deep sense how to pray; and in the light of His practice, they perceived the poverty and unreality of their own.

From **The Life of the Spirit** *by* Herbert Waddams

If we chase after fulfilment and satisfaction we shall never find them: they only come as a result of doing something else which is really worth while, into which we can put our whole heart ... When we look out to God there is only one response to make to Him, that is to offer ourselves completely to Him, to surrender, to lose our life without any hidden reservations or attempts to use Him. For we can't have a relationship to God which is not based on His holiness and our position as creatures depends on Him.

This has two sides – prayer and action – prayer, our time put aside for opening our hearts and our inner selves to God; and action towards others in our everyday life. Some recent writers have suggested that prayer consists entirely in our relationship with our neighbour and that it is this alone that is important. But this is bad advice, though we must be ready to agree that any prayer which does not come out in our relations with others is no true prayer.

Prayer is not a means of escaping or withdrawing from the world but just the opposite, a means of bringing God and our vision of Him into our world. Both prayer and action are needed, they are two sides of the same coin, both affect each other.

We must see how they make up one whole, each in due proportion, for both are part and parcel of our attempt to give our whole personalities to God – and it is in these two ways that we gradually more and more do so – of course with His help.

So our time of prayer is one in which we look to and towards God, and just because of that, we acquire a deeper engagement with other people and with the world. Moreover this is not something which we produce out of our own inner resources as we realise as soon as we begin to see the facts.

The engagement with the world at a deeper level of understanding comes out of the contact which God has given us with Himself: it is in fact the action of the Spirit of God in our lives; just as the contact is the action of that Spirit within us. It is only as we share God's love and care, however feebly, that we can penetrate beneath the surface in meeting and helping others in their deepest needs ...

Our intercession can be seen to have two sides. We bring other people to God in our prayer, and they bring us. For we cannot bring them to God without coming to God ourselves. Their needs force their way into our prayer, and so they should. And in so doing they force us more persistently to turn to the source where they can alone be met, when we rest them in the calm centre of God's love ... God frees the self from itself by giving life meaning, the meaning which is His love, and it is this alone which can provide the fulfilment of the personality which He wills for each one of us ...

The man or woman who prays regularly day in and day out with absolutely nothing in the way of experience and with a feeling of uselessness much of the time, is often, perhaps always, growing in the life of the Spirit more than another who finds delight in prayer.

Why should this be? It is very simple. In the seemingly useless prayer the will is tested and strengthened; patience is instilled and built up; and in these and other ways it becomes possible to make that fuller offering of self which is the heart of prayer.

That is why regularity, persistence and self-discipline are so basic. It is not these things which themselves achieve the result, but they open our personalities to be formed by God in His own likeness as we give away to Him our self-centredness, and penetrate the mystery of love in which loss is all gain.

St Paul tells his readers to pray without ceasing, so that the attitude of prayer and of reliance on God and offering to Him becomes as permanent a part of our lives as the breathing of oxygen into our bodies. In order to reach this happy condition we have to fix times in our lives, set times which shall not be interfered with unless it is quite necessary. This little space in our lives of say 15 minutes each day is not meant to be the whole of our prayer: it is the way in for God into our lives, so that our whole lives may be suffused with the spirit of prayer. It is the means by which the rhythm of prayer becomes an integral part of the rest of our daily activities. And in giving our time in this particular way we make a gesture which is symbolic of our desire to give all our time: and indeed we do more than that, for as we have seen, we begin to do that very thing.

From **This World and Prayer** *by* Sister Edna Mary

The task of the Christian is to be deeply involved in the world, but to see the involvement always in the light of his relationship with God. There can never be two parts of his life, labelled respectively "God" and "The World", for he ought never to be able to see the one apart from the other.

St Gregory the Great is reported to have said, "As often as I go to God I am sent to men; as often as I go to men I am sent back to God"; but the unity is closer even than this swing of the pendulum. There must be the constant recognition of God as one has dealings with other people, the constant bringing of other people with one in every approach to God. The "going to men" may be of very varied kinds. For the slaves to whom St Peter wrote, and those who came after them, it meant a willing and cheerful, loving fulfilment of the duties that were imposed upon them. For many Christians today duties are still imposed, and still to be accepted in the same frame of mind as that about which St Peter wrote. For others there is a greater choice, and involvement in the world may mean the voluntary acceptance of tasks which for others are involuntary, or the acceptance of some task which is peculiarly open to them. Whether or not the task naturally is congenial makes not the slightest difference – just as St Peter emphasises that the attitude of the slave is to be the same whether his master is considerate or difficult.

Involvement means more than actual physical action, though this may be its most obvious expression. It means concern for others, and the expression of that concern in whatever ways are open. The priest who used to assert that he spoke out for the drains of the slums because he believed in Incarnation, was expressing this concern in his efforts to get the authorities to provide reasonable drainage as much as (and much more efficiently than) if he had been digging the drains himself with his own hands. For others the task is not direct social action but the analysis of the assumption on which life is based, and the effort to ensure that the voice of Christ is heard in politics, economics, social theory, and so on as well as in private life. Those who are called to prophesy may further God's will in Church and State more by the voice of their prophecy than by actual deeds.

From **Vision, Jan-Jun 1968:** *the sixth article in the series on* The Spiritual Life *by* D. E. Shapland

CONTEMPLATION, MISSION AND VOCATION

Once a soul has awoken to Christ, to its own reality as made by God for God, then two attractions are born within it, two desires begin to move its life. First, there is the desire to penetrate more deeply the mystery of this new-found relationship, to turn from all creatures and to sit at the feet of the Master, looking at Him and waiting upon Him, the desire to be utterly and completely His. Secondly, there is the desire to embrace all creation, to make the fullest possible sacrifice of self for the one purpose of bringing all others to the knowledge of that same saving mystery.

The Two Desires

Broadly speaking, we can label these two movements of the awakening soul as the desire for contemplation and the desire for mission. These two desires, however, are not experienced as two amicable yoke-fellows. On the contrary, there is at least a certain tension between them, at worst a veritable torment born of their dual polarity. Is one then to choose the one and reject the other? Or should one try to find a delicate balance between them? Is there no resolution to be hoped for? Or is a lifetime to be spent swinging forever from one to the other?

Christ alone can answer these questions for us, for in Christ alone there is unity, the unity of love.

Jesus was the contemplative, the missionary, but Jesus knew no tension, no disunity, no dual polarity of desire. He knew the agony which is born from the separation, the disunity which is sin, our sin, but that is something which He freely took to Himself. He knew no other separation. His life was a single unity within the person and purpose of the Father. His life was love. The night alone on the mountain was love, the supper party with the tax collector was love, the cleansing of the temple was love.

Contemplation and Mission are words that cannot be used meaningfully when the perfection of love is present. At this point the contemplative soul is utterly apostolic, the apostolic soul utterly contemplative. That is why the great contemplatives have been the great apostles, drawers of others to Christ; and why the great apostles have been the great contemplatives, their lives totally and solely focused upon God in Christ.

Separation and Sin

We only experience these two God-implanted desires in separation, and so know the tension between them, simply because we have not arrived at that end, that perfection of love. In other words, we only experience them as separated because we are sinful, because we live in a state of separation – separation, disunity, from God, from our true selves, and from one another.

This side of sanctity, Christ-likeness, then, and all the way of the approach to sanctity, the way of dying to fallen self, we shall feel the pull and the pain between them.

But if that is so, if the tension is only fully and finally resolved at the point of sanctity, it is yet also true that the tension is ever more consistently contained, resolved, as we grow in union with our Lord.

One Way but Many Paths

To bring about such growth requires but one thing from our side, that we should "stay awake" to Jesus. "What I say to you I say to all, stay awake." This is the basic and unifying principle of inner order, the fundamental attitude of spiritual life, and the one way of continuing in the Way which is Christ. Vigilance, attention, watching, the heart of man constantly turned to God in Jesus.

It is only as we stay awake to Christ like that, that vocation becomes clear at all. Vocation, both in the general sense of an overall pattern of life, and vocation in the detailed sense of the daily, hourly, minute by minute, ordering of life.

God draws the vigilant soul to that particular life, the life which embraces those two basic desires of the soul in a particular way, so that He can use those very desires to bring the soul to purity of heart and so assimilate it utterly to His re-creating work in Christ.

Many Paths but One Goal

That is why there are such varieties in the balance of actual contemplation and mission in different vocations, and at different periods within a particular vocation. For God alone knows how best the soul can be drawn to purity and sanctity and how best the soul can sanctify others. Vocation in every sense, is God's concern not ours.

Stay awake, that is our concern. "Stay awake." Then no matter where we start from, no matter what particular path He calls us along, what different terrains that path traverses, He will bring us to that contemplative apostolate, that spiritual paternity, which is everything. We shall become all love, one unity with the energy of God which embraces all men, all creation.

John Burns
They never sought in vain that sought the Lord aright.

From **The Call to the Religious Life** *by* Sister Edna Mary

The Christian life in any form cannot be understood without this tension between the this-worldly and the other-worldly, between what the Christian already is and what he is becoming, between the present lived as the eternal "now" of God and the present as anticipation of the final consummation.

And if the Christian life cannot be understood without these dualities much less can the religious life.

This is why it is impossible to make sense of the religious life in terms of this world.

The primary task of religious life is the service of God through the offering to him of liturgical worship in the name of the whole Church and the whole world. If prayer has any place in the Christian life – and even for the most secularised of Christians today it is hard to imagine what could be meant by the Christian life without prayer – then the place of the religious life within the Church must be judged by this corporate life of prayer lived by religious not only as the means of their own sanctification but as their specific task within the Church. If the doctrine of the body of Christ is taken seriously and due significance given to the variety of tasks within the body, none more important than another, then the religious life can be seen as one of these tasks, complementing others and complemented by them. For everyone there is prayer and other activity, but the relationship of these two sides of the Christian life will vary from individual to individual.

There will be many within the body who, if they are doing the tasks to which they have been called, will have little time for the conscious offering of prayer and worship to God; and it is because this is so (and should be so – such active lives are not a second best but just as valid a vocation within the whole body) that religious are pledged to the offering of this worship on behalf of those who may not be able to spend on it the time they would wish.

From **The Call to the Religious Life** *by* Sister Edna Mary

More important than the expectation is the anticipation, for to the religious heaven is not merely something future but a present reality – as it should be to every Christian who has meditated on St John's Gospel or understood what is meant by the baptismal life.

What does this mean? It certainly does not mean that religious contract out of their responsibility to "the present age", to the world in which they live. Like any other Christian they are caught between the two ages and feel the tension of their double loyalty.

But the very form of their life is a foreshadowing of the life of heaven, and this in several ways. First of all, it is primarily a life of worship, and the life of heaven can only be expressed in terms of sheer worship and adoration. For all Christians on earth, prayer (liturgical and private) and other forms of work have to alternate; but the religious life is so planned that worship has obviously and explicitly that priority which in principle it has in all Christian life, and therefore there is the constant reminder that this is the eternal element of life, which continues when other needs which have to be met on earth have ended. This is the point of the Mary and Martha episode in Luke 10:39-42. Some have seen this as a justification for regarding the contemplative as a higher form of life than the active. But Augustine saw in this story (as in that of Rachel and Leah) a parable of the two forms of life, neither of which is more meritorious than the other: the active, fruitful in good works; and the contemplative, sterile unless it bears fruit in other souls, but commended by Christ because to sit at His feet and listen to Him is the life of heaven begun on earth, and therefore is the "good part" which Mary chose and which would not be taken away. Martha's works of mercy are necessary in our human state, and most Christians must be prepared to leave their prayers and contemplation and answer the call to active works; but the need for these works will disappear, there will be no hungry to feed or bereaved to comfort in heaven – whereas Mary's part will continue. The allocation of time between prayer and other works varies for different Christians according to their vocation, and varies even within the religious life; but for all it is the life of prayer which is primary as being the anticipation of the life of heaven and carried over unbroken into that life. And the structure of the religious life makes this primacy clear.

Advent Letter to members of the Watchers' and Workers' Society
from Mark Meynell

Jesus is the revelation of God.

The same Jesus appears to shepherds and to wise men, but the way of each to Him was different. The Shepherds found Him without looking, the wise men found Him by looking. To each his way, but it is Our Lord alone who is common to all.

The sequel to Revelation is vocation, which is the theme of this letter. What I say can, I think, be understood for both. My first point is its surprise. It either finds you when you did not know it existed; or you are filled with such restlessness, where you are, that you begin to look around for something that satisfies. We learn to choose the good by learning to refuse the bad. The search for Jesus is long and arduous, whichever way we are called to Him, and there are no short cuts. But His discovery is pure surprise, for He is unimaginable.

Surprising, too, is vocation.

A sense of vocation is sometimes inhibited by a mental barrier, which we are either encouraged to build or which we have allowed to be built in our own mind. I may know my education to be limited and my gifts few. The thought of God wanting me to come into an intimate working relationship with Him simply does not occur to me, because it seems both ludicrous and impossible. That it is neither comes as a shock, which forces us to look at Jesus, in order to discover His mind and His will for our lives. This is the whole point. With God nothing is impossible.

Let all the people of God hold to this faith for the world today greatly needs the shock of faith.

The second point is its marvel.

I do not think that it matters very much to what specific position and work within the Body of Christ, God is calling us. Whether it be to a life of prayer, of service, of suffering, or of priesthood, He is calling us to Himself – to a deeper knowledge, a deeper love, a deeper sacrifice. We must get and keep this straight. Self-importance dislikes it, as does impatience, but it is the truth. Here again we find a mental barrier which must be overcome. Let there be in our minds neither limit nor ceiling to what faith sees in Jesus. Jesus in whose presence we are, is "the wonderful Counsellor, the mighty God, the everlasting Father, the Prince of Peace". Give Him a bit of credit. Look at Him. Listen to Him. Let His majesty silence you. "Whatever He says to you, do it." In His light we see light, which includes the way in which He is calling us to follow Him. So let us be still and know that He is God.

Have you ever thought that Jesus in the manger, Jesus on the Cross, Jesus in the Eucharist, is where He Himself is still? At all other times He is on His way. We have our work cut out to follow Him. Make no mistake, Jesus is very hard indeed to follow. But here we have Him. Here He lets us catch up with Him. Here He is still. And He is here in stillness, in beauty, in the love of humanity, and in peace. Jesus – Saviour – Our Lord and Our God – The Beloved. Let us never ever lose the sense of marvel at the presence of God in the person of Jesus. Let us contrive, mentally at least, always to be in it. Never to be without it. May God give you this grace.

The third is its security. The security of revelation is expressed in the great Pauline phrase "Our life is hidden with Christ in God." The security of vocation is simply the doing of what God wants us to be doing, where He wants us to be doing it, and in the way He wants us to be doing it. This can be thought of in a high or low way. The high way is that this status and function is where I as a cell in Christ's body can be doing the greatest good. The low way is to think of it as where I can be doing the least harm. Of course my vocation, my calling, my life, my business, my work, my place is tied up with my salvation – which is perhaps only a big and religious word for security. Look at it like this. There is no safety outside my place. I am safe – eternally safe, that is – only when I am doing my job, in my place. This is vocation.

Conversely, therefore, there is no safety in doing what I ought not, however good it is, wherever I should not be, however attractive it is. Believe me, this business of vocation is no matter for the playboy. If you are such get out. Equally there is danger in forcing the issue of vocation because of the intensity of our desire for it. We must beware of this. God is not mocked. Vocation is a matter in which neither resistance, nor desire can be allowed to sway the judgement. My judgement in all things must give place to Christ, for it is in Him and in Him alone that God calls us to Himself and to His work. May His will be done. Speaking for myself it is the low road that I must walk, the way in which I can do the least evil. Evil is that which destroys others as well as myself. We can use two great vocational clauses of the Lord's Prayer – "Lead us not into temptation but deliver us from evil."

God forbid that I or any other of His sons or daughters should seek anything of or for themselves. His name, His Kingdom, and His will are what I want. We must look to Him to supply the meat, medicine and the mind, for all to do it.

It Takes Two To Make Prayer *by* Eva Pinthus (Quaker Publication)

There are innumerable definitions of prayer, but all imply a dialogue. One of the problems of modern man living in a technological era is: with whom does one have a dialogue? It is not really a question of to whom do I pray, but *with* whom do I pray, with whom do I hold the dialogue, who confronts me? Leo Baeck would say that in prayer every individual encounters "his people", and the people encounter every individual; life encounters itself. Such meeting is the deepest and most intrinsic sense of prayer, it is much more than self-recognition. One begins by learning to understand oneself and is then enabled to cope with the pattern of the day. In prayer one holds a dialogue with life and is enabled to cope with it.

The first stage of prayer, then, is self-knowledge. One faces oneself as one really is, with all one's shortcomings. One ceases to pull the wool over one's own eyes. In contact with other people, most of us try to give a good impression; we hide our dark sides, often so successfully that we cease to be aware of them. Prayer at its lowest, in the stages of its infancy, is akin to depth psychology, to acquiring real self-knowledge; and we do this by matching ourselves against life, against him who has the fullness of life, against him who was and is most fully man: for the Christian this is Jesus Christ. There emerges then gradually not only self-knowledge, not • only the recognition of one's weaknesses, the relationships one has broken, the situations one cannot cope with, but also the Other who shows one the way out, the way of humility to mend relationships, the reality of the situation which seems impossible and the strength and the power to find a way through which is consistent with the life of the Other.

The Christian in the prayer dialogue is confronted by three different but related realities. First and foremost he is confronted by the Infinite, the Ultimate, that which is beyond him. He who Is – God, the depth of being, that which embraces, that which upholds, which is above and below and round about. To the Christian this reality is the Father of our Lord Jesus Christ, because the little we know of God is that which has been revealed to us by the law and the prophets, the life, teaching, death and resurrection of Jesus. He referred to this reality as our Father, indicating thereby that this infinite, wholly other is nevertheless someone with whom one can have a relationship, with whom one can have a dialogue and who cares to the uttermost, even if I crucify him, as most of us do in our loveless way. He is the only one who will not let me go, never mind what I do; who loves and suffers with me; who knows my shame before even I become aware of it, so that I need not hide it. He knows already and forgives it as soon as I am willing to acknowledge it to myself.

He is *our* Father, not only mine; and so we come to the second reality that confronts us in prayer: "my people". To begin with my people may be only those nearest and dearest to me, but as in the dialogue understanding grows, so the concept of my people grows. God is our Father; we, all of us, all human beings are his children, my people. All human beings, indeed all creation, past, present and as yet unborn are my people, and in prayer they confront me. Their hopes and fears and needs, loves and hates stand over against me, and ask me where do I stand? What have I done to alleviate some of the suffering in the world? Am I treating others as fully personal, as a Thou, or are they merely there for my convenience, are they so many Its which I pass by on the other side as of no concern to me? Am I willing to take up my priestly office on their behalf and mediate for them before the Father who is mine and theirs? Am I willing conversely to mediate the Father to them, to enter into their joys and fears, hopes and pains? What have I done to ease their lot or confront them with the challenge to cease from oppression? Mediation is a two-way traffic: on behalf of my people, but also on behalf of God. This involves us not only in giving succour but also in confronting others with the will of God for his people. From this it follows that meaningful prayer is bound to be followed by action.

This leads straight on to the third reality that confronts me in prayer: the wholeness of life in general and my little bit of life in particular. Here one examines one's job, one's political allegiances, one's use of money and resources, one's use of time, pleasure and leisure, one's contribution to life. As one's comprehension of the Other grows, as one's relationship with God deepens, so one's role in life may change, one's allegiances and obligations alter. What may be the right course of action today, may be wrong next year or in ten years' time. Prayer ensures that one's life remains flexible in its response to the larger life in which we are set.

How does all this work out in practice? Here each individual must find his own path, another can only give guidelines which may be helpful to some and not to others. This is why prayer manuals may be congenial to some and anathema to others. There is no one way, only many different paths.

I find it worth while spending time recollecting with whom I am holding the dialogue. I do this when I walk the dog and drive the car, when washing up or with any other task that does not really require the whole of my mind. I do this many times a day. For many set times and places are helpful, for discipline is required in the matter of prayer. But discipline is much easier to achieve in community and when left to myself I rarely use a set time except Sunday morning meeting. I recollect his presence and often get lost in the wonder, awe and amazement – "hallowed be thy name". I thank him for beautiful things I can see and the eyesight I still have to see with, for lovely things to hear and the hearing I have been given, the upbringing that gave me perception, the strange thing of the thrill of touch, in fact anything I happen to be thankful about, not least his presence when I am truly conscious of him, which is not always. I examine myself, try to be honest and not to make excuses for my sins. I ask for strength to control my evil impulses, for being shown the way to make amends where I have done wrong and for humility to act as I ought.

This has already made me conscious before God of "my people". I bring him all those I know in need, asking what I can do to help, which practically for instance may mean writing innumerable letters; to me, letter writing is often a form of intercession and an upholding of people, for in writing I remember an individual before God. Intercession inevitably implies action not just talking, so one is confronted by the totality of life and looks at its demands together with God.

Thus prayer becomes the daily unifying factor in one's life. It is a stillness that leads to intense activity, it is contemplation which must lead to action if prayer is not to be hypnotic, a selfish preoccupation with oneself. It is that which integrates the individual, reconciles him to himself, to his people, to life in this world and finally to the ground of being which is God.

From **Readings from St John's Gospel** *by* William Temple

The gift of God cannot be received to be merely enjoyed. It must always be shared. Its very nature involves that; for it is Himself, His own Spirit, the Spirit of Love. To receive that does not mean to enjoy the knowledge that God loves us. It means that His active love is present in our hearts; and if so it must go out to others. If we are not sharing with others the gift of God, that is proof that we have not received it.

From the **Bhagavad Gita,** *quoted in* **Mysticism** *by* F. C. Happold

The world is imprisoned in its own activity, except when actions are performed as worship of God. Therefore you must perform every action sacramentally, and be free from all attachment to results.

> *In the beginning*
> *The Lord of beings*
> *Created all men*
> *To each his duty.*
> *"Do this" he said*
> *"And you shall prosper.*
> *Duty well done*
> *Fulfils desire."*

The ignorant work
For the fruit of their action:
The wise must work also
Without desire
Pointing man's feet
To the path of his duty.
Let the wise beware
Lest they bewilder
The minds of the ignorant
Hungry for action:
Let them show by example
How work is holy
When the heart of the worker
Is fixed on the Highest.

Seer and leader,
Provider and server:
Each has the duty
Ordained by his nature
Born of the gunas.

The seer's duty
Ordained by his nature,
Is to be tranquil
In mind and in spirit,
Self-controlled,
Austere and stainless,
Upright, forbearing;
To follow wisdom,
To know the Atman,
Firm in faith
In the truth that is Brahman.

The leader's duty,
Ordained by his nature,
Is to be bold,
Unflinching and fearless,
Subtle of skill
And open-handed,
Great-hearted in battle,
A resolute ruler.

Others are born
To the tasks of providing:

These are the traders,
The cultivators,
The breeders of cattle,
To work for all men,
Such is the duty
Ordained for the servers:
This is their nature.

All mankind
Is born for perfection;
And each shall attain it
Will he but follow
His nature's duty.

From **The Sufi Path of Love,** *quoted in* **Mysticism** *by* F. C. Happold

THE VISION OF GOD IN EVERYTHING

In the market, in the cloister – only God I saw.
In the valley and on the mountain – only God I saw.
Him I have seen beside me oft in tribulation;
In favour and in fortune – only God I saw.
In prayer and fasting, in praise and contemplation,
In the religion of the Prophet – only God I saw.
Neither soul or body, accident nor substance,
Qualities nor causes – only God I saw.
I opened mine eyes and by the light of His face around me
In all the eye discovered – only God I saw.
Like a candle I was melting in his fire:
Amidst the flames outflanking – only God I saw.
Myself with mine own eyes I saw most clearly,
But when I looked with God's eyes – only God I saw.
I passed away into nothingness, I vanished,
And lo, I was the All-living – only God I saw.

by Baba Kubi of Shiraz,
trans. by R. A. Nicholson

From **The Prophet** *by* Kahlil Gibran

And an old priest said, Speak to us of Religion. And he said:
Have I spoken this day of aught else?
Is not religion all deed and all reflection,
And that which is neither deed nor reflection, but a wonder and a surprise ever springing in the soul, even while the hands hew the stone or tend the loom?

Who can separate his faith from his actions, or his belief from his occupations?

Who can spread his hours before him, saying, "This for God and this for myself; This for my soul and this other for my body"?

All your hours are wings that beat through space from self to self.

He who wears his morality but as his best garment were better naked.

The wind and the sun will tear no holes in his skin.

And he who defines his conduct by ethics imprisons his song-bird in a cage.

The freest song comes not through bars and wires.

And he to whom worshipping is a window, to open but also to shut, has not yet visited the house of his soul whose windows are from dawn to dawn.

Your daily life is your temple and your religion.

Whenever you enter into it take with you your all.

Take the plough and the forge and the mallet and the lute.

The things you have fashioned in necessity or for delight.

For in reverie you cannot rise above your achievements nor fall lower than your failures.

And take with you all men:

For in adoration you cannot fly higher than their hopes nor humble yourself lower than their despair.

And if you would know God, be not therefore a solver of riddles.

Rather look about you and you shall see Him playing with your children.

And look into space; you shall see Him walking in the cloud, outstretching His arms in the lightning and descending in rain.

You shall see Him smiling in flowers, then rising and waving His hands in trees.

8

On Suffering

"He who suffers most has most to give"

---

2 Corinthians 1:3-7

Source Unknown. "He who has found his soul's life in God is happy"

Revelation 22:1-2

From **The True Wilderness** *by* H. A. Williams. Christ's sufferings

St Francis of Assisi. Praised be my Lord for all who pardon

From **Jesus, a Dialogue with the Saviour** *by* Father Lev

From **The True Wilderness** *by* H. A. Williams. Happiness and misery experienced for mankind

From **Living Prayer** *by* Metropolitan Anthony Bloom. One life and one death

A Prayer for Fellowship in the Cross *from* **The Book of Prayer for Students**

From **Palm Sunday to Easter** *by* William Temple. CREATIVE SUFFERING

Poem *by* C. L. Drawbridge, *taken from* **The Mystery of Suffering** *by* Hugh Evan Hopkins

Teilhard de Chardin *from* **Teilhard de Chardin: Pilgrim of the Future** *edited by* Neville Braybrooke. *Trans. by* Noel Lindsay. THE MEANING AND CONSTRUCTIVE VALUE OF SUFFERING

From **The Spirit of Discipline** *by* Francis Paget

Poem *by* A. E. Hamilton, *taken from* **Christ in Isaiah** *by* F. B. Meyer. COMFORT YE, COMFORT YE

Matthew 26:40

From **Jesus, a Dialogue with the Saviour** *by* Father Lev

From **The Bible Reading Fellowship.** O God, who knowest the needs of every heart

From **Freedom, Faith and the Future** *by* Archbishop Michael Ramsey. FAITH

From **The Use of Praying** *by* Neville Ward. SUFFERING

From **The Sermon in the Hospital** *by* Eleanor Hamilton King. FACING PAIN

From **The Sermon in the Hospital.** THE TOUCH. THE END

My God, My God, Why Hast Thou Forsaken Me? *by* E. B.

From **Markings** *by* Dag Hammarskjöld

From **Five for Sorrow Ten for Joy** *by* J. Neville Ward

From **Christ Our Priest** *by* C. R. Bryant, S.S.J.E.

From **The Times.** The Society of Compassionate Friends

The Healing *by* Virginia Thesiger

Prayer: We beseech Thee O Lord, remember all for good

From **Edges of His Ways** *by* Amy Carmichael. Before the winds that blow do cease

From **A Child Possessed** *by* R. C. Hutchinson

The Inviolate Soul *by* Leslie D. Weatherhead, *taken from* **Time for God**

From **Five for Sorrow Ten for Joy** *by* J. Neville Ward

From the **Chhandogya Upanishad,** *quoted in* **Mysticism** *by* F. C. Happold

---

2 Corinthians 1:3-7

Praise be to the God and Father of our Lord Jesus Christ, the all-merciful Father, the God whose consolation never fails us. He comforts us in all our troubles, so that we in turn may be able to comfort others in any trouble of theirs and to share with them the consolation we ourselves receive from God. As Christ's cup of suffering overflows, and we suffer with Him, so also through Christ our consolation overflows. If distress be our lot, it is the price we pay for your consolation, for your salvation; if our lot be consolation, it is to help us to bring you comfort, and strength to face with fortitude the same sufferings we now endure. And our hope for you is firmly grounded; for we know that if you have part in the suffering, you have part also in the divine consolation.

Source Unknown

But he who has found his soul's life in God is happy, not in truth with perfect happiness, that is not granted to men in this world, but a foretaste thereof. He has a secret joy which is beyond the realms of temptation, unrest and sorrow, a quiet confidence and steadfastness which abide even while the waves and storms of life sweep over him.

God has promised not that he shall be free from crosses, rather do they form the ladder by which the soul mounts upwards, but that He will abide with His faithful servant through them all, and be his rock, his castle, his strong foundation.

Revelation 22:1-2

And he showed me a pure river of water of life, clear as crystal, proceeding out of the throne of God and of the Lamb. In the midst of the street of it, and on either side of the river, was there the tree of life, which bare twelve manner of fruits and yielded her fruit every month: and the leaves of the tree were for the healing of the nations.

From **The True Wilderness** *by* H. A. Williams

In page after page of the New Testament we are told that in so far as we share in Christ's sufferings we are made partakers here and now of His resurrection. This is the great and glorious paradox of Christian experience: that it is by dying that we live, that it is by sharing with Jesus the horror of His agony that we live with Him reigning indestructibly in peace. Once we are willing to see and feel the desert in which we live, the desert becomes fertile, bringing forth every tree whose fruit shall be for meat and the leaf thereof for healing. Once we know that we are poor, the Kingdom of Heaven is ours. So when our lot is cast with somebody who is finding his cross, his desert, his poverty overwhelming, we are on holy ground. For it is precisely here that God is present to save, to save us as well as them. So our identification with the other person brings to our lives and to theirs the power, the joy, the victory which is already ours and all mankind's in Christ Jesus our Lord.

That, I believe is the message which our age is waiting to hear – a realistic recognition of suffering and evil in the universe, not trying apologetically to pretend that things are better than they are, together with the first-hand affirmation of this suffering and evil as the place where the Son of Man is glorified and with Him all mankind.

St Francis of Assisi

Praised be my Lord for all who pardon one another for love's sake, and who endure weakness and tribulation; blessed are they who peacefully shall endure, for Thou, oh most high, will give them a crown.

From **Jesus, A Dialogue with the Saviour** *by* Father Lev

The Saviour takes possession of the souls of those who love Him, and He does so with all His might, because these souls were once able to open their hearts to more hostile influences. O souls whom the devils have possessed, take courage. If among the Saviour's words, I had to choose one of them, only one, which could sum up for unbelievers all the good news, I would choose without hesitation these words: "Come to Me all you who labour and are burdened, and I will refresh you." Would you call this simply humanism? No, because it is a question of seeing who dares to speak in such a way. This text really says everything. It is a call directed at all the suffering in the world, at all those whom evil weighs down. This is the proclamation of a person – Christ – that He is Himself the remedy. The only remedy for men's suffering. Would a man who is only a man say these things? These are the gifts of the liberator of all who come to Him; comfort, consolation and rest.

All the truths of divine revelation are not explicitly formulated in these words but all of them are found there implicitly in germ. My Saviour I see the vast suffering mass of people crushed to the ground; I see the mass stretch forth its arms towards You, crawl along, get up, try to go on towards You, groping, tottering. You are drawing them without their knowing You. In You they have a foreboding of the one who cures, who consoles, who pardons.

From **The True Wilderness** *by* H. A. Williams

In all works of love which we do and in all works of love which we receive, there is God Himself creating harmony. And the work of love includes attitude – the atmosphere created by a person's outlook. The work of God's love in redemption thus goes on through the medium of the accepting community . . .

I want to end by speaking of something which I find very hard to put into words. In so far as we live for others – I am aware of how little I myself do – but in so far as we live for others, we do so not only by our actions and attitudes, but also by (what is inseparable from them) our interior state, what we are and what we experience most deeply inside us. The happiness and misery which come to us, the exulting and the agony, we experience as in individuals alone. But they are not for us alone. They are for mankind. When we thank God in our joy or cry to Him in our pain, we articulate the prayers of the World – prayers which for this reason or that, perhaps cannot be articulated in some hearts. So we find ourselves offering our joy or our pain to God to be used to help others. There have been periods in my life – and it must also be true of all of us here – periods of black despair when the only thing that we could do with our distress was to ask God however half-heartedly and fitfully to use it to bring light and peace to others. After all Christ has called us, invited us to share His cross. And this doesn't mean merely putting up with it. It means offering it for the salvation of souls. These are extreme moments. But we can do much the same when we are on a more even keel. Talking to people in a pub or at supper we find their most hidden desires for goodness and love revealed beneath the surface of what they say. It may simply be a chance remark or an immediately forgotten exclamation. But they show what the person is feeling after, and in our own hearts, as we continue the conversation, we can seize upon this desire of theirs (hidden to a large extent even from themselves) and articulate it in a silent movement of our heart to God; for it is Christ in them, the hope of glory. It is revelation of God at work redeeming. It owes nothing to our words or deeds, so the prayer is really an act of worship for God's own goodness and love thus manifested in those we are talking with. It is another way in which we are allowed to participate in the redemptive process.

From **Living Prayer** by Metropolitan Anthony Bloom

But to share with Christ His passion, His crucifixion, His death, means to accept unreservedly all these events, in the same spirit as He did, that is to accept them in an act of free will, to suffer together with the Man of Sorrows, to be there in silence, the very silence of Christ, interrupted only by a few decisive words, the silence of real communion; not just the silence of pity, but of compassion which allows us to grow into a complete oneness with the other so that there is no longer one and the other, but only one life and one death.

A Prayer for Fellowship in the Cross *from* The Book of Prayer for Students

Almighty God, who hast shewn us in the life and teaching of thy Son the true way of blessedness, thou hast also shewn in His suffering and death that the path of love may be a crown of thorns.

Give us grace to learn these hard lessons. May we take up our cross and follow Christ in the strength of patience and the constancy of faith; and may we have such fellowship with Him in His sorrow that we may know the secret of His strength and peace, and see even in our darkest hour of trial and anguish the shining of the eternal light.

From **Palm Sunday to Easter** by William Temple

CREATIVE SUFFERING

What is the meaning of pain? How does it find a place in a world created by a loving God? If we are to face that tormenting question as Christians we must take care that we are not prejudiced by our natural attitude to pain. For we naturally tend to think of it as the first, if not the worst of evils. In recent discussion of the problem of evil, suffering has bulked larger than sin. But here at the foot of the Cross, we learn once for all that pain – agonising pain – may find a place in the perfect life. It did have place there. But no sin has any place there – no form of selfishness, whether hatred, lust or greed. The perfect life and death were sinless; they were not painless.

On the contrary, the pain directly contributed to the perfection of the life and death. It was in the endurance of the pain that the supreme courage was perfected. Take away pain from life, and you take heroism with it: the result is to make life poorer not richer. Of course this truth must never be made an excuse for lack of sympathy towards sufferers; we must relieve them if we can; so we show love – the very best thing in life. But here paradoxically is another justification of pain. It is the chief occasion of sympathy. Our hearts are not easily drawn to others by their joy or their laughter, their virtue or their talents; but pain claims sympathy wherever it occurs. It is the great binder of hearts. And sympathy being a form of love, is so precious that the cost of pain is not worthy to be compared with it.

We see how false our standards are when we reflect how much of our perplexity about pain is due to the suffering of the innocent. The assumption is that pain is at all costs to be avoided and averted unless it comes as a just penalty for wrong-doing. But this ignores the refining power of pain for those who accept it in gentleness and love. Observations show that the pain either purifies or coarsens the character, according to the degree of its development towards selfishness. From a Christian stand-point it is harder to justify the pain that coarsens a brutal character, than the pain which comes to an innocent sufferer and is used as the material of spiritual growth. For there is no unselfishness so great as the unselfish endurance of pain; and when it is so used it becomes something for which the sufferer gives thanks.

The world is full of pain today; each of us has a share; for some it is but a slight burden, for others it is crushing. But every Christian can turn it into a blessing if he will seek the companionship of Christ in his suffering; then the pain becomes a new point of fellowship with Christ; and even our suffering becomes part of the price of the world's redemption as we fill up what is left over of the suffering of Christ.

Pain does not then cease to be pain; but it ceases to be barren pain; and with fellowship with Christ upon the Cross we find new strength for bearing it and even making it the means by which our hearts are more fully cleansed of selfishness and grow towards perfect love.

Poem *by* C. L. Drawbridge, *taken from* **The Mystery of Suffering** *by* Hugh Evan Hopkins

> *The cry of earth's anguish went up unto God,*
> *Lord, take away pain!*
> *The shadow that darkens the world Thou hast made;*
> *The close coiling chain*
> *That strangles the heart; the burden that weighs*
> *On the wings that would soar.*

> Lord take away pain from the world Thou hast made,
> That it loves Thee the more!
>
> Then answered the Lord to the world He had made
> Shall I take away pain;
> And with it the power of the soul to endure,
> Made strong by the strain?
> Shall I take away pity, that knits heart to heart,
> And sacrifice high?
> Will you lose all your heroes that lift from the flame
> White brows to the sky?
> Shall I take away love that redeems with a price?
> And smiles through the loss?
> Can ye spare from the lives that would climb unto mine
> The Christ on His Cross?

Teilhard de Chardin *from* **Teilhard de Chardin: Pilgrim of the Future**
edited by Neville Braybrooke. *Trans. by* Noel Lindsay

THE MEANING AND CONSTRUCTIVE VALUE OF SUFFERING

Illness, by its very nature, tends to give those who suffer from it the impression that they are no use, or even that they are a burden on the face of the earth. A sick man is almost inevitably bound to feel that, in the main stream of life, he is by sheer misfortune, set apart from all the endeavour and all the stir; his condition seems to have no sense; in the midst of universal action it seems to doom him to inaction.

The object of the following reflections is to try to dispel these saddening thoughts by showing, from a tenable point of view, the place and efficacy of suffering in building the world, even the visible world itself.

First and foremost, the world is still building.

That is the basic truth which must be grasped at the outset and assimilated so thoroughly that it becomes part of the very habit and nature of thought. At first sight we might be tempted to think that created beings and their destinies are dispersed at random, or at any rate arbitrarily, over the face of the earth. We could almost believe that each one of us might equally well have been born earlier or later, here or there, richer or poorer, as though the universe from start to finish of its history were some vast pleasure garden in time and space, in which the gardener could change the flowers about at his own sweet will. But ideas of this kind will not hold water. The more we reflect, in the light of the lessons to be learned from science, philosophy and religion, each in its own sphere, the more we realise that the world is to be likened, not to a gathering of individual elements assembled with art, but rather to some organic system, animated by a broad movement of growth, special to itself. Over the centuries an all-embracing plan seems in truth to be unfolding around us. Something is afoot in the universe, some issue is at stake, which cannot be better described than as a process of gestation and birth: the birth of the spiritual reality formed by the souls of men and by the matter which they bear along with them laboriously, through the medium and by virtue of human activity; the new earth is gathering its forces, emerging and purifying itself. No. We are not like the blooms in a bunch of flowers, but rather the leaves and blossoms of some great tree on which all things appear in due season and due place, in time and at the behest of the All.

It may be thought that this conception of the world in a state of growth is ingenious but abstract. In fact it has immediate practical consequences, since its whole tendency is to give new strength to our mental concept, either of the value of the individual human effort (enhanced by all the universal labour with which it is united) or (and this is all that concerns us here) of the price of individual suffering. Let us expand this point a little, bearing in mind the comparison between the tree and the bunch of flowers.

In a bunch of flowers it would be surprising to find imperfect or sickly blooms, because they have been picked one by one and assembled with art. On a tree, by contrast, which has had to fight the internal hazards of its own growth, and the external hazards of rough weather, the broken branches, the bruised blossoms and the shrivelled, sickly or faded flowers are in their rightful place; they reflect the amount of difficulty which the trunk which bears them has undergone before attaining its growth. Similarly, in a universe where every created being formed a small self-contained whole, willed for its own sake and theoretically transposable at will, we should find some difficulty in justifying in our own minds the presence of individuals painfully cut short in their possibilities and their upward flight. Why this pointless inequality, these meaningless restrictions?

... In contrast, if the world really represents a conquest still under way, if at our birth we are really thrown into the thick of the battle, then we can well understand that, for the success of the universal effort, in which we are at the same time the partners and the stake, pain in inevitable. The world looked at empirically on our scale, is an immense groping, an immense search, an immense attack, it can only progress at the cost of many failures and many casualties. The sufferers, whatever the nature of their suffering, are the reflection of this austere but noble condition. They are not useless and diminished elements. They are merely those who pay the price of the universal progress and triumph. They are the ones who have fallen on the field of honour.

Let us go a little deeper. In the entity formed by mankind as a whole, and subordinate to Christ in the "Mystical body" there are, as St Paul tells us, different functions, different members. What member can we conceive to be more especially charged with sublimating and spiritualising the labour of progress and conquest. The contemplatives and those who pray, no doubt. But also very certainly the sick and suffering. By their nature, by their complexion, the sufferers find themselves as it were driven out of themselves, forced to emigrate into the present forms of life. Are they not therefore, by the very fact, predestined and elected for the task of elevating the world above and beyond immediate enjoyment toward an ever more lofty light? It is their part to tend toward the divine more explicitly and with greater purity than the rest. It is their part to give breath to their brothers who labour like miners in the depth of matter. Thus it is exactly those who bear in their enfeebled bodies the weight of the moving world, who find themselves, by the just dispensation of providence the most active factor in that very progress which seems to sacrifice and shatter them.

If this assessment is right, the sick man, in his apparent inaction, is faced with a most noble human task. No doubt he must never cease seeking betterment or cure with all his might. No doubt he must employ his remaining strength in the various forms of work which are still open to him, sometimes very fruitful. It goes without saying that Christian resignation is the very converse of capitulation. But once this amount of resistance to evil is secured, the sick man should understand that, to the very extent of his sickness, he has a special task to fulfil in which no-one else can take his place – namely, to co-operate in the transformation (it might be called the conversion) of human suffering.

What a vast ocean of human suffering is represented by the whole of the suffering on earth at any moment! But what makes up that suffering? Blackness, deficiency, waste? No! We repeat, but rather potential energy. In suffering is concealed, with extreme intensity, the world's power of ascension. The whole problem is to liberate it by making it conscious of what it means and what it can achieve. What a leap forward the world would make toward God if all sick people at the same time converted their pain into a common desire that the reign of God should rapidly mature through the conquest and organisation of the earth. All the sufferers on earth uniting their suffering so that the world's pain became a great and unique act of conscience – would not that be one of the highest forms which the mysterious work of creation could take in our eyes?

And is it not exactly for that reason that creation, in the eyes of the Christian, is consummated in the Passion of Jesus? – We are perhaps apt to see nothing more on the Cross than individual suffering and expiation. The creative force of that death eludes us. If we looked with a larger view we should see that the Cross is the symbol and the focus of an action whose intensity is inexpressible. Even from an earthly point of view, fully understood, Jesus crucified is not outcast or defeated. He is on the contrary the One who bears the weight and bears always higher toward God, the progress of the universal advance. Let us do likewise, that we may be united with Him all the days of our life.

From **The Spirit of Discipline** by Francis Paget

Surely it has been the secret of some of the highest, noblest lives that have helped the world, that men have refused to make allowances for themselves; refused to limit their aspirations and effort by the disadvantages with which they started: refused to take the easy tasks which their hindrances might seem to justify or to draw premature boundaries to the power of their will.

As their are some men to whom the things that should have been for their wealth are, indeed, an occasion for falling, so there are others to whom the things that might have been for their hindrance, are an occasion of rising: who going through the vale of misery use it for a well, and the pools are filled with water: "And they shall go from strength to strength – in all things more than conquerors through Him that loveth them: wresting out of the very difficulties of life a more acceptable and glorious sacrifice to lift to Him: welcoming and sanctifying the very hindrances that beset them as the conditions of that part which they, perhaps, alone can bear in the perfection of His Saints, in the edifying of the Body of Christ.

And in that day when every man's work shall be made manifest, it may be found, perhaps, that none have done Him better service than some of those who, all through this life, have been His ambassadors in bonds.

Poem by A. E. Hamilton, *taken from* **Christ in Isaiah** by F. B. Meyer

COMFORT YE, COMFORT YE

> *Ask God to give thee skill*
> *In comfort's art;*
> *That thou mayst consecrated be*
> *And set apart,*
> *Into a life of sympathy.*
> *For heavy is the weight of ill*
> *In every heart;*
> *And comforters are needed much*
> *Of Christlike touch.*

Matthew 26:40

Verily I say unto you. Inasmuch as ye have done it unto one of the least of these My brethren, ye have done it unto me.

From **Jesus, a Dialogue with the Saviour** *by* Father Lev

It is through suffering that God triumphs over suffering. Suffering souls are better disposed to the promises of joy. To the Mother who has just lost her only son, to the wife who has just lost her husband, we can say "Jesus Himself at this very moment, is suffering what you are suffering, and He triumphs over it for you forever. The cross which you are carrying, as Simon of Cyrene carried it, is your Saviour's cross. Jesus carries it at this moment with you.

You do not yet see that this bearing of the cross by you two together expresses a triumph. Your eyes will be opened and you will see ... My wounds have also another meaning. Since My Ascension, you can touch My open side only if you bend down in compassion over the wounds of man. In times of doubt, look for someone lower than yourself, comfort that unfamiliar pain. I am the one you will touch. My living presence will become certain for you in this contact with the suffering members of My Body.

From **The Bible Reading Fellowship**

O God, who knowest the needs of every heart, look in mercy on all who are beyond human help, all whose hope is gone, and all whose sickness finds no cure, all who feel beaten by the storms of life. Grant them Thy strength, and uphold them with the assurance of Thy light and love.

From **Freedom, Faith and the Future** *by* Archbishop Michael Ramsey

FAITH

Yet there is also the vast amount of suffering which seems attributable to no human fault or cause. There can be none of us whose heart has not sometimes been broken by tragedies through accidents of nature or through sickness or disease which bring pain and grief. There have been speculative explanations, like the theory of a demonic force working in nature in rebellion against the creator's good purpose; but none of these explanations, however plausible, are proved or revealed. But there are two considerations which experience has found to bring some comfort and conviction when the problem agonisingly presses on us.

One consideration is that in the midst of apparently insoluble suffering some of the most heroic of human qualities have been seen: a seemingly supernatural patience, courage, sympathy, gentleness, a power to turn pain to good account such as the biblical word "transfigure" describes. And when this is experienced we find that in the abyss of the problem of evil it is the problem of good which invades the scene and makes its own challenge.

The other consideration is this. As long as we are a race collectively sinful and selfish, there would be little chance of our growing out of sinfulness and selfishness if the world of nature were uniformly comfortable and free from accident. Because this world contains hazards we are discouraged from settling down with our horizons limited to it as if it were all, and we are spurred on in the path of unselfish brotherhood and in the hope of heaven beyond life. At once I sense the protest that I am invoking heaven as a compensation for an insoluble problem. If so, I reply that heaven is in its essence a state of unselfish goodness and sacrificial love, no compensation for our frustration but rather a fulfilment of those qualities as lived and practised in this world.

I claim no more than that those two considerations, which add up to no theoretical solution, have braced men and women to endure and to find God near to them in times of pain and sorrow. For the answer of faith we turn to the biblical writers. Their method is not to try to explain the problem or to explain it away, but somehow to carry it into the presence of God and to see what happens to it in that context. Prophets, psalmists, poets, dramatists like the author of the Book of Job, proclaimed in a crescendo of prophecies that God is one, God is righteous, God is loving, God is ruler, God is ruler of all, God is saviour, God is saviour of all; and the more they thus proclaimed the more exposed were they to sensitivity about the agonies of suffering. In sum, their answer was this. Do not argue, do not theorise, keep near to God, in nearness to him things become different. "I will hold me fast by God." Keep near to him and see what happens. That is the experience and the advice. "I will hold me fast to God." Keep near to him and see what happens. That was the way of faith, and it is the way of faith still. "See what happens to you, and to the suffering, through God's nearness to you." It is a summons to a practical experience. But faith moves on to hope; and the men of faith in the Old Testament look forward, and they say: "Keep near to God. See what difference that makes. But also wait. God is going to act; look forward, God is going to do something."

From **The Use of Praying** *by* Neville Ward

SUFFERING

. . . The believer who is seeking God and God's meaning in his suffering should attempt to put his suffering in the right category. Is what I am going through part of the normal pain that accompanies the growth and fulfilment of the self, so that what is required of me primarily is understanding of the situation and appropriate decision? Or is it a major experience of adversity in which I need to draw on the deepest spiritual assurances and convictions I have?

If it is real suffering, two steps at least are clear for the praying Christian. He needs to accept the situation, reject his resentment and self-pity, and receive into his life this unbelievable incarnation of God, because every experience is a form of God's presence. The second step is to wish to do God's will in this situation as in any other. The thought of doing the will of God renders many distinctions void; there is, in the Christian, essentially no difference between a man of 70 dying of cancer and a man of 20 at the height of his intellectual and physical power deciding his career. Both have an infinite future before them and both can want to do God's will here and now – the patient to endure the restriction and termination of his earthly life in faith and love, the young man to sustain the competition of the many earthly opportunities before him and decide between them in faith and love.

The basic Christian posture would seem to be the same for everyone, young or old, fortunate or unfortunate, and it is decided by the conviction that in God's will is our peace. "Thy will be done" is wrongly interpreted in a merely backward-looking sense of resignation to what has happened; its full significance is that it is a creative and forward-looking act – "in this situation that has come to me I want to know and do God's will as fully as I can." The result of adopting this attitude is not that the struggle ceases but that what it is all about changes completely. For the Christian believer, in suffering, the struggle is not "about" enduring the suffering but serving God in it.

The doing of God's will is what gives meaning to every situation whether it is happy or revolting. Suffering is given a Christian meaning by being accepted as the sphere in which it is appointed that I serve God at this time.

We may not be able to see what God is doing or going to do with our service, but our faith is that to serve Him is the meaning of life and that ultimately this will be clear in a fulfilment of understanding and joy that may well be unimaginable here and now though occasionally people have flashes of conviction here and now that is the truth.

But normally in great suffering it is not possible to see any good that can ever come out of it. It feels like being in hell or at best an indefensible waste of human experience. It does not look as if Jesus saw what God was doing or would do with what He was suffering. The darkness deepened and He did not feel that the Lord was abiding with Him. Indeed He almost died in despair, feeling outrageously deceived, as though all He had done and suffered meant nothing at all and His faith should not have been put in God but in something else if humanity had had the wit to think up an alternative. But at the last minute the pure faith of the man shone out again like the sun struggling round the edge of a cloud.

But even though suffering often seems like a waste of time, the fact is that no time in which God is served is wasted. The service of God is the sanctification of time, and this is true with a particular solemnity of painful and apparently meaningless time.

Exactly how God makes use of our services we can never understand fully and often have no clue at all. We can never understand this fully because what God is doing extends beyond this world of time into eternity so that even if we think we can see the meaning of some earthly suffering here and now, that certainly does not exhaust the meaning.

The wounds of Jesus "in time" have revealed the love of God to millions of human beings, and indeed go on doing this in the most stupendous spiritual harvest this world has ever seen gathered. But that does not exhaust their meaning, because God's purpose is only finally completed beyond time. What Jesus's sufferings mean beyond time we do not know but we believe that they have a mysterious and culminating meaning there ... But when we are presented with suffering that seems to have borne no fruit in time at all, that of the criminal, the dead who went out young, the complete failures who never got into satisfying relationship with anyone and felt outside every joy, the always starving whose existence is a standing reproach to God who has given them life in such an outrageous form, it is time to say that in the Christian understanding of life its meaning is not confined to this life but is developed, purged, clarified, worked out in range upon range of significance the other side of death (which, as Rilke says, is but the side of life that is turned from us).

In this faith there is the conviction that nothing need be wasted and every evil is not finally and forever itself but can and will be made into good.

... The Christian faith makes possible an attitude to suffering in virtue of which it is not wasted experience and useless pain but a giver of life. (When Baudelaire spoke of "la fertilisante douleur" he spoke with Christian understanding.) This attitude is one of faith that God wills in the situation both as asker and giver (giver of what He asks), that the situation therefore can be and should be realistically accepted, and that what is to be done "about" it is the doing of God's will "in it".

Again and again we are faced with situations in which in some sense life is testing us with the challenge to give or give up something valuable, even priceless, even absolutely necessary to us. Sometimes we can side-step the sacrifice asked of us; but then we inevitably lose, though this may not become immediately obvious to us. We shall do all our thinking in that region less efficiently, more evasively, after this refusal to face things. On the other hand we can accept the situation and go through with it, even though "it" is catastrophe. Then we immediately gain in honesty and strength and our sense of reality, even if we cannot for the time being answer the questions the ghastly situation raises. And, much more importantly, again and again it is found that something that the situation requires is provided, that we are given the power to give what it appears we are asked to give. In this sense when dark experience approaches it is normally the case, on this view, that the only way out is the way further in. All experience refused is a true waste of time; and there follows an impoverishment of the personality, which becomes bitter, self-centred, backward-looking, resenting life, indeed the most boring condition into which anyone can degenerate. But when experience is lived through without regrets and reservations, lived through with the whole of one's being, it is found that what looked unendurable as it appeared on the horizon of possibility, proves itself quite a different thing, as though someone shared the load when the moment comes for taking it on. Readiness for experience gives people access to a new level of life on which what they suffer is absorbed in a much deeper range of feeling and understanding. What looked, as it was approached, as the place of sacrifice, turns out to be the place where it is found that the Lord provides, the truth about God being that He is not a taker but a giver.

... In suffering it is hard to be objective enough to want to do God's will, so that suffering is that experience par excellence that both tests faith and enables faith to prove itself. And Christians have found again and again that when suffering is lived through without resentment, as an experience in which God particularly, nervously, hopefully asks us to do His will, it becomes unexpectedly fruitful, it makes a new life. It is of course not always so. Sometimes suffering destroys faith, destroys the whole self, and not one hopeful word can be said about it. But there is so much of the other evidence that Christians will always argue that handled by faith, suffering has a special relation to the presence of God in the world.

Until we have some knowledge of this depth in the Christian way of experiencing life we shall find it extremely hard to believe the teaching it has produced, and we shall continue our subterfuges and evasions, our futile playing with experience on the border of the only realm in which we may conceivably find peace and power. But once we have proved this Christian truth in experience, we shall know that even in pain the only prayer that is worth praying is the Gethsemane prayer of Jesus. This kind of prayer is honest: it does not pretend a bravery of faith it does not possess. It is ready to admit into consciousness whatever lurks below the surface of the mind. But it moves forward, not easily but successfully, through fear and honesty, to the single desire that in whatever one must go through now one will have the power and discernment to do the will of God.

FACING PAIN

"Abide ye in My Love"

John 15:1

> *"I am the True Vine," said our Lord, "and ye,*
> *My Brethren, are the branches"; and that vine,*
> *Then first uplifted in its place, and hung*
> *With its first purple grapes, since then has grown,*
> *Until its green leaves gladden half the world,*
> *And from its countless clusters rivers flow*
> *For healing of the nations, and its boughs*
> *Innumerable stretch through all the earth,*
> *Ever increasing, ever entwined*
> *With each, all living from the Central Heart.*
> *And you and I, my brethren, live and grow,*
> *Branches of that immortal human stem.*

"He that doth not take his cross and follow after Me, is not worthy of Me"

Matthew 10:37

> *And now, what more shall I say? Do I need here*
> *To draw the lesson of this life; or say*
> *More than these few words, following up the text:*
> *The vine from every living limb bleeds wine;*
> *Is it the poorer for that spirit shed?*
> *The drunkard and the wanton drink thereof;*
> *Are they the richer for that gift's excess?*
> *Measure thy life by loss instead of gain;*
> *Not by the wine drunk, but the wine poured forth;*
> *For love's strength standeth in love's sacrifice*
> *And whoso suffers most hath most to give.*

Pain is an interesting subject for discussion between people who are not suffering. Those who do suffer have not time to discuss. They have all their work cut out to cope.

These poems may help those in pain to cope with it. Drugs and anaesthetics relieve it: gritting the teeth goes a short way to mastering it but to cope with it – that's another matter.

The desperate need is for someone to share the unsharable; to be right inside these shattering waves of pain with a power more shattering still. Jesus Christ is the only conceivable possibility.

Eleanor Hamilton King, who wrote these poems, was a devoted disciple

136

of the heroes who freed Italy a hundred years ago by astounding feats of
endurance, pain and martyrdom. Among them was a Barnabite Friar,
Fra Ugo Bassi; and these poems are his hospital sermon said to have been
preached the year before he was executed by the Austrian Army.

The sermon is not great poetry, but it is utterly honest; and the preacher
faces the real agonies of the prospect of lifelong pain, the apparent uselessness of so much suffering and the injustice of inherited disability. He does
not offer any glib or easy answer; he is only original in one respect – his
speculation that this planet has a particular vocation to suffering – and
that originality may be too much for us; but he preaches a gospel, not a
theory; a Saviour, not a consultant; a Victor in glory, not a dying
idealist.

From **The Sermon in the Hospital**

THE TOUCH

"The Hand of God has touched me"

Job 19:21

> But if pain be the hardest ill of all
>   For mortal flesh and heart to bear in peace,
> It is the one comes straightest from God's hand,
>   And makes us feel him nearest to ourselves.
> God gives us light and love, and all good things
>   Richly for joy and power, to use aright;
> But then we may forget Him in His gifts:
>   We cannot well forget the hand that holds,
> And pierces us, and will not let us go,
>   However much we strive from under it.
> If God speaks to thee in the summer air,
>   The cool soft breath thou leanest forth to feel
> Upon thy forehead; dost thou feel it God?
>   Nay but the wind: and when heart speaks to heart,
> And face to face, when friends meet happily,
>   And all is mercy, God is also there,
> Yet thou perceivest but thy fellow's part.
>   But when the sharp strokes flesh and heart run through,
> For thee and not another; only known
>   In all the universe, through sense of thine;
> Not caught by eye or ear, not felt by touch,
>   Not apprehended by the spirit's sight,
> But only by the hidden tortured nerves,
>   In all their incommunicable pain –

God speaks Himself to us, as mothers speak
  To their own babies, upon the tender flesh
With fond familiar touches close and dear;
  Because He cannot choose a softer way
To make us feel that He Himself is near,
  And each apart His own beloved and known.
. . . Is it not God's own finger-tips
  Laid on thee in a tender steadfastness?
The light and careful touches which to thee
  Seem heavy, because measured to thy strength,
With none to spare; and yet He does not fail
  For thy impatience, but stands by thee still.
Patient unfaltering, till thou too shalt grow
  Patient – and wouldst not miss the sharpness grown
To custom which assures Him at thy side,
  Hand to thy hand, and not far off in heaven.
And when the night comes, and the weariness
  Grows into fever, and thy anguish grows
Fiercer, and thou beseechest Him with tears,
  "Depart from me O Lord, and let me rest!"
He will not leave thee, He will not depart,
  Nor lose thee, nor forget thee; but will clasp
Thee closer in the thrilling of His arms,
  No prayer of ours shall ease before their time.
He gives His angels charge of those who sleep:
  But He Himself watches with those who wake.

"The cup which my Father hath given me. Shall I not drink it?"
John 18:11

. . . . But if Himself He come to thee, and stand
  Beside thee, gazing down on thee with eyes
That smile and suffer: that will smite thy heart,
  With their own pity, to a passionate peace;
And reach to thee Himself the holy cup
  (With all its wreathen stems of passion-flowers
And quivering sparkles of the ruby stars),
  Pallid and royal, saying "Drink with Me";
Wilt thou refuse? Nay not for paradise!
  The pale brow will compel thee; thou shalt take
Of that communion through the solemn depths
  Of the dark waters of thine agony,
With heart that praises Him, that yearns to Him

The closer through that hour. Hold fast His hand,
Though the nails pierce thine own! Take only care
Lest one drop of the sacramental wine
Be spilled, of that which ever shall unite
Thee, soul and body to thy living Lord!

THE END

"I have been crucified with Christ; Yet I live; And yet no longer I, but Christ liveth in me: And that life which I now live in the flesh I live in faith, the faith which is the Son of God, who loved me, and gave Himself for me."

Galatians 2:19–20

Therefore gird up thyself, and come, to stand
Unflinching under the unfaltering hand
That waits to prove thee to the uttermost.
It were not hard to suffer by His hand,
If thou couldst see His face – but in the dark!
That is the one last trial – be it so:
Christ was forsaken, so must thou be too;
How couldst thou suffer, but in seeming else?
Thou wilt not see the face nor feel the hand,
Only the cruel crushing feet,
When through the bitter night the Lord comes down
To tread the wine press. Not by sight, but faith,
Endure, endure – be faithful to the end!

*   *   *

O the depth of the riches
Both of the wisdom and knowledge of God!
How unsearchable are His judgements,
And His ways past tracing out!
Of Him and through Him and unto Him
Are all things
To Him be the glory for ever.
Amen.

(Romans 11:33 and 36)

My God, My God, Why Hast Thou Forsaken Me? *by* E. B.

The most awe-ful words in the Bible spoken by Jesus on the Cross. If proof were needed of the complete humanity of our Lord surely it is here in these words.

I believe they speak especially to those of us who have had some great sorrow to bear. When tragedy comes into our lives, when we need most of all to be able to pray and so draw on the well of our spiritual resources, it is so often just then that we find it almost impossible to pray with any real sense of being in touch with God. We are stunned and shocked into a feeling of hopelessness.

Our Lord must have experienced this feeling of separation a thousand-fold. He was one with His Father; throughout His life on earth we know that He was in constant communion with Him. How unbelievable it must have seemed to Him. How can we compare our moments of dere-liction with those He endured? He was sinless, there was no question of His deserving what was happening to Him.

But the desolation passed and He was able to say at last "Into Thy hands I commend my Spirit". He was with His Father again and God grant that it may always be the same with us, and that we may be enabled to echo His words.

When these words are said, then gradually the agony will lessen, and by God's grace we shall be able to see that what seemed to be unbearable can through Him become able to be borne.

"Thy strength is sufficient for my weakness."

Possibly what is needed most of all at these times is a feeling of positive constructiveness. On the face of it, it seems there is nothing we can do, it has happened and all the countless things we could have done and have left undone are no longer possible. I believe that in offering our distress to God we are doing the one constructive thing left to us to do, quite possibly the most constructive thing we have ever done. What has oc-curred cannot be undone, but through this positive offering I believe God is enabled to use our tragedy to help others and to His greater glory. He can, I believe, bring good out of something which has seemed totally evil and against His perfect will.

From **Markings** *by* Dag Hammarskjöld

It did come, the day when the grief became small. For what had be-fallen me and seemed so hard to bear became insignificant in the light of the demands which God was now making. But how difficult it is to feel that this was also, and for that very reason, the day when the joy became great.

From **Five for Sorrow Ten for Joy** *by* J. Neville Ward

The Christian life is more than enduring. Something has to be done in and with what has to be endured, and a grace received from God for the doing. Without anxiety, and with gratitude we are to ask what God's will is and be made ready to learn.

Believers find that through this kind of openness and honesty and trust the senseless situation takes on meaning, becomes endurable for that reason; they are given a more productive view of their difficulties, they abandon certain mistaken expectations about them.

It does not often happen in this world that a problem is fully solved. There are improvements, loosenings, so that after some standstill, movement becomes possible again.

Occasionally, for all our insight and effort and the grace received, things seen to deteriorate, but only seem. It all depends on the principle of measurement.

Do we think Christ was in fact forsaken? We do not. We believe he entered into the only kingdom that matters, the kingdom of love and truth, and we do not care who forgets us if we are remembered there.

From **Christ Our Priest** *by* C. R. Bryant, S.S.J.E.

The Epistle to the Hebrews declares "Ours is not a high priest unable to sympathise with our weaknesses, but one who, because of his likeness to us, has been tempted every way, only without sin." Christians while paying lip service to the true humanity of Christ have often failed to think of him as fully human. People have thought of him as physically human but psychologically divine. They have thought that he suffered intensely in body but was sustained by a more than human perception of what he had to do and how things would turn out. It seems to me that if this had been so he would have been spared one of the sharpest trials a good man has to endure, uncertainty as to what will be the effect of his actions and the nagging fear that he may have made the wrong decision. It seems to me both more compatible with the reality of our Lord's manhood and with such indications that the Gospels give that Christ though he saw plainly the human probabilities did not know clearly what was going to happen, that the unborn future was hidden from him. I believe that we grasp better both what actually happened and its meaning for our own lives, if we understand him as suffering not with a clear vision of the good that would flow from his endurance but in human weakness, in uncertainty and in ignorance of the outcome of it all; clinging only to the Father's will, relying solely on the Father's power; trusting the Father, even at that moment near the end when he felt as though forsaken.

He was pulled in two by his utter devotedness to the Father and his complete openness to his fellow men. When we say that Christ was sinless we are using much too negative a term to describe the wholeness and completeness of his humanity. Because he was totally devoted to the Father and wholeheartedly trusted him, he was able to accept and live out, as we are quite unable to, the whole of his humanity. He has shown what man can be when he lives in complete harmony with his Maker. He has shown what the Creator was working towards in the slow, patient evolution of our species. In him we see a combination of human qualities rarely found together: we see courage and compassion, gentleness and daring, holiness and companionability, a capacity for intense moral indignation and yet sympathy for human weakness. It was because he was so at one with God that he was able to be open to his fellows. Because he was secure in the knowledge of the Father's love he was able to make friends with hard-fisted tax-collectors and notorious loose-livers. Because he was rooted in the Father's peace he could be at one with every type of human being.

In his passion Christ our high priest was tested to the uttermost. He became the link between the all-holy, all-loving God and mankind estranged from him.

From **The Times**

Fate deals out some cruel blows, but surely none could be worse than the tragedy that hits 27,000 families in Britain a year – the death of a child, sometimes their only child.

Only those who have lost a child can know the terrible heartbreak and sheer physical pain of such a loss. And while some do discover consolation in their religious beliefs, the rest find themselves isolated and alone in a world that does not want to recognise the inevitability of death and therefore cannot help by sharing their grief or even allowing them the consolation of mourning.

"We must not talk about it: we don't want to reopen the wound: we must not remind them," people say when a child dies, so they put the parents into a kind of quarantine, not realising that the wound does not heal so easily: that they never forget, and that talking is the therapy that helps people work through their grief and accept their loss. Time *can* be a great healer once the healing process has properly begun, but bottled up unresolved grief only becomes more bitter and more soul-destroying as time goes on.

Two years ago a young chaplain in a big accident hospital in Coventry befriended the parents of two boys who lay dying, one from cancer, the other as the result of a road accident. He told the parents about each other, but it was not until both boys had died that they met for the first time. Immediately a friendship developed, and being based on mutual understanding of heartbreak and sorrow, it had an enormously therapeutic value to both families; through sharing their grief they found new hope and courage.

Observing and meeting with these two families gave the young chaplain, the Rev. Simon Stephens, the idea of expanding their little group to help other bereaved parents in the city, and this in turn proved so helpful and so welcome that he decided to try to organise self-help groups of bereaved parents as well as doctors, nurses, psychiatrists, and others professionally involved, all over the country.

He called his organisation The Society of Compassionate Friends. There are now 37 separate groups up and down the country. They comprise people who themselves have known the despair of losing a child and are prepared to help others, more recently bereaved, who may need to call on them at any hour of the day or night. And for those out of reach of personal contact there are people who will try to help by letter.

The Healing *by* Virginia Thesiger

> *After so long, so long*
> *in my tight prison,*
> *with my familiar shackles*
> *heavy on head and heart;*
> *after so long, so long,*
> *suddenly I see the bars*
> *with the eyes God gave me,*
> *touch the chains*
> *with the hand God made me,*
> *and suddenly, suddenly*
> *(oh, but my heart flies out of the dream*
> *like a singing bird!),*
> *suddenly I am free.*

Prayer:

We beseech Thee O Lord, remember all for good: have mercy upon all, O God. Remember every soul, who being in any affliction, trouble or agony, stands in need of thy mercy and help, all who are in necessity or distress, all who love or hate us.

Thou, O Lord, art the Helper of the helpless, The Saviour of them who are tossed with tempests, the Haven of them that sail, be Thou all to all . . .

Lord, be Thou within us, to strengthen us; without us, to keep us; above us to direct us; behind us to keep us from straying; round about us, to defend us.

Blessed be Thou, O Lord our Father, for ever and ever. Amen.

From **Edges of His Ways** *by* Amy Carmichael

> *Before the winds that blow do cease,*
> *Teach me to dwell within Thy calm;*

Before the pain has passed in peace,
  Give me, my God, to sing a psalm.
Let me not lose the chance to prove
  The fullness of enabling love.
    O love of God, do this for me:
    Maintain a constant victory.

Before I leave the desert land
  For meadows of immortal flowers,
Lead me where streams at thy command
  Flow by the borders of the hours,
That when the thirsty come, I may
Show them the fountains in the way.
    O love of God do this for me:
    Maintain a constant victory.

From **A Child Possessed** *by* R. C. Hutchinson

"Tell me," he said, "What do you really mean when you talk about things which are permanent? We've agreed that Russia as a nation will last for ever. Is that all you mean?"

"It's something I came to see in my early times of imprisonment," Stepan answered slowly . . . "As a prisoner you live so close to the rest that the boundaries disappear. The ordinary distinctions don't operate because there's nothing to preserve them – you've lost everything you took a pride in, what you're ashamed of can't be hidden. So you know men far better than you can in any other phase of life; you get to see how much you have in common – being hungry the whole time for food and women and nicotine, always rather frightened, frightened of dying slowly or of some new, unthought-of humiliation . . ."

"What struck me most about my fellow-prisoners," he said, "was their stupendous goodness. Most of them were kind without any reason, they shared whatever came their way, they helped you all the time." His eager eyes were travelling now between Rozanov and his hostess, his voice had warmed with a gentle excitement. "Listen – you won't easily believe this, but it's true, I swear it is. My feet were agonisingly cold one night – it was in a frozen lumber camp, somewhere in Yakutsk Province – I dreamt they'd gone gangrenous and a surgeon was sawing off the toes. Then after a while the torture passed and my feet got blissfully warm. When it was light I found what had happened – it was due to the man next to me, a fresh arrival, an old Jew from Vilna who hardly knew me at all. I suppose he'd heard me squealing, I may have called out something about my feet. At any rate he'd taken off his old coat and wrapped it very carefully round my legs. And before morning he'd died."

"I was so young then," he continued, "so childish in mentality that I simply accepted those things – it was not till later that I started to reason about them. I was doing my first spell of solitary confinement – I'd been sent to Veslich, after getting wrong with the district soviet – and when you're in darkness with no one to speak to all day long you follow your thoughts as far as they'll go, just to use up time. That was when I tried to see where it came from, this power I'd found in other men of deserting themselves, surrendering their own advantage. I hunted in my own nature – where else had I to hunt! – and there I saw nothing but a midden of appetites and self-regard. Then I had an odd experience, I found myself crying with pity – actually weeping – for one of my guards, a big ugly bastard who'd done me out of a day's rations. That seemed so senseless that I had to look outside myself for the reason. And then I saw it quite plainly – as if I'd stumbled on the solution of a problem in mathematics. I saw that the goodness of God can only work by means of His creation, it uses even the degenerate and feeble, it can find a passage through every human absurdity and every corruption . . . I say it came like the answer to a problem. But it was also a vision. I did – in those days of endless darkness – I did see God's goodness as a thing entirely different from anything I'd learnt or imagined. It was a waterfall of light, but it was also close and personal – not a vague and misty thing but tangible, like Mussorgsky's music or the taste of wine . . ."

"What I lacked", he said pensively, "was the physical means to make a record of that experience there and then, for other people's use as well as mine. If I could have done that, I'd have ceased to worry whether my life had any sense or purpose . . . The trouble is that one sees nothing so clearly in daylight – there are too many distractions. Too much noise and anger, too many voices, including one's own. I read a lot of books; I thought that other men's philosophy might lead me back to the truth I'd once held in my hands. It hasn't up to now. So I make do with other occupations! But it's hard to take it seriously, this transient business of getting money for tobacco and food. What I really live for is to recover that vision – to go where it leads, to make it operate."

The Inviolate Soul *by* Leslie D. Weatherhead, *taken from* **Time for God**

A man wrote to me recently, troubled because his wife had been persuaded to undergo an operation which, he said, had changed her character. "It worries me", he said, "that the self can be changed, and her way of looking at things altered by surgery or even by drugs." People whose relatives suffer from mental illness worry similarly: "Is the innermost self mad?"

Here is a parable. Imagine a man locked in a room with crinkly glass in its window. He, looking out, sees a distorted world. Others, looking in, see a distorted person. But the cause of the distortion is the window not the person.

Similarly, after certain treatments, surgical or sedative, or in certain conditions, mental or emotional, the patient seems to his friends abnormal, and the world seems different to him. But the cause of the distortion is the condition of brain and nerve and disturbed feeling which separate the real self of the patient from his world and his friends. He, himself, his soul, is as untouched as the man in our parable is unaffected by the glass through which he looks out and others look in.

Here is another relevant parable: imagine a man whose only means of communicating with others is by playing a violin. If his violin is taken away and smashed, he is still a violinist. He still loves music. His ability is not destroyed. No one can touch that. "Fear not them that kill the body", said Jesus, "and after that have no more that they can do" (Lk 12:4). The soul is inviolate and goes on into another phase of being, picks up another instrument, which Paul called "the spiritual body" (1 Co 15:44) and plays even more glorious music than the physical body and brain could express.

Death, disease, mental disharmony and emotional disturbance may affect the body, the brain and the senses which depend on it. But all these were only instruments which the soul used on this plane of being. The inviolate soul will not have suffered deprivation let alone annihilation. God has had access to the soul all the time.

To those whose loved ones are dead, or mentally ill, or physically worn out, or ravaged with disease, I would say "Be of good cheer! The soul is inviolate. It dwells in the innermost sanctuary of being. God keeps its key on His girdle, and none may enter but He."

From Five for Sorrow Ten for Joy by J. Neville Ward

God cannot want from us what is not possible. When we are as personalities, so reduced that we cannot entertain the thoughts and intuitions of faith and love, God no longer wants his will done by us, he wants it done for us by others.

From the Chhandogya Upanishad, quoted in Mysticism by F. C. Happold

In this body, in this town of Spirit, there is a little house shaped like a lotus, and in that house there is a little space. One should know what is there.

What is there? Why is it so important?

There is as much in that little space within the heart as there is in the whole world outside. Heaven, earth, fire, wind, sun, moon, lightning, stars; whatever is and whatever is not, everything is there.

If everything is in man's body, every being, every desire, what remains when old age comes, when decay begins, when the body falls?

What lies in that space does not decay when the body decays, nor does it fall when the body falls. That space is the home of Spirit. Every desire is there. Self is there, beyond decay and death; sin and sorrow; hunger and thirst; His aim truth. His will truth.

9

Blessed Are Those Who Mourn

"Blessed are those who mourn for they shall be comforted"

Romans 8:38, 39

From **Address at a Memorial Service** *by* William Temple

Prayer: God grant us the courage to stay with Jesus

Passage by George Eliot

Wisdom 11:26

Prayer *found in* Father Bede Jarrett's **Prayer Book.** We give them back to Thee, dear Lord

Prayer *by* George Eliot. May I reach that purest heaven

Prayer: O Thou that hast prepared a place for my soul

From **The Use of Praying** *by* J. Neville Ward

From **The Book of Common Prayer**

Poem *by* Amy Carmichael, *taken from* **The Mystery of Suffering** *by* Hugh Evan Hopkins. In acceptance lieth peace

De Profundis *by a correspondent to* **The Times.** STRENGTH IN THE FACE OF CALAMITY

2 Maccabees 1:3–5

Psalm 84:4

O Love that will not let me go *by* G. Matheson

Wisdom 3:1–9

From **The Book of Common Prayer.** Lord support us all the day long

Circular Letter *written by* Mark Meynell *for the* Watchers' and Workers' Society, Christmas 1970

In Time of War, source unknown. They served their King and Country

Prayer for the Fallen, source unknown. Unto Thee, O God, be praise and thanksgiving for all those

To the Givers of the Conquering Dead: August 1914–November 1918

From **The Mystery of Suffering** *by* Hugh Evan Hopkins

From **Jesus of the Scars and other Poems** *by* Edward Shillito. HE SHOWED THEM HIS HANDS AND HIS SIDE

Romans 8:38, 39

For I am persuaded, that neither death, nor life, nor angels, nor principalities, nor powers, nor things present, nor things to come, nor height,
nor depth, nor any other creature shall be able to separate us from the
love of God which is in Christ Jesus our Lord.

From **Address at a Memorial Service** *by* William Temple

Christ who died and is alive for evermore has overcome the world.
By faith in Him we share His triumph. In the assurance of that faith we
banish sadness. Sorrow indeed we are bound to feel but the sorrow is lit
with hope and at its very heart is a thrilling joy. For though our friend is
gone from our side, we know that he is only gone to a closer union with
his Lord, and whenever we lift up our hearts to the Lord we join with
Angels and Archangels and all the company of Heaven and there find our
friend again. In that faith in that union with the Master and through the
Master with all His followers, we turn back to serve God by serving
men until the time comes for us to go home.

Prayer:

God grant us the courage to stay with Jesus so that we may know the power of His resurrection and the fellowship of His sufferings and thereby transmit to those we meet some of the riches of His compassion.

Passage by George Eliot

Those children of God to whom it has been given to have communion together can never more be sundered though the hills should lie between, for they bear one another about in their thoughts continually as it were a new strength.

Wisdom 11:26

> *They are Thine, O Lord,*
> *Thou Lover of Souls.*

Prayer *found in* Father Bede Jarrett's **Prayer Book**

We give them back to Thee, dear Lord, Who gavest them to us. Yet as Thou dost not lose them in giving, so we have not lost them by their return.

Not as the world giveth, givest Thou, O Lover of souls. What Thou gavest, Thou takest not away: for what is Thine is ours always, if we are Thine. And Life is eternal and love is immortal, and death is only a horizon, and a horizon is nothing save the limit of our sight.

Lift us up, strong Son of God, that we may see further. Cleanse our eyes that we may see more clearly.

Draw us closer to Thyself that we may know ourselves nearer to our beloved who are with Thee. And while Thou dost prepare a place for us, prepare us for that happy place, that where they are and Thou art, we too may be: through Jesus Christ our Lord. Amen.

Prayer *by* George Eliot

> *May I reach*
> *That purest heaven, be to other souls*
> *The cup of strength in some great agony,*
> *Enkindle generous ardour, feed pure love,*
> *Be the sweet presence of a good diffused,*
> *And in diffusion ever more intense:*
> *So shall I join the choir invisible*
> *Whose music is the gladness of the world.*

Prayer:

O Thou that hast prepared a place for my soul, prepare my soul for that place; prepare it with holiness; prepare it with desire; and even while it so journeyeth upon earth, let it dwell in heaven with Thee beholding the beauty of Thy countenance and the glory of Thy Saints now and for evermore. Amen.

From **The Use of Praying** *by* J. Neville Ward

It is natural to reserve a special place for those who mean much to us but happen to have died. Faith in the communion of saints is much attenuated in current Protestantism and hardly gets out of the Creed into life where alone, of course, it can be any use. Indeed, Protestant Christianity has not very much to say to any Christian who has been through the crucial experience of seeing the face he loves most in the world recede into the inaccessible mystery of death. The embarrassed silence we offer the bereaved (who usually and naturally want very much to talk about their beloved dead) is outrageous – the stone with which our scepticism and inadequate sympathy respond to their request for bread.

It may be that we shall be helped in this matter by cultures not as atomised as ours, nor as afraid of death. J. V. Taylor's book, *The Primal Vision*, in the beautiful chapter titled "The Tender Bridge", makes one reflect on the superiority of African sensitiveness to the thought of death.

"Surely the 'tender bridge' that joins the living and the dead in Christ is prayer. Mutual intercession is the life-blood of the fellowship and what is there in a Christian's death that can possibly check its flow? To ask for the prayers of others in this life, and to know that they rely on mine, does not show any lack of faith in the all-sufficiency of God. Then, in the same faith, let me ask for their prayers still, and offer mine for them, even when death has divided us. They pray for me, I may believe, with clearer understanding, but I for them in ignorance, though still with love. And love, not knowledge, is the substance of prayer."

It is not right that this natural expression of Christian love be confined to confirmed members of the Church. One of the commonest questions asked of ministers in times of bereavement is how the widow or widower is to think of husband or wife who was not a member of the Church or even an attender at its worship. The answer is simply that death does not kill love; in some ways it deepens it. Love wants to express itself, without inhibition, in prayer and faith.

The words, "In Adam all ..." included the whole family of Man in death, the promise, "In Christ all ..." cannot include less than that in life. The genealogies in the Gospel linking Christ himself with unnumbered myriads of the dead are a symbol of the unbroken cord with which God will finally draw Adam back to Paradise. The Christian link with his ancestors, in remembrance and unceasing intercession, may be part of that ultimate redemption: for as Cesaire the Martiniquean poet puts it "there is room for all of us at the rendezvous of victory" (*The Primal Vision*).

Once again it is in the Eucharist that this use of praying is given characteristically Christian form. The sacraments are like poetry to theology's prose; they give the essence, the complexity, the mystery of Christian faith in a concentrated immediacy which theology needs volumes to expound. In the Eucharist the Sanctus is said in a positively excited conviction that in prayer, distance, death and time are completely transcended. We share in all the supernatural life of the whole Body, immersed in the one great stream of grace which God uses to refresh and cleanse and invigorate us as we seek to serve him in the world of distance, death and time. And it has been part of Christian praying from earliest times to relate this point in Holy Communion especially with vanished smiles and household voices gone, so that it is a moment of great intensity at which public liturgy and the most private prayer can meet and blend. Both the living and the dying depend on this.

From **The Book of Common Prayer**

Go forth upon thy journey from this world, O Christian soul. In the name of God the Father Almighty who created thee. Amen.
In the name of Jesus Christ who suffered for thee. Amen.
In the name of the Holy Ghost who strengtheneth thee. Amen.
In communion with the blessed Saints, and aided by Angels and Archangels and all the armies of the heavenly host. Amen.
May thy portion this day be in peace, and thy dwelling in the heavenly Jerusalem. Amen.

Poem *by* Amy Carmichael, *taken from* **The Mystery of Suffering** *by* Hugh Evan Hopkins

> He said, "I will forget the dying faces
> The empty places –
> They shall be filled again;
> O voices mourning deep within me cease."
> Vain, vain the word: vain, vain;
> Not in forgetting lieth peace.
>
> He said, "I will crowd action upon action,
> The strife of faction
> Shall stir my spirit to flame;
> O tears that drown the fire of manhood, cease."
> Vain, vain the word: vain, vain;
> Not in endeavour lieth peace.

He said, "I will withdraw me and be quiet,
Why meddle in earth's riot?
Shut be my door to pain.
Desire thou dost befool me; thou shalt cease."
Vain, vain the word: vain, vain;
Not in aloofness lieth peace.

He said, "I will submit; I am defeated;
God hath depleted
My rich life its gain.
O futile murmurings; why will ye not cease?"
Vain, vain the word: vain, vain;
Not in submission lieth peace.

He said, "I will accept the breaking sorrow
Which God tomorrow
Will to His son explain."
Then did the turmoil deep within him cease.
Not vain the word, not vain:
For in acceptance lieth peace.

De Profundis by a correspondent to **The Times**

STRENGTH IN THE FACE OF CALAMITY

The progress of science and technology has virtually removed many calamities from the human scene. In western countries childbirth has been practically robbed of its terrors. Modern transport brings speedy relief to areas stricken by famine, which only a few decades ago would have sentenced thousands to death. Radar has greatly reduced, though not abolished, the perils of the sea. But in spite of all this, human tragedy still haunts both nations and families.

Some great natural forces have not yet been tamed or adequately guarded against. Typhoons and hurricanes still sweep hundreds to their deaths. Earthquakes can kill their thousands. The tide of modern transport which saves the lives of many carries off its daily toll of some twenty dead in our country alone. If TB is tamed, a cure for cancer still eludes us. The advertisements for life assurance remind us that the happiest home may at a moment lose its Father or its Mother, while the loss of a young son or daughter may take all, or almost all the joy from parents who are already seeing their own lives recapitulated in those of their children. It is all very well for Wordsworth to write of

that blessed mood
In which the burden of the mystery,

153

In which the heavy and the weary weight
Of all this unintelligible world is lightened.

But that mood is not for all, and even for those who sometimes catch it, it will not be there all the time. "The visionary gleam" is all too transient.

At least for the whole of the Christian era, Christian faith has been the strength and stay of those who find themselves overwhelmed by tragedy. God's suffering children have called upon God out of the deep – *de profundis* – and have been convinced that he has heard their voice. To some courage has come from the fact that "Christ our Redeemer passed the self-same way"; to some, from the vision of Christ's empty grave on an Easter morning; to some from the poetic picture of a world in which all fears shall be wiped away, and sorrow and sighing shall be no more. The fact that many no longer share the premises from which such comforting conclusions can be drawn has presented a problem to sociologists and humanists. Statistical surveys are mounted to bring detailed knowledge of human reactions to bereavement. Some have suggested civic funerals in order to provide the bereaved with a secular ceremony that makes no credal demands. Where shall the ordinary Christian take his stand in all this, the Christian who at his best cannot get much further than to pray, like the man in the Gospel, "Lord I believe, help thou mine unbelief"?

First he must realise that the cup of life is "fullmixed", filled with joy and sorrow. Some seem to have more of the one than the other, but most people seem to get their share of both. Then he must by imaginative sympathy bear his share of others' troubles. Whatever strength is available for those in need may have to pass through him. And he must pray that when his turn comes to be in the centre of the storm and not at the circumference he will find God's grace sufficient for him, and his strength made perfect in weakness.

Those whose duty and privilege it has been to minister to many stricken souls know that most frequently such people reveal a quite unexpected power to absorb, rise above and overcome the bereavement that seemed to threaten the very springs of life itself. Happy are they who can still discern in such resources the signs of a more than human provision for an all too human need.

2 Maccabees 1:3-5

God give you all an heart to serve Him and do His will with a good courage and a willing mind ... and send you peace ... and hear your prayers and be at one with you and never forsake you in time of trouble.

Psalm 84:4

Blessed are they that dwell in Thy house: they will be always praising Thee.

Blessed is the man whose strength is in Thee: in whose heart are Thy ways.

Who going through the vale of misery use it for a well: and the pools are filled with water.

They will go from strength to strength: and unto the God of Gods appeareth every one of them in Sion.

O Lord God of hosts, hear my prayer: hearken O God of Jacob.

O Love that will not let me go *by* G. Matheson

O Love that will not let me go,
            I rest my weary soul in Thee:
I give Thee back the life I owe,
That in Thine ocean depth its flow
            May richer, fuller be.

O Light that followest all my way,
            I yield my flickering torch to Thee:
My heart restores its borrowed ray,
That in Thy sunshine's blaze its day
            May brighter, fairer be.

O Joy that seekest me through pain,
            I cannot close my heart to Thee:
I trace the rainbow through the rain,
And feel the promise is not vain
            That morn shall tearless be.

O Cross that liftest up my head,
            I dare not ask to fly from Thee:
I lay in dust life's glory dead,
And from the ground there blossoms red
            Life that shall endless be.

Wisdom 3:1–9

The souls of the righteous are in the hands of God, and there shall no torment touch them. In the sight of the unwise they seemed to die: and their departure is taken for misery. And their going from us to be utter destruction: but they are in peace. For though they be punished in the sight of man, yet is their hope full of immortality. And having been a little chastised, they shall be greatly rewarded: for God proved them, and found them worthy for Himself. As gold in the furnace hath He tried them, and received them as a burnt offering. And in the time of their visitation, they shall shine, and run to and fro like sparks among the stubble. They shall judge the nations, and have dominion over the people, and their Lord shall reign for ever. They that put their trust in Him shall understand the truth: and such as be faithful in love shall abide with Him: for grace and mercy is to His saints, and He hath care for His elect. The righteous live for evermore: their reward also is with the Lord, and the care of them is with the most High. Therefore shall they receive a glorious kingdom and a beautiful crown from the Lord's hand: for with His right hand shall He cover them and with His arm He shall protect them.

From **The Book of Common Prayer**

Lord support us all the day long of this troublous life, until the shades lengthen, and the evening comes, and the busy world is hushed, the fever of life over, and our work is done. Then, Lord, in Thy mercy grant us safe lodging, a holy rest and peace at the last, through Jesus Christ our Lord. Amen.

Circular Letter *written by* Mark Meynell *for the* Watchers' and Workers' Society, Christmas 1970

For a long time now, the Psalmist's "When my father and my mother forsake me, the Lord taketh me up" has become for me a principle of life. We could call it a principle of transference from earth to heaven – or of exchange of heaven for earth – or of co-inherence of heaven in earth.

The word "forsake" is important, for it is not only in the traumatic times of death or divorce or desertion, not in the creeping paralysis of disinterest, in which we find ourselves on our own. "Forsake" can equally describe the isolation into which our own reaction to home or family or parents can cast us. I suppose all of us leave our homes for work or marriage or life, with some legacy of unsolved relationship in our locker – son with father, daughter with mother, or vice versa, or both, or with brother or sister. There can be no life which does not have some deprivation. Even an inferiority complex can sometimes cripple us as surely as a missing leg. But the importance of "forsake" is not HOW it happens but THAT it happens. We MAY need help, we SHALL need courage and generosity, yet separation is a blessing, because it frees us for God. For father and mother, family and home are an image of God, more or less true, but still only an image. The truth is that imagery and reality cannot co-exist. One must be given up. The more we can thank God for father, for mother, for family and for home, the better, the truer and the easier the transference, because the common coin of relationship – love – flourishes only where gratitude and forgiveness are growing.

Prayer then becomes a loving converse of relationship with the living Lord. And here it is wise to remember the divine initiative, for it is the Lord who takes me up.

In Time of War, Source unknown

They served their King and Country with all their strength and gave their lives to save their friends. "Whosoever leads such a life need not care upon how short a warning it be taken from him."

> *Courage and fortitude are lovely words,*
> *And lovely are the virtues they define,*
> *Yours was the courage, laughing soldier,*
> *May the fortitude be mine.*

Prayer for the Fallen, Source unknown

Unto Thee, O God, be praise and thanksgiving for all those who have been faithful unto death: into Thy merciful keeping we commend their souls, beseeching Thee to grant unto all of us for whom they died, that their love and devotion may bear fruit in us in more abundant love for others, through Him, who by His death hath destroyed death – Thy Son our Lord, Jesus Christ.

To the Givers of the Conquering Dead: August 1914–November 1918

> *To you, who in these years have given your all;*
> *To you, who gave your men at Honour's call;*
> *To you, who saw them dare the fiercest fight,*
> *Right through the gates of death, beyond your sight,*
> *Homage from us, who ready to give,*
> *By God's grace are allowed to see our fighters live*
> *Midst thundering guns, grim sounds of war that cease;*
> *From elsewhere comes your victor's song of Peace,*
> *Our Peace of victory that crowns the strife*
> *Won by their sacrifice of dauntless life.*
> *In silent prayer we kneel, and with bowed head*
> *We watch you share the triumph of your dead.*

From **The Mystery of Suffering** *by* Hugh Evan Hopkins

The writer to the Hebrews tells us that Jesus was "touched with the feeling of our infirmities" (Heb 4:15). Whenever He came in contact with those who suffered His heart went out to them in loving compassion and He brought help, healing and forgiveness. We believe that Our Lord is still the same and that the picture He gave in His Own Person of the way God cares for His children when they are in trouble, is a true picture of the character and nature of our God still. That is the lesson Studdart Kennedy so graphically put into the mouth of his soldier in the trenches, a lesson we can learn to our infinite comfort: it matters to God about us.

> How can it be that God can reign in glory
>   Calmly content with what His love has done,
> Reading unmoved the piteous shameful story,
>   All the vile deeds men do beneath the sun?
>
> Are there no tears in the heart of the Eternal?
>   Is there no pain to pierce the soul of God?
> Then must He be fiend of Hell infernal,
>   Beating the earth to pieces with His rod.
>
> Father, if He, the Christ were the revealer,
>   Truly the first begotten of the Lord,
> Then must Thou be a sufferer and a healer,
>   Pierced to the heart by the sorrow of the sword.
>
> Then must it mean, not only that the sorrow
>   Smote Thee that once upon the Lonely tree,
> But that today, tonight and on the morrow
>   Still it will come, O gallant God to Thee.

From **Jesus of the Scars and other Poems** *by* Edward Shillito

HE SHOWED THEM HIS HANDS AND HIS SIDE

> If we have never sought, we seek Thee now;
>   Thine eyes burn through the dark, our only stars;
> We must have sight of thorn-pricks on Thy brow,
>   We must have Thee, O Jesus of the Scars.
>
> The heavens frighten us; they are too calm;
>   In all the universe we have no place.
> Our wounds are hurting us, where is Thy balm?
>   Lord Jesus by Thy Scars, we claim Thy grace.
>
> If when the doors are shut, Thou drawest near,
>   Only reveal Thine hands, that side of Thine;
> We know today what wounds are, have no fear,
>   Show us Thy Scars, we know the countersign.
>
> The other gods were strong: but Thou wast weak:
>   They rode, but Thou didst stumble to a throne;
> But to our wounds only God's wounds can speak,
>   And not a god has wounds but Thou alone.

From **Safety** *by* Rupert Brooke

> *Safe shall be my going,*
> *Secretly armed against all death's endeavour;*
> *Safe though all safety's lost, safe where men fall;*
> *And if these poor limbs die, safest of all.*

From **The Lost Leader** *by* Robert Browning

> *We that loved him so, followed him, honoured him,*
> *Lived in his mild and magnificent eye,*
> *Learned his great language, caught his clear accents*
> *Made him our pattern to live and to die.*

From a wartime **Speech** *by* Sir Winston Churchill

"How proud we ought to be, both young and old, to be living in a tremendous, thrilling, formative epoch in the human story, and how fortunate it was for the world that when these great trials came upon us, there was a generation that terror could not conquer and brutal violence could not enslave. Let us rise to the full level of our duty and of our opportunity, and let us thank God for the spiritual reward He has granted for all forms of valiant and faithful service."

From **The Desert Warrior** *by* Pat Hore Ruthven

> *Take not high courage, Lord,*
> *From a world ever fearing;*
> *Leave light and laughter, Lord,*
> *Where life needs cheering.*

Tribute to General Fairfax, *written by his son-in-law* the Duke of Buckingham

> *He never knew what envy was, nor hate,*
> *His soul was filled with worth and honesty,*
> *And with another thing quite out of date called modesty.*

An Irish Airman Foresees his Death *by* William Butler Yeats

> *Nor law, nor duty made me fight,*
> *Nor public men, nor cheering crowds.*
> *A lonely impulse of delight*
> *Drove to this tumult in the clouds;*
> *I balanced all, brought all to mind,*
> *The years to come seemed waste of breath,*
> *A waste of breath the years behind*
> *In balance with this life and death.*

Theophan the Recluse *from* **The Art of Prayer:** An Orthodox Anthology

Our whole object is to acquire the habit of keeping our attention always on the Lord, who is omnipresent and sees everything, who desires the salvation of all of us and is ready to help us towards it. This habit will not allow you to grieve, whether your sorrow be within or without; for it fills the soul with a sense of perfect contentment, which leaves no room for any feeling of scarcity or need. It makes us entrust ourselves and all we have into the Lord's hands, and so gives birth to a sense of His paramount protection and help.

From **Edges of His Ways** *by* Amy Carmichael

Sorrow is one of the things that are lent, not given. A thing that is lent may be taken away; a thing that is given is not taken away. Joy is given; sorrow is lent. We are not our own, we are bought with a price, "and our sorrow is not our own" (Samuel Rutherford said this a long time ago), it is lent to us for just a little while that we may use it for eternal purposes.

Then it will be taken away and everlasting joy will be our Father's gift to us, and the Lord God will wipe away all tears from all faces. So let us use this "lent" thing to draw us nearer to the heart of Him who was once the Man of Sorrows (He is not that now, but He does not forget the feeling of sorrow). Let us use it to make us more tender with others, as He was when on earth and is still, for He is touched with the feeling of our infirmities.

From **Life Together** *by* Dietrich Bonhoeffer

THE MINISTRY OF BEARING

The Bible speaks with remarkable frequency of "bearing". It is capable of expressing the whole work of Jesus Christ in this one word "Surely he hath borne our griefs, and carried our sorrows" . . . "The chastisement of our peace was upon him" (Isaiah 53:4–5). Therefore, the Bible can also characterise the whole life of the Christian as bearing the Cross. It is the fellowship of the Cross to experience the burdens of the other.

If one does not experience it, the fellowship he belongs to is not Christian. If any member refuse to bear the burden, he denies the law of Christ.

It is, first of all, the freedom of the other person of which we spoke earlier, that is the burden to the Christian. The other's freedom collides with his own autonomy, yet he must recognise it.

He could get rid of this burden by refusing the other person his freedom, by constraining him and thus doing violence to his personality by stamping his own image in him. But if he lets God create His image in him, he by this token gives him his freedom and himself bears the burden of this freedom of another creature of God. The freedom of the other person includes all that we mean by a person's value, individuality, endowment. It also includes his weaknesses and oddities, which are such a trial to our patience, everything that produces frictions, conflicts and collisions among us. To bear the burden of the other person means involvement with the created reality of the other, to accept and affirm it, and, in bearing with it, to break through to the point where we take joy in it.

This will prove especially difficult where varying strength and weaknesses in faith are bound together in fellowship. The weak must not judge the strong, the strong must not despise the weak. The weak must guard against pride, the strong against indifference. None must seek his own rights. If the strong person falls, the weak one must guard against malicious joy at his downfall. If the weak one falls, the strong one must help him rise again in all kindness. The one needs as much patience as the other. "Woe to him who is alone when he falleth; for he hath not another to help him up" (Ecclesiastes 4:10). It is doubtless this bearing of another person in his freedom that the Scripture means when it speaks of "forbear one another" (Col 3:13). "Walk with all lowliness and meekness, with long suffering, forbearing one another in love" (Ep 4:2).

The service of forgiveness is rendered by one to the others daily. It occurs without words in the intercession for one another. And every member of the fellowship, who does not grow weary in this ministry, can depend upon it that this service is also being rendered him by the brethren.

He who is bearing others knows that he himself is being borne, and only in this strength can he go on bearing.

Then where the ministry of listening, active helpfulness, and bearing with others is faithfully performed, the ultimate and highest service can also be rendered, namely the Ministry of the Word of God.

Letter *from* Samuel Palmer, to a bereaved friend, *taken from* **Visionary and Dreamer** *by* Lord David Cecil

If we will but be still and listen, I think we shall hear these sad trials talking to us: saying as it were, 'You have known life and enjoyed it, you have tried it and suffered from it; your tent has been pitched in pleasant places among those of dear relations and tried friends, and now they are disappearing from around you. The stakes are loosened one by one, and the canvas is torn away, with no vestige left behind, and you want something which will not be taken away. You want something large enough to fill your heart, and imperishable enough to make it immortal like itself. That something is God.

From **An Address** *given by* Dr Patricia Graeme, M.B., B.S., M.R.C.P.

When we glimpse Man's part in the Divine Plan and when we remember God's infinite love for each one of us it seems inconceivable that the mere accident of the death of the body should be anything but an incident in the continuing life of the soul.

But I know well that it is easy to be objective like this about death when we are not actually facing it. It is not so easy when it concerns ourselves or those nearest to us. It becomes startlingly difficult in illness when all our strength and energy are gathered to fight against it. Even though we have faith, even though we believe and trust the promises and teachings of Christ, it does not follow that we shall be unafraid when the time comes. Fear is one of Nature's most powerful weapons to preserve life from extinction, and anything which threatens the life of the body, almost automatically brings fear to the mind. Our bodies are marvellously equipped to resist death by every possible means and the mind of Man has an infinite capacity for hope. Together, these two present a formidable barrier against allowing a sick person to accept death as the inevitable outcome of his illness even when the hopelessness of the situation is obvious to those around him. The somewhat hackneyed observation that "while there's life there's hope" remains profoundly true.

Do not be dismayed, therefore, if someone whom you know to have accepted the fact of death with serenity throughout his lifetime, suddenly seems totally unable to accept it during his last illness. This paradox has to be recognised and understood for what it is. It is part of his bodily illness, part of his fight for life, and it in no way detracts from his courage or from his spiritual stature. Death for us may come swiftly and unexpectedly or the road to it may be long and weary. For some it comes finally as a friend, for others it is "the last enemy" to be fought every inch of the way. We do not know and we cannot know how it will be with us, and when we are well we do not know how we should react to the pain or discomfort, the fears, the weakness, the depressions, the restriction of activity, both mental as well as physical, all of which are inseparable from any serious illness, especially a long illness. And if we *are* afraid, if we feel isolated and alone, if it seems to us that God has deserted us, there is no need to feel ashamed (as some do) or to wonder whether our faith has failed to endure the test. In the Garden of Gethsemane and on the Cross, Jesus Himself knew all these and showed us that following the desolation and despair of Good Friday there are the joy and triumph of Easter Day.

In these sort of circumstances when prayer is often difficult and when we cannot seem to find that inner tranquillity which was formerly the root of all our strength, I am sure that God means us to recognise Him in the other ways in which He comes to us. We can find and receive Him in the hands of those who nurse and care for us, in the courage of those who love us and who conceal their anxiety for our sake, in the kindliness of friends and acquaintances and even in the medicines, developed by many through long years of patient endeavour, which ease our pain and help us to fight our disease.

When we think about death, it is inevitable that we should also wonder about life after death. It is with considerable hesitation that I speak, even briefly, on this the greatest of all mysteries, but I think it is helpful if one can find some conception, however vague, which is real for oneself.

In the deepening and enriching of our spiritual lives we feel that we are progressing towards something, moving towards some sort of goal. Although in our earthly lives we are committed to involvement in the world we are aware that complete fulfilment can only be found beyond this life. It is reasonable to suppose that this fufilment will somehow follow on our experience here, be a continuation of it. Therefore it seems logical to regard the deepest moments in our spiritual lives here as the nearest points to that which we shall experience hereafter.

We have all known these moments – moments of increased perception and awareness – and in a way they are the foundations on which our faith has been built, because they are our own personal revelations of God and, as such, are for us totally valid.

It may have been on a mountain at sunrise, or standing in silence under the vast beauty of a night sky that we were first stirred by a strange indescribable longing; it may have been when we beheld the miracle of a new-born baby or the first spring blossom on the bare trees of winter and were suddenly overwhelmed by a sense of awe and wonder; it may have been when a deep and lasting truth was revealed to us through Scripture or art or poetry or great music; it may have been in the experience of human love when our hearts overflowed with joy and gratitude in the utter astonishment of loving and realising that we were loved, or even in the bewilderment of grief and sorrow when we came unbelievably close to another person. It may have been in our quiet times of prayer and meditation when we found release in the sudden sure knowledge of for-giveness, or at times of great strain and stress when we discovered deep within ourselves a profound peace and tranquillity. Or it may have been in the shared experience of worship together when we knew the real meaning of communion because there was at one and the same time a deep personal encounter with God and with one another.

In all these moments – moments which T. S. Eliot has described as "in and out of time", moments in which we saw "all things new", we reached out and touched the mystery at the heart of life, and in so doing, did we not also touch the mystery beyond death? Did we not on these occasions see, however imperfectly and incompletely, the image of God, and experience momentarily the unutterable joy of being made one with Him?

It stretches the mind to its uttermost limit to try to comprehend how, in the fullness of union with God after death, we shall be able to retain our separate identities and to recognise our loved ones. But perhaps we can derive some measure of understanding from those occasions known to most if not all of us when someone we loved, although separated from us by distance, or even by death, suddenly seemed very near to us. We could not have explained to anyone how we recognised it to be that particular person and none other. We just knew that it was so. This is doubtless only a shadow of the truth, but it is at least conceivable that it will be on this kind of deep and mysterious level that we shall know one another in the life beyond death.

I would like to conclude with some words of Kahlil Gibran, taken from his book *The Prophet*.

> *You would know the secret of death,*
> *But how shall you find it unless you seek it in the heart of life?*
> *The Owl, whose night-bound eyes are blind unto the day, cannot unveil*
> *the mystery of light.*
> *If you would indeed behold the spirit of death, open your heart wide into*
> *the body of life,*
> *For life and death are one, even as the river and the sea are one.*

From **A Child Possessed** *by* R. C. Hutchinson

ON THE DEATH OF THE CHILD

"You see, it was such a burdensome body she had to go about with. I keep rejoicing that she's done with that. I keep thanking God that she's rid of it for always."

... "In a way," he said slowly, "the break's a good thing, for me as well as for her. I don't manage my life very sensibly, as you know. It was getting to be a kind of self-indulgence – I enjoyed so much being everything to her, it was getting to be all I ever thought of." Helene said, "But you'll need some other interest to take her place."

He nodded with deliberation, as if this came to him as a novel point of view. "Well, there's Marseilles to start with – half a million people. I adore Marseilles. Have you ever seen the very old women in the Place Jean-Jaures? So brave and beautiful. Sometimes I think God meant the

Marseillais to be Russian – they accept their lives so gallantly, with so few comforts to feed this courage." "Yes," he said reflectively, "I feel closer to them now. Because of her, I mean. Did you ever read Father Lluis Heredia? To me the Spanish philosophers are difficult, up to now I've never quite grasped that dictum of his, 'Private loves are mere self-interest unless they're a cure for spiritual blindness; the use of loving one person is to be educated in finding one's way to all the rest.' At last I begin to see that. But for me education's a slow business, I've always to start again at the beginning."

Heard *in the Anglican Church, Monte Carlo*

> *Remember, O Lord, for good the needs of all who cry to Thee; and as Thou seest best, make known to each and all of us our need for loving Thee.*
>
> > *In all that we ask may we seek Thee;*
> > *In all that we do may we honour Thee;*
> > *In all that we suffer may we find Thee;*
> *For all in which we grieve Thee may Thy Sacred Passion avail,*
> > *till all pardoned souls shall know Thee*
> > *and follow Thee unto the end,*
> > *our only Prince and Saviour, Jesus Christ.*
> > > > *Amen.*

The Bible: Wisdom

"Where shall wisdom be found?"

From **The Coronation Service.** Hear the Word of God

Prayer for Wisdom *by* Queen Elizabeth I. Give me, O eternal Father, a docile heart

Motto for a Bible *by* Lord Byron. FOUND IN AN OLD BIBLE

Job 11:7-9

Job 28: 12, 21-28

Job 33: 31, 33 and 42: 1-6

Letter 117 *by* St Francis de Sales *from* **Selected Letters.** O that I might receive the gift of understanding

From **Worship** *by* Evelyn Underhill

Thomas à Kempis, *quoted in* **Our Knowledge of God** *by* John Baillie

Genesis, *spoken by three Astronauts while orbiting the Moon on* Christmas Day 1968

Light Looked Down *by* Laurence Housman

From **God & Sons** *by* Dewi Morgan

From **Living Prayer** *by* Metropolitan Anthony Bloom. Prayer is an adventure

Prayer: Eternal God, whose glorious life is far beyond our sight

From **The Journey Inwards** *by* F. C. Happold. THE UNKNOWABILITY OF GOD BY THE MIND. THE KNOWABILITY OF GOD BY THE HEART

The Hidden Man of the Heart *by* Theophan the Recluse, *taken from* **The Art of Prayer:** An Orthodox Anthology

A Prayer for Enlightenment *from* **Daily Prayers** *by* John Baillie

From **God & Sons** *by* Dewi Morgan. FERMENT IN THE SOUL

From **Sacred and Secular** *by* Archbishop Michael Ramsey

Genesis 9:12-17

From **Areopagitica** *by* John Milton. Books are not absolutely dead things

From a **Letter** *from* Dr Coggan, Archbishop of York, *in* **The Times**

From **The Prophet** *by* Kahlil Gibran

From **The Coronation Service**

Hear the Word of God written in the Holy Bible, the most valuable thing that this world affords.

Prayer for Wisdom *by* Queen Elizabeth I

> *Give me, O eternal Father, a docile heart that I may know what is acceptable with Thee.*
>
> *Send from heaven the spirit of Thy wisdom and rule my heart by Thine own command.*
>
> *Blessed is he whom Thou dost instruct, O Lord, and make learned in Thy will. Without this I lack the strength either to purpose well for myself or to be of service to others.*

Motto for a Bible *by* Lord Byron

FOUND IN AN OLD BIBLE

> *Within this sacred volume lies*
> *The mystery of mysteries;*
> *Oh happiest thing of human race,*
> *To whom our God has given grace,*
> *To hear, to read, to fear, to pray,*
> *To lift the latch, to force the way.*
> *But better had they ne'er been born*
> *Who read to doubt, or read to scorn.*

Job 11:7-9

> *Can you find out the deep things of God?*
> *Can you find out the limit of the Almighty?*
> *It is higher than heaven – what can you do?*
> *Deeper than Sheol – what can you know?*
> *Its measure is longer than the earth,*
> *and broader than the sea.*

Job 28:12, 21-28

> *But where shall wisdom be found –*
> *And where is the place of understanding?*
>
> *It is hid from the eyes of the living*
> *and concealed from the birds of the air.*
> *Abaddan and death say*
> *We have heard a rumour of it.*
> *God understands the way to it*
> *and He knows the place.*

For He looks to the ends of the earth
and sees everything under the heavens.
When He gave to the wind its weight,
and meted out the waters by measure;
when He made a decree for the rain
and a way for the lightning of the thunder;
He established it and searched it out.
And He said to man:
Behold the fear of the Lord, that is wisdom,
and to depart from evil is understanding.

Job 33:31, 33 and 42:1-6

Be silent and I will speak,
listen to me, be silent and I will teach you Wisdom;
Then Job answered the Lord:
I know that Thou canst do all things,
And that no purpose of Thine can be thwarted.
Who is this that hides counsel without knowledge?
Therefore I have uttered what I did not understand:
things too wonderful for me, which I did not know.
Hear and I will speak; I will question you, and you declare to me.
I had heard of Thee by the hearing of the ear,
but now my eye sees Thee,
therefore I despise myself,
and repent in dust and ashes.

Letter 117 *by* St Francis de Sales, *from* **Selected Letters**

O that I might receive the gift of understanding as I ought . . . so as to get a clearer and deeper insight into the holy mysteries of our faith! For the intelligence has a marvellous power to subject the will to God's service, our understanding is committed to Him and plunged in Him recognising Him as wonderfully and perfectly good.

And the mind ceases to think anything else good in comparison with this goodness, even as when our eyes look deep into the sun we can no longer see any other light. But because we can only show our love in this world by doing good, because our love must act in some way, please God, we need counsel so as to see what we ought to do to put this love which presses us into action; for it is heavenly love itself which urges us on to do good.

And the Holy Ghost gives us His gift of counsel, so that we may find out how to do good, which good to choose and in what way to express our love in action. So that we can say that our soul shares in good measure in heaven's sacred gifts.

May the Holy Ghost show us favour and ever be our consolation. My soul and spirit adore Him for all eternity! I entreat Him always to be our wisdom and our understanding, our counsel, our fortitude, our knowledge, our piety: and may He fill us with the spirit of the heart of the eternal Father.

From **Worship** *by* Evelyn Underhill

While all things abode in tranquil silence and the night was in the midst of her swift course, thine Almighty Word, O Lord leapt down out of thy royal throne, Alleluia.

Thomas à Kempis, *quoted in* **Our Knowledge of God** *by* John Baillie

How much thou knowest, and how much the better thou understandest, so much the more grievously shalt thou be judged, unless thy life be also more holy.

Genesis, *spoken by three Astronauts while orbiting the Moon on* Christmas Day 1968

In the beginning God created the heavens and the earth. The earth was without form and void, and darkness was upon the face of the deep; and the Spirit of God was moving over the face of the waters ... Then God said, "Let us make man in our image, after our likeness; and let them have dominion over the fish of the sea, and over the birds of the air, and over the cattle and over all the earth and over every creeping thing that creeps upon the earth." So God created man in his own image, in the image of God he created him; male and female created he them. And God blessed them and God said to them, "Be fruitful and multiply, and fill the earth and subdue it; and have dominion over the fish of the sea and over the birds of the air and over every living thing that moves upon the earth." And God said, "Behold, I have given you every plant yielding seed which is upon the face of all the earth, and every tree with seed in its fruit; you shall have them for food. And to every beast of the earth, and to every bird of the air, and to everything that creeps on the earth, and everything that has the breath of life, I have given every green plant for food." And it was so. And God saw everything that he had made, and behold it was very good.

Light Looked Down *by* Laurence Housman
> *Light looked down and beheld darkness,*
> *Thither will I go, said Light.*

Peace looked down and beheld War,
Thither will I go, said Peace.
Love looked down and beheld Hatred,
Thither will I go, said Love.
So came Light and shone;
So came Peace and gave rest;
So came Love and brought Life.
And the Word was made Flesh and dwelt among us.

From **God & Sons** *by* Dewi Morgan

Man has embarrassed himself by his own riches. He has learned, even if he is unwilling to acknowledge the fact even to himself, that being given a talent is an obligation to stewardship. The twentieth century cannot bury its gifts in the ground and escape the consequences. Knowing that, it discovers that to be equipped to govern the future is to be saddled with a terrible burden.

Long ago, Jesus told men who were weary to come to Him and He would give them rest. Was He offering a pious opiate, a stained glass escapism? And in any case, was His offer of short duration and limited only to Middle Eastern peasants whose burdens were very different?

Jesus was perfect man. Few people in history have wanted to dispute that statement in that form. And as perfect man, he was always deeply aware, and he always demonstrated his awareness, that he was at all times dependent on God. Twentieth century man is right in believing he has gained, or rapidly is gaining, mastery over nature. Where he goes wrong is in assuming that such a mastery confers upon him an independence which makes God superfluous. On the contrary, that very mastery over nature is a validation of God and God's first order to man – subdue the earth and have dominion. The answer to man's anxiety about his degree of control over tomorrow is not to try and lose that control and forget all the scientists have taught him. Rather is it to exercise that control as a creature who is responsible to his creator, thus recognising that while man is responsible, he is not on his own in a lonely and bleak universe. When Jesus called men to him he was not calling men out of the world but rather into a richer and more creative relationship with the world through its Creator. The sort of rest that Jesus offered was not inertia but the rest that a body has when all the forces acting upon it are perfectly stabilised and harmonised.

The formula for twentieth-century man, then, is to acknowledge and accept your responsibility but remember you are not on your own but in a family business, "God & Sons", and its potential is limitless. Your function is to get on with what lies immediately to hand, giving it all you have got. Take the future into consideration by all means, but always remember that what you are responsible for is the right choice at this moment in the light of what this moment reveals.

Man is responsible for his world, for God commanded him to be so. But the responsibility is a given one. That is to say, it is not something man invented or acquired, it comes from a decision external to man. The decider, God, does not change His mind, so this responsibility remains man's. But always man must exercise it with awareness of its source.

From **Living Prayer** *by* Metropolitan Anthony Bloom

Prayer is an adventure which brings not a thrill but new responsibilities. As long as we are ignorant, nothing is asked of us, but as soon as we know anything, we are answerable for the use we make of that knowledge. It may be a gift, but we are responsible for any particle of truth we have acquired as it becomes our own, we cannot leave it dormant but have to take it into account in our behaviour and in that sense we are to answer for any truth we have understood.

Prayer:

Eternal God, whose glorious life is far beyond our sight: have mercy upon us and when our minds stretch out unto Thee, do Thou stoop down and bless us with understanding and wisdom.

From **The Journey Inwards** *by* F. C. Happold

THE UNKNOWABILITY OF GOD BY THE MIND

When the great Christian saint, St Bernard, was asked the question "Who is God?" he replied that the only answer he could give was "He who Is". It is not possible to "think" about God; all that one can think about is some idea or image of God. For God is the Inexpressible, the Unknowable, the Unconditional, the Ultimate reality, the One "before whom all words recoil", ungraspable by the human intellect.

In saying this I am not saying anything new. It is as old as the hills. Hinduism has known it for thousands of years. In the Hindu Scriptures, the Upanishads, which date back to the millennium before Christ, it is written: "There is nothing in the world which is not God . . . It is undying, blazing Spirit, wherein lay hidden the world and all its creatures", and also "He who says that Spirit is not known, knows; who claims that he knows, knows nothing. The ignorant think that Spirit lies within knowledge, the wise man knows it beyond knowledge."

Nor is what I have written from the Christian standpoint in the least unorthodox. The spiritual geniuses of Christendom have said very much the same thing. We have already quoted St Bernard. St Augustine wrote

"There is in the mind no knowledge of God except that it does not know Him." St Augustine is echoed by St Thomas Aquinas, "What God actually is always remains hidden from us. And this is the highest knowledge we can have of God in this life, that we know Him to be above every thought that we can think of Him." While that great mystic and Doctor of the Church, St John of the Cross, who wrote the most exquisite poems on the union of the soul with God in the whole of Christian literature, could write: "One of the greatest favours bestowed on the soul transiently in this life is to enable it to see so distinctly and to feel so profoundly that it cannot comprehend God at all." He goes on, "These souls are herein somewhat like the saints in heaven, where they who know Him most perfectly perceive most clearly that He is infinitely incomprehensible; for those who have less clear vision do not perceive so clearly as do those others how greatly He transcends their vision . . . Never has the truth of the unknowability of the That we call God been put more succinctly and vigorously than by the fourteenth century German mystic, Meister Eckhart, when he said: "Why dost thou prate of God? Whatever thou sayest of Him is untrue." While the unknown author of *The Cloud of Unknowing* wrote:

Of all creatures and their works, yea, of all the works of God's self, may a man through grace have full head of knowing; but of God Himself no man can think . . . for why? He may well be loved but not thought. By love may He be gotten and holden, but by thought never.

Finally let me quote a passage from the great Father of Christian negative (or apophatic) theology, the so-called Dionysius the Areopagite: "Neither can any affirmation or negation be applied to Him, for though we may affirm or deny the things below Him, we can neither affirm nor deny Him."

THE KNOWABILITY OF GOD BY THE HEART

Let us go back to Dionysius. True he says God is unknowable to the human intellect. Nevertheless, there is in man a higher faculty, which can be developed, whereby he may be united "to Him who is wholly unknowable; thus by knowing nothing he knows That which is beyond his knowledge". Dionysius is, of course, using the word "know" in two different senses. What, in effect, he is saying is that man has at his disposal two organs of perception, two ways of knowing. We may call them intellectual or rational and intuitive or spiritual knowing, the knowing of the "head" and the knowing of the "heart". One writer has written: "God is neither perceptible to our senses, nor conceivable by our intellects, but He is sensible to the heart." While another carries us a step further: "The essential meaning of religion is not to know God as one knows a friend; it is to become God, for to know Him is to take Him into our inmost self as the fulfilment of that self; and it is only in becoming Him that we know Him." Do not be afraid, you of my readers, who have been brought up in that complex of ideas and images which make up so much of popular Christian theology of this idea of man becoming God. Did not that great champion of Catholic orthodoxy against the Arian heresy, St Athanasius, use (in his *De Incarnatione*) this striking phrase: "Christ became man in order that man might become God."

The Hidden Man of the Heart *by* Theophan the Recluse, *taken from* The Art of Prayer: An Orthodox Anthology

The spirit of wisdom and revelation, and a heart that is cleansed, are two different matters; the former is from on high, from God, the latter is from ourselves. But in the process of acquiring Christian understanding they are inseparably united, and this understanding cannot be gained unless both of them are present together. The heart alone, despite all purification – if purification is possible without grace – will not give us wisdom; but the spirit of wisdom will not come to us unless we have prepared a pure heart to be its dwelling place.

The heart is to be understood here, not in the ordinary meaning, but in the sense of "inner man". We have within us an inner man, according to the Apostle Paul, or a hidden "man of the heart", according to the Apostle Peter. It is the God-like spirit that was breathed into the first man, and it remains with us continuously, even after the Fall. It shows itself in the fear of God, which is founded on the certainty of God's existence, and in the awareness of our complete dependence on Him, in the stirrings of conscience and in our lack of contentment with all that is material.

A Prayer For Enlightenment *from* Daily Prayers *by* John Baillie

O Thou who art the source and ground of all truth. The Light of Lights, who hast opened the minds of men to discern the things that are, guide me today, I beseech Thee in my reading. Give me grace to choose the right books and to read them in the right way.

Give me wisdom to abstain as well as to persevere.

Let the Bible have proper place; and grant that as I read I may be alive to the stirrings of Thy Holy Spirit in my soul.

From God & Sons *by* Dewi Morgan

FERMENT IN THE SOUL

There is a great awakening potential in the soul of contemporary man ... We live in an era of scientific triumph yet it is also an era of growing realisation of inadequacy. The very achievements of the scientist have confronted him with some of the most intractable dilemmas of human experience – the discoverers of the Bomb, for example, are still pondering whether the right moral course would not have been to strangle their infant at birth.

Scientific advance is in one way the greatest assurance of frustration. As Robert Oppenheimer said in a broadcast, in science you constantly find how wrong you are; scientific explanations can never be more than partial and each new explanation uncovers new arrears of ignorance so that, in a way, ignorance and knowledge grow together (in parenthesis there is an echo here of a Teacher who said, let the wheat and the tares grow together until the harvest).

The experience of the scientist is the experience of all men. The artist, for example, can regard each masterpiece he can produce not as the end of his artistry but only as the challenge to greater heights and it is the masterpiece itself which discloses regions beyond. It all points to the fact that man is incomplete and that incompleteness is not an accident of our present state but the substance of our nature. What the scientist or artist reveals by glorious dissatisfaction is equally revealed by lesser mortals in their sometimes terrifying ability to create some object of veneration if they are unable to find one ready to hand. The idol may be a film star or a dictator, a pop singer or a footballer. Always it is evidence that man, being incomplete, must have something on which to project himself. It is a deep underlying need of all human life. It is the intimation that however creative man may be, ultimately he is a creature and is dependent on something beyond himself. When St Augustine said "Thou hast made us for Thyself and our heart is restless till it finds its rest in Thee" he was making a statement which was true not only for Christians but for all mankind. If it is not true for mankind it is not true for Christians. Contemporary events are providing proof of Augustine's statement because the very religiousness of our age is evidence that all the earthly gadgets we have discovered and all our human reasonings can do little to solve the problems those very reasonings delineate or to fill up what has been called "the God-shaped gap in our lives".

From **Sacred and Secular** by Archbishop Michael Ramsey

We are compelled to attempt what is unattainable, to climb where we cannot reach, to speak what we cannot utter.

Instead of the bare adoration of faith we are compelled to entrust the deep things of religion to the perils of human expression.

The beyondness in the knowledge of God is realised in the silence of adoration, and in the place of mystical experience which is beyond words and images.

Genesis 9:12-17

God said, "Here is the sign of the Covenant I make between myself and you and every living creature with you for all generations. I set my bow in the clouds and it shall be a sign of the Covenant between me and the earth. When I gather the clouds over the earth and the bow appears in the clouds, I will recall the Covenant between myself and you and every living creature of every kind. And so the waters shall never again become a flood to destroy all things of flesh. When the bow is in the clouds I shall see it and call to mind the lasting Covenant between God and every living creature of every kind that is found on the earth."

From **Areopagitica** by John Milton

Books are not absolutely dead things, but do contain a potency of life in them. To be as active as that soul was whose progeny they are; nay they do preserve as in a vial the purest efficacy and extraction of that living intellect that bred them.

From a **Letter** from Dr Coggan, Archbishop of York, in **The Times**

The highest education is that which brings the student face to face, not simply with something great but with someone great, namely Christ.

... I believe that the same principles which apply in a university and which are in peril of going by default, apply also in our schools. I would go further: I believe that many of our present ills both in universities and in schools, are due precisely to this lack of "availability" on the part of teachers to their students ...

It sounds strange to say so, but many of our students are desperately lonely. Almost without realising it, generally without being able to articulate it, they are seeking from their school or university not merely enough to enable them to earn a living in a competitive society, but a way which will help them to live.

They flounder – of course they do. They cannot unaided begin to find an answer to the iniquities and inequities which scream at them from newspaper and television set. To whom shall they go? All too often, father and mother haven't a clue; they may even be frightened of them, and so they give them everything they want but little of what they need.

No wonder if the young shout ... no wonder if they rebel. No wonder if they experiment, often to the severe damaging of their own persons and of others. To whom shall they go? To whom?

You will see the answer that I am pointing towards. Coming as our students often do, from homes where no guidance is given as to the meaning of life and personality and destiny, they must seek that guidance from us. We are back again at the doctrine of "availability". It is a hard doctrine and a costly one.

I know the problems of classes that are too big, of buildings that are too old, of timetables that are far too heavy, and sometimes of salaries that are too low. And because I know this, I know the costliness of availability in terms of sheer tiredness. I know the patience, the insight, the tenacity of purpose that are called for. But unless somewhere close to the student there is someone available in the floundering days of adolescence and young manhood what hope is there of strong character tomorrow?

Many of our young people at school and university – more than the press often suggests – are finding the moral and spiritual guidance they need in the clergy and those who immediately help them. Many are not. Hence the onus on the teacher if, to revert to Dante, the pupil is to come "face to face with something great, so that he experiences first awe and then curiosity". The calling of a teacher, defined in those terms, is indeed a great one, great enough to make any man or woman tremble.

But then you see, I should want to go further than Dante, though I don't think he would have disagreed with my extension of his wording. I would want to say that the very highest, most wonderful education is that which brings the student face to face, not simply with something great, but with someone great, namely Christ. If before him the student can experience awe and curiosity, if he can get some glimpse of Christ crucified and risen, alive and present, he will have his feet put on the road, not merely of earning a living but of entering into life, splendid life in the here and now, life eternal.

And I can imagine no more wonderful vocation (I use the word intentionally) than that of a teacher who is available to help, to guide the student's feet in that direction – no forcing, no compelling, but guiding just at that period of life when a strong, steady, positive lead is desperately needed . . .

St John records how, at a crisis in the ministry of Jesus, "many of his disciples withdrew and no longer went about with him, so Jesus asked the Twelve 'Do you also want to leave me?' Simon Peter answered him, 'Lord to whom shall we go? Your words are eternal life.'" It was a good answer to a direct question. That day Simon Peter's education took a leap forward. He found himself face to face with someone so great that he experienced awe and curiosity. Awe led him to worship and to whole-hearted service. He could not be neutral when he looked into the eyes of Christ. Curiosity led him on imperiously, relentlessly. Who was this who was calling him, holding him, remaking him?

The journey led, if tradition be reliable, eventually to martyrdom, but every mile of the journey was worthwhile, for every mile proved to him the availability of the risen Christ, and in that availability, in the impact of the great one on the little, he discovered the meaning of life.

From **The Prophet** *by* Kahlil Gibran

Then said a teacher, Speak to us of Teaching. And he said:

No man can reveal to you aught but that which already lies half asleep in the dawning of your knowledge.

The teacher who walks in the shadow of the temple, among his followers, gives not of his wisdom but rather of his faith and his lovingness.

If he is indeed wise he does not bid you enter the house of his wisdom, but rather leads you to the threshold of your own mind.

The astronomer may speak to you of his understanding of space, but he cannot give you his understanding.

The musician may sing to you of the rhythm which is in all space, but he cannot give you the ear which arrests the rhythm, nor the voice that echoes it.

And he who is versed in the science of numbers can tell of the regions of weight and measure, but he cannot conduct you thither.

For the vision of one man lends not its wings to another man.

And even as each one of you stands alone in God's knowledge, so must each one of you be alone in his knowledge of God and in his understanding of the earth.

I I

Children, Awareness, Beauty, Nature

"God reveals Himself through these"

Matthew 19:13-15

From **Auguries of Innocence** *by* William Blake. To see the world in a grain of sand

From **Centuries** *by* Thomas Traherne. THE THIRD CENTURY

Matthew 18:1-7, 10, 14

Blest are the pure in heart by J. Keble, 1792-1866

From **Our Knowledge of God** *by* John Baillie

Speech of welcome to Christopher Columbus *by one of the Chiefs of Cuba*

On **The Australian Aborigines.** Source unknown

From **The Listening Heart** *by* Sister Jeanne d'Arc, O.P.

From **The Prophet** *by* Kahlil Gibran

From **A Child Possessed** *by* R. C. Hutchinson. MARSEILLES

From **The Pity of Love** *by* W. B. Yeats. A pity beyond all telling

From **Land of Heart's Desire** *by* W. B. Yeats. Where beauty has no ebb

The Young Man *by* Caryll Houselander, *taken from* **Let there be God,** an anthology of religious poetry *compiled by* T. H. Parker *and* F. J. Teskey

From the introduction to **Let there be God,** an anthology of religious poetry *compiled by* T. H. Parker *and* F. J. Teskey

The Power and the Glory *by* Siegfried Sassoon, *taken from* **Let there be God,** an anthology of religious poetry *compiled by* T. H. Parker *and* F. J. Teskey

John Coburn *from* **Spirituality for Today** (ed. Eric James)

From **Visionary and Dreamer:** William Blake *by* Lord David Cecil

Awareness. Source untraced. The Painter

Comfort *by* Elizabeth Barrett Browning. Earth's crammed with heaven

From **A Child Possessed** *by* R. C. Hutchinson

Mary of Nazareth *by* Clive Sansom, *taken from* **Let there be God,** an anthology of religious poetry *compiled by* T. H. Parker *and* F. J. Teskey

From **Markings** *by* Dag Hammarskjöld

From **Readings from St John's Gospel** *by* William Temple. THE SPIRIT
OF TRUTH

Micah 6:8

Isaiah 33:17, 21-22

God Abides in Men *by* Caryll Houselander, *taken from* **Let there be
God,** an anthology of religious poetry *compiled by* T. H. Parker *and*
F. J. Teskey

From **Visionary and Dreamer:** Edward Burne-Jones *by* Lord David
Cecil

From **The School of Prayer** *by* Olive Wyon. Beauty

Evelyn Underhill, *quoted in* **Shepperd's Pie** *by* H. R. L. Shepperd.
I come in the little things

From **Centuries** *by* Thomas Traherne. THE FIRST CENTURY

The Green Veil *from* **Punch.** Anon. It was the Willow who first wore it

Sunrise: a description, *by* Elizabeth Goudge

The Cloud *by* P. B. Shelley. I bring fresh showers

From **The Story of a Life** *by* Konstantin Paustovsky

From **Only One Year** *by* Svetlana Alliluyeva. THE GANGES AT NIGHT

From **Childe Harold** *by* Lord Byron. The moon is up and yet

From **The Story of a Life** *by* Konstantin Paustovsky. THE DEMON

From **Markings** *by* Dag Hammarskjöld. In a dream I walked with God

From **Markings** *by* Dag Hammarskjöld. LONELINESS

From **Intimations of Immortality** *by* William Wordsworth

From **Rabbi ben Ezra** *by* Robert Browning. Grow old along with me!

From **The Ring and the Book** *by* Robert Browning. All that is at all

Salutation to the Dawn *from* **Martha's Prayer Book.** Look well to
this day

The Glory of Life. Source unknown

From **Freedom, Faith and the Future** *by* Archbishop Michael Ramsey.
THE FUTURE

From **The Story of my Heart** *by* Richard Jefferies, *taken from* **Mysticism**
by F. C. Happold

Sunset *by* Edwin Muir, *taken from* **New Fire.** Fold upon fold of light

From **An Essay on Man** *by* Alexander Pope. All are but parts of one
stupendous whole

From **The Shaking of the Foundations** *by* Paul Tillich. NATURE, ALSO,
MOURNS FOR A LOST GOOD

Isaiah 11:6-9

Job 39:19-25. THE HORSE

The Dog's Prayer *by* Piero Scanziani

From **Markings** *by* Dag Hammarskjöld. ELEGY FOR MY PET MONKEY
From **Chronicles of Brother Wolf** *by* Tertius Mowbray, *found in*
The Burrswood Herald. WAITING
Song to David *by* Christopher Smart. He sang of God

Matthew 19:13-15

Then some little children were brought to him, so that he could put
his hands on them and pray for them. The Disciples frowned on the
parents' action but Jesus said "You must let little children come to me,
and you must never stop them. The Kingdom of Heaven belongs to
little children like these!" Then he laid his hands on them and went
away.

From **Auguries of Innocence** *by* William Blake

> *To see a world in a grain of sand*
> *And a Heaven in a Wild Flower;*
> *Hold Infinity in the palm of your hand,*
> *And Eternity in an hour.*

From **Centuries** *by* Thomas Traherne

THE THIRD CENTURY

All appeared new and strange at first, inexpressibly rare and delightful
and beautiful. I was a little stranger, which, at my entrance into the world,
was saluted and surrounded with innumerable joys. My knowledge was
Divine. I knew by intuition those things which since my apostasy, I
collected again, by the highest reason. My very ignorance was advan-
tageous, I seemed as one brought into the Estate of Innocence. All things
were spotless and pure and glorious: yea and infinitely mine and joyful
and precious. I knew not that there were any sins or complaints or laws.
I dreamed not of poverties, contentions or vices. All tears and quarrels
were hidden from my eyes.

Everything was at rest, free and immortal. I knew nothing of sickness or
death or rents or exaction, either for tribute or bread. In the absence of
these I was entertained like an angel with the works of God in their
splendour and glory. I saw all in the peace of Eden; Heaven and Earth
did sing my creator's praises, and could not make more melody to Adam
than to me. All time was eternity, and a perpetual Sabbath. Is it not
strange that an infant should be heir to the whole world and see those
mysteries which the books of the learned never unfold.

The corn was orient and immortal wheat, which never should be reaped, nor was ever sown. I thought it had stood from everlasting. The dust and stones of the street were as precious as gold: the gates were at first the end of the world. The green trees, when I first saw them through one of the gates, transported and ravished me, their sweetness and unusual beauty made my heart to leap, and almost mad with ecstasy, they were such strange and wonderful things. The Men! O what venerable and reverend creatures did the aged seem! Immortal Cherubims! And young men glittering and sparkling Angels. And maids strange seraphic pieces of life and beauty! Boys and girls tumbling in the streets and playing, were moving jewels. I knew not that they were born and should die; but all things abided eternally as they were in their proper places. Eternity was manifest in the Light of Day, and something infinite behind everything appeared: which talked with my expectation and moved my desire. The city seemed to stand in Eden, or to be built in Heaven. The streets were mine, the temple was mine, the people were mine, their clothes and gold and silver were mine, as much as their sparkling eyes, fair skins and ruddy faces. The skies were mine, and so were the sun and moon and stars, and all the world was mine; and I the only spectator and enjoyer of it. I knew no childish proprieties, nor bounds, nor divisions: but all proprieties and divisions were mine; all treasures and the possessors of them. So that with much ado I was corrupted, and made to learn the dirty devices of this world; which now I unlearn, and become as it were, a little child again that I may enter into the Kingdom of God.

Matthew 18:1-7, 10, 14

It was at this time that the disciples came to Jesus with the question, "Who is really greatest in the Kingdom of Heaven?" Jesus called a little child and set him on his feet in the middle of them all. "Believe me," he said, "unless you change your whole outlook and become like little children you will never enter the Kingdom of Heaven. It is the man who can be as humble as this little child who is greatest in the Kingdom of Heaven.

"Anyone who welcomes one child like this for my sake is welcoming me. But if anyone leads astray one of these little children who believe in me he would be better thrown off into the depths of the sea with a millstone hung round his neck! Alas for the world with its pitfalls! In the nature of things there must be pitfalls, yet alas for the man who is responsible for them . . .

" . . . Be careful that you never despise a single one of these little ones – for I tell you that they have angels who see my Father's face continually in Heaven.

"... You can understand then that it is never the will of your Father in Heaven that a single one of these little ones should be lost."

Blest are the pure in heart *by* J. Keble, 1792–1866

> *Blest are the pure in heart,*
> *For they shall see our God;*
> *The secret of the Lord is theirs,*
> *Their soul is Christ's abode.*
>
> *The Lord, who left the heavens*
> *Our life and peace to bring,*
> *To dwell in lowliness with men*
> *Their pattern and their King;*
>
> *Still to the lowly soul*
> *He doth himself impart,*
> *And for his dwelling and his throne*
> *Chooseth the pure in heart.*
>
> *Lord, we thy presence seek;*
> *May ours this blessing be;*
> *Give us a pure and lowly heart*
> *A temple meet for thee.*

From **Our Knowledge of God** *by* John Baillie

Are there men or have there ever been men in whose experience religion has played no part? Is there a consciousness which, while already fully human, is yet merely human, and has never been invaded by the Divine?

It is clear to me that I cannot find such a consciousness by going back to the beginning of my experience. No matter how far back I go, no matter by what effort of memory I attempt to reach virgin soil of childish innocence, I cannot get back to an atheist's mentality.

As little can I reach a day when I was conscious of myself but not of God as I can reach a day when I was conscious of myself but not of other human beings. My earliest memories have a definitely religious atmosphere. They are already heavy with the numinous. They contain as part of their substance a recognition – as vague and inarticulate as you will, yet quite unmistakable for anything else – of what I have now learned to call the divine as a factor in my environment ...

Clearly, however my infant experience was determined for me, to an extent which it is difficult to set a limit, by the long tradition in which I stood. I was born into a christian home and God's earliest disclosure of His reality to my infant soul was mediated to me by the words and deeds

182

of my parents. Had I been born into the first generation of human infants, or into a society of the most primitive kind of which we have any knowledge or record, my experience could not possibly have been what it was. But would it still have had some religious quality? One way of seeking an answer to this question is to ask, Are the most primitive human societies known to us already aware of some such confrontation? And there seems little doubt that they are. It seems nowadays to be a matter of almost unanimous agreement among those competent to judge, that neither history nor geography can show us any tribe or people which is devoid of all religious awareness.

We know no human society however savage and backward, which does not already find itself confronted with the divine. It may be a matter of dispute whether all peoples are aware of deity as personal, or even as spiritual being but it is not disputed that all peoples have such an awareness of the divine as is sufficient to awaken in them what it is impossible to regard otherwise than as a typically religious response.

Speech of welcome to Christopher Columbus *by one of the Chiefs of Cuba*

Whether you are divinities or mortal men we know not. You have come into these countries with a force against which were we inclined to resist it, resistance would be folly: we are all therefore at your mercy. But if you are men subject to mortality like ourselves you cannot be unapprised that after this life there is another, wherein a very different portion is allotted to good and bad men. If therefore you expect to die and believe with us that everyone is rewarded in a future state according to his conduct in the present, you will do no hurt to those who do no hurt to you.

On The Australian Aborigines. Source unknown

There seems to have been a continual preoccupation with the mystery of life and death, and all that was unknown or not physically present at any given moment was referred to as being "in the dreaming".

From The Listening Heart *by* Sister Jeanne d'Arc, O.P.

There is another privileged period in our lives when the gifts of the Holy Spirit have free play, though, in the case of very many Christians, it often passes unnoticed. I am referring, of course, to childhood. Before they reach the age of reason, little children are very often under the influence of the Holy Spirit. The mechanism of the virtues has not been fully developed; they still do not possess full freedom of judgement or the ability to assess objectively the value of their actions. Nevertheless, they retain the unsullied grace of baptism and the Lord himself can easily work in their souls. Thus the Spirit moves them to act in accordance with the divine life which they have received, so much so that their spiritual judgement, their taste for the things of God, their understanding, the openness of their intelligence and their heart, are far more advanced supernaturally than they are in the natural order.

Once they attain the "use of reason", they will have to practise the virtues patiently, with fortitude and over a very long period before they can once more regain that familiarity with the supernatural, that feeling for divine realities, that ready docility to grace which was so spontaneous in them when they were small.

From **The Prophet** *by* Kahlil Gibran

And a woman who held a babe against her bosom said, Speak to us of Children.

And he said:

Your children are not your children.

They are the sons and daughters of Life's longing for itself.

They come through you but not from you,

And though they are with you yet they belong not to you.

You may give them your love but not your thoughts.

For they have their own thoughts.

You may house their bodies but not their souls,

For their souls dwell in the house of to-morrow, which you cannot visit, not even in your dreams.

You may strive to be like them, but seek not to make them like you.

For life goes not backward nor tarries with yesterday.

You are the bows from which your children as living arrows are sent forth.

The archer sees the mark upon the path of the infinite, and He bends you with His might that His arrows may go swift and far.

Let your bending in the Archer's hand be for gladness;

For even as He loves the arrow that flies, so He loves also the bow that is stable.

From **A Child Possessed** *by* R. C. Hutchinson

MARSEILLES

More and more he realised how his old fondness for the sprawling conurbation had been heightened by her coming. It had always commanded his admiration: immeasurably old but delighting in modern fripperies, proof against men's and nature's violence, breathing the scents

184

of Africa and the wasted arrogance of Rome, this slatternly Queen of the Mediterranean had bewitched him with her inexhaustible vitality. But now her face had become more motherly. For at any crossing of her myriad lanes, in any pattern of hour and season, he would recall some small excursion with Eugenie, some turn of conduct which had revealed another facet of her nature. Here in the Boulevard Mirabeau she had escaped from him to wander off and seat herself in the middle of the road, and now he could seldom pass this way without a recollection of the scene – the street in a fan of yellow light split from the storm clouds massing over Fort St Jean, the child a figure of extreme composure staring with what he believed to be conscious impudence at the several drivers she had wantonly alarmed. Likewise he had come to think of the church of St Theodore, so long his private refuge, as Eugenie's own; since there instead of promenading noisily and clambering over chairs as she did in other Churches, she would stand so still, in awe of its dark immensity, that he often forgot her presence, and once when his devotion had lasted longer than usual, he had found her lying in the Misericorde chapel peacefully asleep.

The headland of Malmousque had become the place where, as they stood to watch the crash of mighty seas on the rocks below, she had taken his thumb and held it with perfect gentleness between her lips; amid the convulsive traffic of the Place des Capucines, one burning afternoon, she had turned her stolid face to his and uttered the peculiar sound which he took to stand for gaiety and joy; and on a winter evening when an offshore breeze set all the lights of the Quai du Port dancing in the water, she too, letting go his hand, throwing her weight from one crooked leg to the other like an old man in his cups, had done her best to dance. He began to see the town of his adoption and the daughter who had been restored to him as possessing more in common than his affection. They had the appearance, both, of careless fashioning, each had grown away from her natural shape, each was supplied too meagrely with those graces which are looked for in a finished work. But he thought they shared as well, a kind of honesty, a calm endurance of their state. Each – with the gleam of morning light on a file of sycamores or on a tumbled lock of hair, with the sudden blaze of flowers at a street corner or the rose perfection of a nipple thrusting from a torn night-dress, the lowing of a ship's siren through the opalescent mist or a queer small cry that greeted the starting of the Berliet's engine – could show such a flash of beauty as would set his heart on fire. And sometimes, now, he could fancy that Notre Dame-de-la-Garde, keeping by day and night her lofty watch over the loaded streets, the hiving ships, the diadem of islands, would yet have in her special care a virgin girl confined by deformity to a separate, twilight world, a child so innocent, so terribly alone.

185

From **The Pity of Love** *by* W. B. Yeats

> A pity beyond all telling
> Is hid in the heart of love.

From **Land of Heart's Desire** *by* W. B. Yeats

Where beauty has no ebb, decay no flood,
But joy is wisdom, time and endless song.
All things uncomely and broken, all things worn out and old,
The cry of a child by the roadway, the creak of a lumbering cart,
The heavy steps of the ploughman, splashing the wintry mould,
Are wronging your image that blossoms a rose in the deeps of my heart.
The wrong of unshapely things is a wrong too great to be told
I hunger to build them anew and sit on a green knoll apart,
With the earth and the sky and the water remade, like a cask of gold;
For my dreams of your image that blossoms a rose in the deeps of my heart.

The Young Man *by* Caryll Houselander, *taken from* **Let there be God**,
an anthology of religious poetry *compiled by* T. H. Parker *and* F. J. Teskey

There is a young man
who lives in a world of progress.
He used to worship a God
who was kind to him.
This God had a long white beard,
He lived in the clouds,
but all the same
He was close to the solemn child
who had secretly
shut Him up, in a picture book.

But now
the man is enlightened.
Now he has been to school
and has learned to kick a ball
and to be abject
in the face of public opinion.
He knows too,
that men are hardly removed from monkeys.
You see he lives in the light
of the twentieth century.

He works, twelve hours a day,
and is able to rent a room,

in a lodging house,
that is not a home.
At night he hangs
a wretched coat
up on a peg on the door,
and stares
at the awful jug and basin,
and goes to bed.
And the poor coat,
worn to the man's shape
round-shouldered and abject
watches him, asleep, dreaming of all
the essential
holy things
that he cannot hope to obtain
for ten pounds a week.

Very soon
he will put off his body
like the dejected coat
that he hates.
And his body will be
worn to the shape
of twelve hours' work a day
for ten pounds a week.
If he had only known
that the God in the picture book,
is not an old man in the clouds
but the seed of life in his soul,
the man would have lived.
And his life would have flowered
with the flower of limitless joy.

But he does not know,
and in him
the Holy Ghost
is a poor little bird
in a cage,
who never sings,
and never opens his wings,
yet never, never
desires to be gone away.

From the introduction to **Let there be God,** an anthology of religious poetry
compiled by T. H. Parker *and* F. J. Teskey

> *Let there be life, said God . . .*
> *Let there be God, say I . . .*
> *Let life be God . . .*

Into those three short sentences Siegfried Sassoon has compressed a
profound religious belief. And with many of his fellow artists, whether
they be painters, sculptors, composers, or poets, he could have postulated,
"Let life be art", thus completing the mystic circle: God, Life, Art.

Religion and the arts have always been naturally complementary.
Temples to Athene Parthenos and Zeus architecturally showed the Greeks'
reverence and fear for their gods; statues of the Roman deities, Jupiter,
Venus and Apollo, were the forerunners of Epstein's Madonna and Child
and St Michael and the Devil. A religion of love and hope was enshrined
in the sublime poetry of the Psalms, and in all ages great music has ennobled man's idea of God.

Enamel and gold of Russian icons depicted Christ in human likeness;
mosaics and marbles of Byzantine churches and stained-glass windows of
mediaeval cathedrals spelled out the Bible story in rich colours for those
who were unable to read. The beauty of Christ's birth and his agony on
the Cross have been portrayed by every Christian nation in painting,
sculpture, or engraving.

In the widest, and possibly truest, sense of the word, all great artists have
been religious in that they have created works which appeal as religion
does, to the best in man. It must be recognised that man has a "best",
and by corollary, a "worst". That is a basic premise whether one's ideals
are Christian, Buddhist, Moslem, Humanist, or even Existentialist.

Perhaps it is that restless "best" in Man that prompts progress. Progress
of any kind implies the existence of a desirable goal, and a recognition of
the defects in an existing system, whether it be an economic, a social, or
a religious system.

The materialistic twentieth century sees a solution to its problems in the
raising of living standards. America is lauded for its prosperity: the
emergent nations of Africa clamour for a greater portion of the world's
goods; Communist Russia and China are equally set on an increasing
affluence.

It would be wrong to attempt to deny the validity of such attitudes;
every man has a natural right to the good things of this earth. And there
is sufficient for everyone, even though many sources may as yet be un-
tapped. It is, however, still pertinent to say "What shall it profit a man if
he gain the whole world and lose his own soul?" Materialism *per se* is

barren and arid. A nation obsessed with materialism must inevitably and ultimately die. Having achieved all its material needs, it has nothing left to live for; the real goal, the ultimate vision, has disappeared. And what else is there for any generation, any country, to hand on to its children except vision, a reason for living, for striving, even for suffering? "Where there is no vision the people perish."

Creative artists have always realised that, either through reasoning or intuitively. But they can also see the misery and suffering, physical and spiritual, that have always been with us. Indeed, because of this sensitivity, the creative artist may be the one who suffers most. Thus arises the dichotomy: on the one hand is the visionary who can see heaven despite this world, or perhaps because of this world; on the other hand is the ordinary citizen of this world, who feels strongly the injustices of life but cannot find hope in the tangle of his frustrations because he has no vision.

One can detect those two attitudes in the poetry, the painting and the sculpture of our times. A work of art is essentially part of God, even though the tone may be bitter, cynical or ironic. The two attitudes are not mutually exclusive; they are, indeed, complementary. Man is of God, although he is but "flesh and bone": "Adam unparadised". He recognises his own sin in that he crucified God the Son; today men are still

onlookers at the crime,
Callous contemporaries of the slow torture of God.

Every generation must find its own values; the present generation is still searching. Man, while recognising the existence of God queries his effectiveness, derides his divinity, sneers at his tenets. But even this is not new; nor is it vital. The fact that man may deny Christianity does not refute the existence of God, who, as D. H. Lawrence said, may exist in a "living unconscious life. If only we were to shut our eyes; if only we were all struck blind, and things vanished from our sight, we should marvel that we have fought and lived for shallow, visual peripheral nothingness. We should find reality in darkness."

It is in the darkness of man's mind that God exists. His spirit is revealed through the agony of creation, whether it be of life, of poetry, of painting, of sculpture, or of music.

The poems and illustrations of *Let there be God* are selected to emphasise the impact that God has made on the twentieth-century creative artist. The mystic circle of God, Life, Art, admits of no systematic philosophy or dogmatic religious creed. God has as many faces as there are poets and painters; religion is a personal feeling, and God reveals Himself in myriads of ways . . .

An equally wide variety of approach and interpretation is apparent in the illustrations. The contemporary artist, whether he is working in oils, tapestry, stone or glass makes his own significant comment on the validity of Bible truths. Unquestioning acceptance is rare; doubt, disillusionment and despair are often evident. But the doubt, disillusionment and despair spring, not from religion, but from man's approach to it and from his treatment of the living God. The artist, in whatever medium he works, depicts what he feels to be right. Society may reject his interpretation, although it cannot ignore it; here it is comment enough to say that society rejected God the Son nearly 2,000 years ago. And yet he still lives, and is honoured and glorified today in art as much as he ever was in the past. God in art represents the best in life.

Not all the poets and painters in *Let there be God* are Christians; some are confessed atheists or agnostics; one is a Buddhist. But each and every contributor is aware of God the Creator, God the crucified, God the Rejected, God in Man, God the Artist. There is implicit in every poem the realisation that Man needs God as much as God needs Man.

The Power and the Glory *by* Siegfried Sassoon, *taken from* **Let there be God,** an anthology of religious poetry *compiled by* T. H. Parker *and* F. J. Teskey

> Let There Be Life, said God. And what He wrought
> Went past in myriad marching lives, and brought
> This hour, this quiet room, and my small thought
> Holding invisible vastness in its hands.
>
> Let There be God, say I. And what I've done
> Goes onward like the splendour of the sun
> And rises up in rapture and is one
> With the white power of conscience that commands.
>
> Let Life Be God. . . . What wail of fiend or wraith
> Dare mock my glorious angel where he stands
> To fill my dark with fire, my heart with faith.

John Coburn *from* **Spirituality for Today** (ed. Eric James)

"I don't know Who – or what – put the question. I don't know when it was put. I don't remember even answering. But at some moment I did answer YES to Someone – or Something – and from that hour I was certain that existence is meaningful and that, therefore, my life, in self-surrender, had a goal" (Dag Hammarskjöld).

To say Yes to Someone – or Something; to be certain that existence is meaningful; to know that the goal of life is self-surrender. That is the new spirituality, as new as Dag Hammarskjöld – and as old as Abraham.

From **Visionary and Dreamer:** William Blake *by* Lord David Cecil

. . . I rest not from my great task. To open the Eternal Worlds, to open the immortal Eyes of man inwards . . .

Awareness. Source untraced.

The painter looks with an enquiring eye. He opens the door of his mind and absorbs in that storehouse all the knowledge he can.

It is not so much knowledge that one acquires but a wider perception of awareness which is infinitely worth while.

It is not the learning of applied brainwork, nor can it be obtained from books.

It is the broadening of the senses: a greater capacity to feel.

Comfort *by* Elizabeth Barrett Browning

> *Earth's crammed with heaven,*
> *And every common bush afire with God;*
> *But only he who sees takes off his shoes,*
> *The rest sit round it and pluck blackberries,*
> *And daub their natural faces unaware*
> *More and more from the first similitude.*

From **A Child Possessed** *by* R. C. Hutchinson

He pressed a switch, and in a corner of the small, shabby room the light from hidden globes broke evenly on an unframed canvas, some eighteen inches square, which showed a Virgin of unconventional youthfulness in a robe and fillet of Aegean blue . . .

"You may get my meaning," he said, "when I tell you that picture does more to me than twenty sermons. For one thing it tells me what religious faith can do with ordinary things. You look at that face – you know that girl's had some experience no other woman had before or since. But the model's nothing unusual – you'll see girls like that today, any time you like to walk around the fields in Tuscany. Look at her skin – look at the freckles. That's not the daughter of a rich storekeeper even. That's a peasant girl."

Mary of Nazareth *by* Clive Sansom, *taken from* **Let there be God**, an anthology of religious poetry *compiled by* T. H. Parker *and* F. J. Teskey

> *It was like music:*
> *Hovering and floating there*
> *With the sound of lutes and timbrels*
> *In the night air.*

It was like waves
Beating upon the shore:
Insistent with a rhythm, a pulsing
Unfelt before.

It was like wind:
Blowing from off the seas
Of other, far other
Lands than these.

It was like wings,
Like whirring wings that fly –
The song of an army of swans
On the dark sky.

It was like God:
A presence of blinding light,
Ravishing body and soul
In the spring night.

From **Markings** *by* Dag Hammarskjöld

Thou takest the pen – and the lines dance. Thou takest the flute – and the notes shimmer. Thou takest the brush and the colours sing. So all things have meaning and beauty in that space beyond time where Thou art. How then can I hold back anything from Thee?

From **Readings from St John's Gospel** *by* William Temple
THE SPIRIT OF TRUTH

Not only in Jesus Christ does the Spirit of Truth touch the hearts of men. He spoke to and through Plato, as the early Christian Fathers fully recognised; and has spoken through many a seer, poet and prophet both within and outside the Canon of Holy Scripture.

Wherever there is response in the hearts of men to the manifested glory of God, whether that manifestation be in nature or in history, there the spirit of truth is at work. He inspires all Science and all Art, and speaks in the conscience of the heathen child. Yet it is also true that the Son sends Him. For only in the Word made flesh is the glory of God truly displayed. We behold the glory; that is the condition of receiving the Holy Spirit in His power. He procedeth from the Father and (or through) the Son.

Micah 6:8

He has showed you, O man, what is good:
and what does the Lord require of you

but to do justice and to love kindness,
and to walk humbly with your God?

Isaiah 33:17, 21-22

> *Your eyes will see the King in his beauty:*
> *they will behold a land that stretches afar.*
> *. . . . But there the Lord in majesty will be for us,*
> *a place of broad rivers and streams,*
> *where no galley with oars can go,*
> *nor stately ship pass.*
> *For the Lord is our judge, the Lord is our ruler,*
> *The Lord is our King; he will save us.*

God Abides in Men *by* Caryll Houselander, *taken from* **Let there be God**, an anthology of religious poetry *compiled by* T. H. Parker *and* F. J. Teskey

God abides in men
Because Christ has put on
the nature of man, like a garment,
and worn it to His own shape.
He has put on everyone's life.
He has fitted Himself to the little child's dress,
to the shepherd's coat of sheepskin,
to the workman's coat
to the King's red robes,
to the snowy loveliness of the wedding garment,
and to the drab
and the sad, simple battle-dress.

Christ has put on man's nature, and given him back his humanness
worn to the shape
of limitless love, and warm from the touch
of His life.

He has given man His crown,
the thorn that is jewelled
with drops of His blood.
He has given him
the seamless garment
of His truth.

He has bound him
in the swaddling bands
of His humility.

He has fastened his hands
to the tree of life.

He has latched his feet
in crimson sandals
that they move not
From the path of love.
God abides in man.

From **Visionary and Dreamer:** Edward Burne-Jones *by* Lord David Cecil

Only this is true, that beauty is very beautiful, and softens and comforts, and inspires, and rouses, and lifts up, and never fails."

From **The School of Prayer** *by* Olive Wyon

The wonder of creation suggests another gateway to worship: the door of Beauty. Whatever kind of beauty stirs us to delight or to painful longing, we can use as a ladder to rise above ourselves. For this love of beauty is divinely implanted. The touch of beauty, when we feel it, is not to be merely a passing delight: it is the call of God, inviting us gently and sweetly to turn to Him. St Augustine says: "Thy whole creation praises Thee without ceasing . . . to the end that, using Thy creatures as stepping stones, and passing on to Him who made them so wonderfully, our soul might shake off its despondence and soar up to Thee. There is refreshment and true courage." To the man or woman who "means only God" the beauty of Creation may become a transparent veil, half concealing and half revealing the presence of Love itself.

Evelyn Underhill, *quoted in* **Shepperd's Pie** *by* H. R. L. Shepperd

I come in the little things,
Saith the Lord:
Not borne on morning wings
Of Majesty, but I have set my Feet
Amidst the delicate and bladed wheat
That springs triumphant in the furrowed sod.
There do I dwell, in weakness and in power:
Not broken or divided, saith our God!
In your strait garden plot I come to flower:
About your porch My Vine
Meek, fruitful, doth entwine:
Waits, at the threshold, love's appointed hour.

I come in the little things,
Saith the Lord:

Yea! on the glancing wings
Of eager birds, the softly pattering feet
Of furred and gentle beasts, I come to meet
Your hard and wayward heart. In brown bright eyes
That peep from out the brake, I stand confest
On every nest,
Where feathery patience is content to brood
And leaves her pleasure for the high emprize
Of motherhood –
There doth My Godhead rest.

I come in the little things,
Saith the Lord:
My starry wings
I do forsake,
Love's highway of humility take:
Meekly I fit My stature to your need.
In beggar's part
About your gates I shall not cease to plead
As man to speak with man
Till by such art
I shall achieve My Immemorial Plan:
Pass the low lintel of the human heart.

From **Centuries** *by* Thomas Traherne

THE FIRST CENTURY

By the very right of your senses you enjoy the World. Is not the beauty of the Hemisphere present to your eye? Doth not the glory of the Sun pay tribute to your sight? Is not the vision of the World an amiable thing? Do not the stars shed influence to perfect the Air? Is not that a marvellous body to breathe in? To visit the lungs, repair the spirit, revive the senses, cool the blood, fill the empty space between the Earth and Heavens and yet give liberty to all objects? Prize these first: and you shall enjoy the residue: Glory, Dominion, Power, Wisdom, Angels, Souls, Kingdoms, Ages. "Be faithful in a little, and you shall be master over much." If you be not faithful in esteeming these; who shall put into your hands the True Treasure. If you be negligent in prizing these, you will be negligent in prizing all. For there is a disease in him who despiseth present mercies, which till it be cured, he can never be happy. He esteemeth nothing that he hath, but is ever gaping after more: which when he hath he despiseth in like manner. Insatiableness is good, but not ingratitude.

. . . Your enjoyment of the World is never right, till you so esteem it, that everything in it is more treasure than a King's exchequer full of Gold and Silver. And that exchequer yours also in its place and service. Can you take too much joy in your Father's works? He is Himself in everything. Some things are little on the outside, and rough and common, but I remember the time when the dust of the streets were as precious as Gold to my infant eyes, and now they are more precious to the eye of reason . . . Your enjoyment of the world is never right, till every morning you awake in Heaven; see yourself in your Father's palace; and look upon the skies, the earth and the air as celestial joys: having such a reverend esteem of all as if you were among the Angels. The bride of a monarch, in her husband's chamber, hath no such causes of delight as you.

You never enjoy the World aright, till the sea itself floweth in your veins, till you are clothed with the heavens, and crowned with the stars: and perceive yourself to be the sole heir of the whole world, and more than so, because men are in it who are every one sole heirs as well as you. Till you can sing and rejoice and delight in God, as misers do in gold, and Kings in sceptres, you can never enjoy the world.

Till your spirit filleth the whole world, and the stars are your jewels, till you are familiar with the ways of God in all Ages as with your walk and table: till you are intimately acquainted with that shady nothing out of which the world was made: till you love men so as to desire their happiness with a thirst equal to the zeal of your own: till you delight in God for being good to all: you never enjoy the world. Till you more feel it than your private estate, and are more present in the hemisphere, considering the glories and the beauties there, than in your own house. Till you remember how lately you were made, and how wonderful it was when you came into it: and more rejoice in the palace of your glory, than if it had been made but today morning.

Yet further, you never enjoy the world aright, till you so love the beauty of enjoying it, that you are covetous and earnest to persuade others to enjoy it. And so perfectly hate the abominable corruption of men in despising it, that you had rather suffer the flames of Hell than willingly be guilty of their error. There is so much blindness and ingratitude and damned folly in it. The world is a mirror of infinite beauty, yet no man sees it. It is a Temple of Majesty, yet no man regards it. It is a region of Light and Peace, did man not disquiet it. It is the Paradise of God. It is more to man since he is fallen than it was before. It is the place of Angels and the Gate of Heaven. When Jacob waked out of his dream, he said "God is here and I wist it not. How dreadful is this place! This is none other than the House of God, and the Gate of Heaven."

The Green Veil *from* **Punch**. Anon.

It was the Willow who first wore it
Until her weaving fingers tore it
On the moss-grown wall,
Weeping, she let it fall.
The Ivy for a shroud intended it,
But Hawthorn with her needle mended it,
Washed it and spread it out to dry.
A March wind, galloping by,
Seized it and threw it over Ash and Oak
Who for a joke,
Tied pale pink ribbons on it
And made the Almond wear it as a bonnet.
Almond ripped off the bows and took a tuck in it
To make a frill for Chestnut's wrist
But Chestnut's treacly thumbs got stuck in it.
Her neighbour, Quince,
Unwound it twist by twist
Gave it a rinse,
And by the ivory moon sat all one night
Embroidering it in stars of white,
For gipsy Cherry, Plum and Pear
To twine in their wild hair.
With the wind's combing
The tangled stars shuffled out,
Weaving a web of thinnest tissue
For Silver Birch
To gather in the April gloaming
And crochet into a lace fichu,
Which (much puffed out)
She wears outside the Church.
So it is passed and passed
Continuously
From tree to tree:
Used now for this, now that –
As garland, coronet, hat
And at the last,
By Poplar, as a broom
To sweep her room,
And then away, away
Into the auction rooms of May

Where all the rags and ribbons of the Spring are sold
For Cowslips gold,
And auctioneering crickets pass
Between the tufty stems of grass
Crying "For sale! For sale!
A green veil."

Sunrise: a description, *by* Elizabeth Goudge

Down below them the valley where they lived was drowned in shadow, about them the mountains were still wreathed in mist, overhead the sky was clear but cold, its ice-blue mirrored in the mountain tarn beside them. They could no longer hear the sheep bells or the voice of the hidden water-falls, for though the music was still there it had fallen away from the consciousness of the watchers, that was focused now upon the music of colour and light. They knew the opening bars of the symphony, or the opening movements of the brush, choosing what analogy they might in their striving for apprehension, by heart now – the silvery lightening of the sky behind the eastern mountains, the corresponding darkening of the peaks that brought their exquisite silhouette into being. Yet the movement into life was never perceptible, never the same, and always there was the shock of surprise at finding in existence a something to whose gradual unfolding one had thought one was raptly attentive, and yet there it was, caught in the moment of perfect attainment and one did not know how it had attained.

And nature, that unlike man admits not even the thought of finality into any of her processes, did not allow the movement even that breath of a pause that comes between the movements of a symphony, the strokes of an artist's brush.

"And now the Sun has stretched out all the hills."

The simplicity of that first statement, the clear-cut contrast of the dark silhouette against the silver sky, was all at once a flood of colour and light that poured over the world as though the eastern mountains were a rampart that had broken letting in the sea. As if the immensity of the sky were a canvas not large enough, the colour came streaming down the mountainside, staining the snows with lilac and rose, brimming the deep ravines with purple and the tarns with gold, down and down until it reached the lower slopes where each rock and tree, each patch of gorse or clump of flowers beside a stream became a dazzling jewel sewn upon the green hem of a garment woven from the height of heaven to the depth of earth without a seam or flaw without even a beginning or end except that arbitrary one of height and depth, man-made because of eyes

that could penetrate neither the blinding light overhead nor the shadows
that would linger in the depths of the valley until mid-day.

The Cloud *by* P. B. Shelley

> *I bring fresh showers for the thirsty flowers*
> *From the seas and the streams;*
> *I bear light shade for the leaves when laid*
> *In their noonday dreams . . .*
>
> *I wield the flail of the lashing hail*
> *And whiten the green plains under,*
> *And then again I dissolve it in rain*
> *And laugh as I pass in thunder.*
>
> *I sift the snow on the mountains below,*
> *And their great pines groan aghast;*
> *And all the night 'tis my pillow white,*
> *While I sleep in the arms of the blast,*
> *Sublime on the towers of my skiey bowers*
> *Lightning my pilot sits;*
> *In a cavern under is fettered the thunder*
> *It struggles and howls in fits.*
>
> *And I all the while bask in Heaven's blue smile*
> *Whilst he is dissolving in rains.*

From **The Story of a Life** *by* Konstantin Paustovsky

Nowhere else have I seen such ancient lime trees. At night their tops
were lost in the sky and if the wind rose the stars darted in and out of the
branches like fireflies. In the daytime it was dark under the trees, while up
above, among the fresh leaves there was the incessant fluttering, chattering
and quarrelling of an immense population of birds.

From **Only One Year** *by* Svetlana Alliluyeva

THE GANGES AT NIGHT

There were no famous temples in Kalakankar, no historical monuments,
no rare sights in this lonely land, with its scorched earth and dirty village.
The colours were not bright, the peasants wore nothing but plain white,
the dusty foliage of the trees was dull. There was nothing exotic about the
place, none of the fairytale quality that tourists sought in India. But
instead, present in everything, permeating everything, there was an
impossible deep sound, like that of an organ. If you remained very quiet,
if you sat still gazing at the river, you too would hear it. You would sense
it coming as a slow, reverberating gong, as the quietly breathing heart of a

mighty, eternal life, in which everything – the earth, the river, the sky, the birds, and man – found itself blended. Even he who knows not God, who does not believe in Him, would, without knowing it, thank Him for the peace that filled his soul, and involuntarily, as though against his will, the words would escape him: "Lord what bliss!"

From **Childe Harold** by Lord Byron

> *The moon is up and yet it is not night;*
> *Sunset divides the sky with her; a sea*
> *Of glory streams along the Alpine height*
> *Of blue Friuli's mountains; Heaven is free*
> *From clouds, but of all colours seems to be –*
> *Melted to one vast Iris of the West –*
> *Where the day joins the past Eternity.*

From **The Story of a Life** by Konstantin Paustovsky

THE DEMON

Moscow was steaming with cold. Clouds of vapour poured out of the open doors of taverns. Against the cosy Moscow snow scene – the frosted trees along the avenues, the windows frosted with rime, the greenish glow of the gas-lights – Vrubel's painting flashed with a diamond flame, like a jewel from the icy summits of the Caucasus. It filled the picture hall with the chilly breath of beauty and the majesty of human discontent.

I stood looking at it for a long time, realising as never before that the contemplation of such a painting is more than visual pleasure – it dredges the mind for ideas one has never before suspected oneself of having.

I thought of Lermontov and imagined him walking in with a discreet jingle of spurs, tossing his greatcoat to the attendant in the hall, stopping in front of the picture and moodily gazing at his Demon. It was about himself that he wrote with bitterness "I am as useless to the world as the blaze of a shooting star." But my God how wrong he was. How great is the world's need of the blaze of shooting stars – since man does not live by bread alone.

He thought of himself as in bondage to the world. He spent himself in the desert. But the desert blossomed, brought to life by his poetry, his anger, his anguish and his conception of joy. And he did, after all, confess to a nodding acquaintance with the shy woodland flowers. Perhaps the rarefied air above the summits sprinkled with the Demon's blood held something of their scent and Lermontov and his Demon were only children refused by life what they so passionately begged of it – freedom, justice, love.

From **Markings** *by* Dag Hammarskjöld

In a dream I walked with God through the deep places of creation; past walls that receded and gates that opened, through hall after hall of silence, darkness and refreshment – the dwelling-place of souls acquainted with light and warmth – until, around me, was an infinity into which we all flowed together and lived anew, like the rings made by raindrops falling upon wide expanses of calm dark waters.

From **Markings** *by* Dag Hammarskjöld

LONELINESS

> *What makes loneliness an anguish*
> *Is not that I have no one to share my burdens,*
> *But this:*
> *I have only my own burdens to bear.*

From **Intimations of Immortality** *by* William Wordsworth

> *Though nothing can bring back the hour*
> *Of splendour in the grass, of glory in the flower;*
> *We will grieve not, rather find*
> *Strength in what remains behind;*
> *In the primal sympathy*
> *Which having been must ever be;*
> *In the soothing thoughts that spring*
> *Out of human suffering;*
> *In the faith that looks through death,*
> *In the years that bring the philosophic mind.*

From **Rabbi ben Ezra** *by* Robert Browning

> *Grow old along with me!*
> *The best is yet to be,*
> *The last of life, for which the first was made:*
> *Our times are in this hand*
> *Who said, "A whole I planned,*
> *Youth shows but half; trust God: see all, nor be afraid."*

From **The Ring and the Book** *by* Robert Browning

> *All that is at all,*
> *Lasts ever, past recall;*
> *Earth changes, but thy soul and God stand sure.*

Salutation to the Dawn *from* **Martha's Prayer Book**

> *Look well to this day, for it is life,*
> *The very life of life!*
> *For yesterday is but a dream, and tomorrow is only a vision,*
> *But today well-lived, makes every yesterday a dream of happiness*
> *And every tomorrow a vision of hope;*
> *Look well therefore to this day.*

The Glory of Life. Source unknown

> *The glory of life,*
> *Is to love, not to be loved,*
> *To serve, not to be served,*
> *To be a strong hand in the dark*
> *To another in the time of need,*
> *To be a cup of strength to any soul*
> *In a crisis of weakness.*
> *This is to know the Glory of Life.*

From **Freedom, Faith and the Future** *by* Archbishop Michael Ramsey

THE FUTURE

What as Christians do we believe about man's relations to nature? Are we free to exploit nature at will? What, for instance, of the abominations of factory farming? We are sent back to the classic doctrine of man and nature found in the eighth Psalm. The psalmist describes how man is given a lordship over nature, to rule it and to use it: a lordship which has grown in ways of which the psalmist never dreamed. But it is a lordship neither absolute nor arbitrary, but under God's own sovereignty and will. Man and nature are together parts of one whole pattern of creation, together serving the glory of God. It is for us to recapture this doctrine, to reaffirm it, and to learn how to apply it in the frighteningly complex world in which we live. Blind exploitation of nature can damage man's future "prospects"; far worse, it can damage man's spiritual life because it damages that which exists to be reverenced by him. Would that we could see again the sensitivity to nature which marked some of the greatest poetry of the past.

From **The Story of my Heart** *by* Richard Jefferies, *taken from* **Mysticism** *by* F. C. Happold

I was utterly alone with the sun and the earth. Lying down on the grass, I spoke in my soul to the earth, the sun, the air, and the distant sea far beyond sight. I thought of the earth's firmness – I felt it bear me up; through the grassy couch there came an influence as if I could feel the great earth speaking to me. I thought of the wandering air – its pureness, which is its beauty; the air touched me and gave me something of itself. I spoke to the sea: though so far, in my mind I saw it, green at the rim of the earth and blue in deeper ocean; I desired to have its strength, its mystery and glory. Then I addressed the sun, desiring the soul equivalent of his light and brilliance, his endurance and unwearied race. I turned to the blue heaven over, gazing into its depth, inhaling its exquisite colour and sweetness. The rich blue of the unattainable flower of the sky drew my soul towards it, and there it rested, for pure colour is rest of the heart. By all these I prayed . . .

Through every grass blade in the thousand, thousand grasses; through the million leaves, veined and edge-cut, on bush and tree; through the song-notes and the marked feathers of the birds; through the insects' hum and the colour of the butterflies; through the soft warm air, the flecks of clouds dissolving – I used them all for prayer . . . I prayed with the glowing clouds of sunset and the soft light of the first star coming through the violet sky. At night now with the stars . . . with the morning star, the light-bringer . . .

All the glory of the sunrise filled me with broader and furnace-like vehemence of prayer. That I might have the deepest of soul-life, the deepest of all, deeper far than all this greatness of the visible universe and even of the invisible; that I might have a fullness of soul till now unknown, and utterly beyond my own conception.

Sunset *by* **Edwin Muir,** *taken from* **New Fire**

> *Fold upon fold of light,*
> *Half-heaven of tender fire,*
> *Conflagration of peace,*
> *Wide hearth of the evening world.*
> *How can a cloud give peace,*
> *Peace speak through a bodiless fire*
> *And still the angry world?*
>
> *Yet now each bush and tree*
> *Stands still within the fire,*
> *And the bird sits in the tree.*
> *Three horses in a field*
> *That yesterday ran wild*
> *Are bridled and reined by light*
> *As in a heavenly field.*
> *Man, beast and tree in fire,*
> *The bright cloud showering peace.*

> All are but parts of one stupendous whole
> Whose body Nature is, and God the soul;
> That, changed through all, and yet in all the same,
> Great in the earth, as in the aethereal frame,
> Warms in the sun, refreshes in the breeze,
> Glows in the stars, and blossoms in the trees;
> Lives through all life, extends through all extent,
> Spreads undivided, operates unspent;
> Breathes in our soul, informs our mortal part,
> As full, as perfect, in a hair as heart;
> As full, as perfect, in vile man that mourns
> As the rapt Seraph that adores and burns:
> To him no high, no low, no great, no small;
> He fills, he bounds, connects and equals all.

From **The Shaking of the Foundations** *by* Paul Tillich

"NATURE, ALSO, MOURNS FOR A LOST GOOD"

Each year when Good Friday and Easter Sunday approach us our thoughts turn toward the great drama of redemption, culminating in the pictures of the Cross and Resurrection. Who is redeemed? Some men alone; or mankind, including all nations; or the world, everything that is created, including nature, the stars and the clouds, the winds and the oceans, the stones and the plants, the animals and our own bodies? The Bible speaks again and again of the salvation of the world, as it speaks of the creation of the world and the subjection of the world to anti-Divine forces. And world means nature as well as man.

So let us ask today: what does nature mean to us? What does it mean to itself? What does it mean in the great drama of creation and salvation? A three-fold answer is contained in the words of the psalmist, the apostle and the prophet: the psalmist sings of the glory of nature; the apostle shows the tragedy of nature; and the prophet pronounces the salvation of nature. The hymn of the psalmist praises the glory of God in the glory of nature; the letter of the apostle links the tragedy of nature to the tragedy of man; and the vision of the prophet sees the salvation of nature in the salvation of the world.

So let us listen once more to the words of the psalmist, about the glory of nature, in their precise meaning.

> The heavens are telling the glory of God,
> And the firmament showeth the work of his hands.
> Day unto day poureth forth the story,

Night unto night announces the knowledge.
There is no speech, no language!
Their voice cannot be heard!
But their music goes out through all the earth,
And their words to the end of the world.

The 19th Psalm points to an old belief held by the ancient world and expressed by poets and philosophers: the heavenly bodies, the sun and the moon and the stars, produce by their movement a harmony of tones, sounding day and night from one end of the world to the other. These voices of the universe are not heard by human ears; they do not speak in human language. But they exist, and we can perceive them through the organs of our spirit. Shakespeare says:

There's not the smallest orb which thou behold'st
But in his motion like an angel sings . . .
Such harmony is in immortal souls;
But whilst this muddy vesture of decay
Doth grossly close it in, we cannot hear it . . .

The psalmist had heard it; he knows that the stars are sounding: the glory of creation and its Divine Ground.

Are we able to perceive the hidden voice of nature? Does nature speak to us? Does it speak to you? Or has nature become silent to us, silent to the men of our period? Some of you may say, "Never before in any period has nature been so open to man as it is today. The mysteries of the past have become the knowledge of children. Through every scientific book, through every laboratory, through every machine, nature speaks to us. The technical use of nature is the revelation of its mystery." The voice of nature *has* been heard by the scientific mind, and its answer is the conquest of nature. But is this all that nature says to us?

I was sitting under a tree with a great biologist. Suddenly he exclaimed, "I would like to know something about this tree!" He, of course, knew everything that science had to say about it. I asked him what he meant. And he answered, "I want to know what this tree means for itself. I want to understand the life of this tree. It is so strange, so unapproachable." He longed for a sympathetic understanding of the life of nature. But such an understanding is possible only by communion between man and nature. Is such a communion possible in our period of history? Is nature not completely subjected to the will and wilfulness of man? This technical civilisation, the pride of mankind, has brought about a tremendous devastation of original nature, of the land, of animals, of plants. It has kept genuine nature in small reservations and has occupied everything for domination and ruthless exploitation. And worse: many of us have lost the ability to live with nature. We fill it with the noise of empty talk, instead of listening to its many voices, and, through them, to the voiceless music of the universe. Separated from the soil by a machine, we speed through nature, catching glimpses of it, but never comprehending its greatness or feeling its power. Who is still able to penetrate, meditating and contemplating the creative ground of nature?

. . . Nature is not only glorious; it is also tragic. It is subjected to the laws of finitude and destruction. It is suffering and sighing with us. No one who has ever listened to the sounds of nature with sympathy can forget their tragic melodies . . . The sighing sounds of the wind and the ever-restless, futile breaking of the waves may have inspired the poetic, melancholic verse about nature's subjection to vanity. But the words of Paul refer also, and in a more direct way, to the sphere of living things. The melancholy of the leaves falling in autumn, the end of the jubilant life of spring and summer, the quiet death of innumerable beings in the cold air of the approaching winter – all this has grasped and always will grasp the hearts, not only of poets, but of every feeling man and woman. The song of transitoriness sounds through all the nations. Isaiah's words, "The grass withereth, the flower fadeth, because the breath of the Lord bloweth upon it," describe the shortness of the lives of individuals and nations. But they could not have been written without a profound sympathy with the life of nature. And then Jesus speaks, praising the lilies of the field: "Even Solomon in all his glory was not arrayed like one of these." In these two sayings about the flowers of the field we perceive both the glory and the tragedy of nature.

Sympathy with nature in its tragedy is not a sentimental emotion; it is a true feeling of the reality of nature. Schelling justly says: "A veil of sadness is spread over all nature, a deep, unappeasable melancholy over all life." According to him this is "manifest through the traces of suffering in the face of all nature, especially in the faces of animals". The doctrine of suffering as the character of all life, taught by the Buddha, has conquered large sections of mankind. But only he who is connected within the ground of his own being with the ground of nature is able to see its tragedy; as Schelling says, "The darkest and deepest ground in human nature is 'longing' . . . is melancholy. This, mainly, creates the sympathy of man with nature. For in nature too the deepest ground is melancholy. Nature also mourns for a lost good." Can we still understand the meaning of such half-poetic, half-philosophic words? We have become incapable of perceiving the harmonious sounds of nature. Have we also become insensitive to the tragic sounds? . . . The tragedy of nature is bound to the tragedy of man as the salvation of nature is dependent on the salvation of man. What does this mean? Always man has dreamed of a time when harmony and joy filled all nature, and peace reigned between nature and man – Paradise, the Golden Age. But man by violating the divine law, destroyed the harmony, and now there is enmity between man and nature, between nature and nature. In Paul's melancholic words this dream resounds. It is a dream, but it contains a profound truth: man and nature belong together in their created glory, in their tragedy and in their salvation. As nature, represented by the "Serpent", leads man into temptation, so men, by trespassing of the divine law, leads nature into tragedy. This did not happen once upon a time, as the story says; it happens within every time and space, as long as there is time and space. So long as there are the old heaven and the old earth, man and nature will be subjected together to the law of vanity. Many profound thinkers within and without Christianity agree that man is determined to fulfil the longing of nature. In so far as he has failed and still fails to come to his own fulfilment, he is unable to fulfil nature – his own bodily being and nature around him. Therefore Jesus is called the Son of Man, the man from above, the true man, in whom the forces of separation and tragedy are overcome not only in mankind but in the universe. For there is no salvation of man if there is no salvation of nature, for man is in nature and nature is in man.

Let us listen once more to the words of the prophet about the salvation of nature.

> Then I saw the new heaven and the new earth. For the first heaven and the first earth had passed away; and the sea was no more ... Then he showed me the river of the water of life, bright as crystal ... on both sides of the river grew the tree of life, bearing twelve kinds of fruit, each month having its own fruit; and the leaves of the tree were for the healing of the nations.

Needless to say, this is not the description of a future state of our world. Like the Golden Age of the past, the Golden Age of the future is a symbol pointing to something mysterious within our present world – namely the forces of salvation. And one thing is made very clear in the visions of the prophets that salvation means salvation of the world, and not of human beings alone. Lions and sheep, little children and snakes, will lie together in peace, says Isaiah. Angels and stars, men and animals adore the child of the Christmas legend. The earth shakes when Christ dies, and it shakes again when He is resurrected. The sun loses its light when He closes His eyes, and it rises when He rises from the tomb ...

Do we not see everywhere the estrangement of people from nature, from their own natural forces and from nature around them? And do they not become dry and uncreative in their mental life, hard and arrogant in their moral attitude, suppressed and poisoned in their vitality? They certainly are not the images of salvation . . .

Therefore commune with nature! Become reconciled with nature after your estrangement from it. Listen to nature in quietness, and you will find its heart. It will sound forth the glory of its divine ground; it will sigh with us in the bondage of tragedy. It will speak of the indestructible hope of salvation.

Isaiah 11:6-9

And the wolf shall dwell with the lamb and the leopard shall lie down with the kid, and the calf and the lion and the fatling together and . . . the lion shall eat straw like the ox. The sucking child shall play over the hole of the asp, and the weaned child shall put his hand in the adder's den. They shall not hurt or destroy in all my holy mountain; for the earth shall be full of the knowledge of the Lord as the waters cover the sea.

Job 39:19-25

THE HORSE

Do you give the horse his might?
Do you clothe his neck with strength?
Do you make him leap like a locust?
His majestic snorting is terrible,
He paws in the valley, and exults in his strength.
He goes out to meet the weapons.
He laughs at fear, and is not dismayed;
he does not turn back from the sword.
Upon him rattle the quiver
the flashing spear and javelin.
With fierceness and rage he swallows the ground;
he cannot stand still at the sound of the trumpet.
When the trumpet sounds he says "Aha";
he smells the battle from afar,
the thunder of the captains, and the shouting.

The Dog's Prayer *by* Piero Scanziani

O Lord of all creatures, make the man, my master, as faithful to other men as I am to him. Make him as loving to his family and friends as I am to him. Make him the honest guardian of the blessings which you have entrusted to him, as I honestly guard his own.

Give him, O Lord, an easy and spontaneous smile, easy and spontaneous as when I wag my tail. May he be as readily grateful, as I am quick to lick his hand. Grant him patience equal to mine, when I await his return without complaining. Give him my courage, my readiness to sacrifice everything for him in all circumstances, even life itself. Keep for him the youthfulness of my heart and the cheerfulness of my thoughts.

O Lord of all creatures, as I am always truly a dog, grant that he may be always truly a man.

From **Markings** *by* Dag Hammarskjöld

ELEGY FOR MY PET MONKEY

Far from the chattering troop,
From the green gloom under the tree-tops
And the branches over the jungle trail
Where the eyes of leopards
Gleamed in the night,
Alone,
In the white-washed room
With the bannisters and the dangling rope,
He sat on the window-sill
Watching the snow fall
And the cars rush by
With their eyes of fire.

Nobody was watching
When, one day, he jumped
For the loop of the rope,
And his chest got caught in its coils
And he choked to death.
Nobody was watching —
And who had ever understood
His efforts to be happy,
His moments of faith in us,
His constant anxiety,
Longing for something
He could only vaguely remember?
Yet all of us had liked him,
And we all missed him,
For a long time.

From **Chronicles of Brother Wolf** *by* Tertius Mowbray, *found in* **The Burrswood Herald**

WAITING

St Francis speaks, "Brother Wolf, what wast thou about yester'een when thou didst lie silent, thy paws crossed, thy body motionless for a long hour, while I was in my cell?"

"My father," said Brother Wolf, "I did but wait at thy door, till thou shouldst come forth again and need thy Wolf."

"What didst thou think upon Brother Wolf?"

"Aye, Father, verily, my heart was full of thee. For thou art my master, and I live but to serve thee. And I did but wait, till thou shouldst bid me serve thee."

"I will ask thee one more question, my wolf. If at the end of thy waiting, I came forth of my cell, and bade thee go away, or come another time, for that I did not need thee, or must be occupied with another – what then?"

"My father, many times has this happened. Why not? For if it is thy bidding that I go, I go gladly, knowing that I shall see thee anon; and if it is thy bidding that I stay and serve, I stay and serve joyfully; that is all a wolf may do. Wouldst thou have it otherwise or have I done amiss?"

"Thou hast not done amiss, my wolf, thou hast but learned truly of prayer. For when I am in my prayer with the brothers, behold, we wait at the door of God. If He delays we wait with love in the heart. If we see Him not, we remember that we shall see Him; if we hear Him not, we remember that we shall hear Him. If He bids us serve Him, we serve with gladness; if He bids us wait, with joy and patience we wait. Yet one thing more, brother Wolf, and thou understandest all. If I bade thee do some work that thou couldst not fulfil perfectly yet awhile, what wouldst thou do?"

"My father, I would wait, with the bidding in my heart, doing for thee such small things as I might, until the time came when I could perform thy will."

"Even so, my son, do we who are servants of the great God. For often He biddeth us do some great thing, and the time is not yet. Then we abide softly, doing His bidding in little things, until the time come when we can go forth to accomplish all His will. Be not afraid that, when thou doest nothing, God is not served; for he who has learned to wait has learned all."

Song to David *by* Christopher Smart

> He sang of God – the mighty source
> Of all things – the stupendous force
> On which all strength depends:
> From whose right arm, beneath whose eyes,
> All period, pow'r and enterprise
> Commences, reigns, and ends.

Tell them I am, Jehova said
To Moses: while earth heard with dread,
And smitten to the heart,
At once above, beneath, around,
All nature, without voice or sound,
Replied, O Lord, Thou art.
For Adoration all the ranks
Of Angels yield eternal thanks,
And David in the midst.
Strong is the horse upon his speed
Strong in pursuit the rapid glede,
Which makes at once his game:
Strong the tall ostrich on the ground;
Strong through the turbulent profound
Shoots xiphias to his aim.
Strong is the lion – like a coal
His eye-ball – like a bastion's mole
His chest against his foes:
Strong the gier-eagle on his sail,
Strong against tide, th' enormous whale
Emerges as he goes.
Glorious the sun in mid-career;
Glorious th' assembled fires appear;
Glorious the comet's train:
Glorious the trumpet and alarm;
Glorious th' almighty stretched-out arm;
Glorious th' enraptured main.
Glorious the northern lights astream
Glorious the song when God's the theme:
Glorious the thunder's roar:
Glorious hosanna from the den
Glorious the catholic amen;
Glorious the martyr's gore.
Glorious – more glorious is the crown
Of Him that brought salvation down
By meekness, called thy Son;
Thou that stupendous truth believ'd
And now the matchless deed's achieved,
Determined, dared, and done.

12

Unity

Union with God. Union within Christianity. Union with all men.

UNION WITH GOD

From **The Art of Prayer: An Orthodox Anthology**. Union with God
From **Lent with William Temple**. UNION WITH GOD
From **The Art of Prayer: An Orthodox Anthology**. Divine love
From **Markings** by Dag Hammarskjöld. Thou who art over us
From **Readings from St John's Gospel** by William Temple. The essence of prayer
John 17. JESUS'S PRAYER FOR HIS CONTEMPORARY AND FUTURE DISCIPLES
Valdivielso from **St Theresa of Jesus** by E. Allison Peers
From **The Journey Inwards** by F. C. Happold. THE OBLATION AND CONSECRATION OF THE WORLD
From **The Journey Inwards** by F. C. Happold. PRAYER IS A SOURCE OF INNER POWER
From **The School of Prayer** by Olive Wyon. True Prayer
The Effect of Christ's Ascension by William Temple, *taken from* **A Treasury of the Kingdom**
From **Christ Our Priest** by C. R. Bryant, S.S.J.E. Address in Canterbury Cathedral, 1970
St Francis of Assisi, 1182–1226

UNION WITHIN CHRISTIANITY

Thanksgiving for the Churches from **A Book of School Worship** by William Temple
From **The Household of God** by Leslie Newbiggin
Prayer for Unity: Pray for Unity such as Christ wills
Psalm 18:28
From **The School of Prayer** by Olive Wyon. PRAYER AND THE PURPOSE OF GOD
From **The School of Prayer** by Olive Wyon. The righting of human wrongs
Frustration from **Daily Readings** by William Temple
From **Readings from St John's Gospel** by William Temple. I AM THE DOOR OF THE SHEEP

212

UNION WITH GOD

From **The Art of Prayer:** An Orthodox Anthology

. . . The first divine decree about man is that he should be in living union with God, and this union consists of living in God with the mind in the heart: thus anyone who aims at such a life, and still more anyone who participates in it to some extent, can be said to fulfil the purpose in life for which he was created. Those who seek this living union should understand what they are trying to do, and not be troubled at their lack of achievement in any specially important external feats. This work by itself embraces all other action.

From **Lent with William Temple**

Praying is speaking to God; so the first necessity is that you should be directing your mind towards God. That is the best part and most important part of prayer anyhow, and without it all the rest is useless. The great aim is union with God and the first need is that you should be, so far as you are capable, with open face gazing upon Him. And then, when you have remembered what you know about God (which is not difficult, because He has given us the portrait of Himself in Jesus Christ, and though you cannot see God you can always remember Jesus Christ; so you should never begin to pray until you have the figure of Christ before your mind, and should pray to God as you see Him there), then you turn to the things you will pray for, and this is to be after the manner of the Lord's Prayer. I wonder where most of you begin to mean business as you say the Lord's Prayer. I used often to ask the boys at school when I was preparing them for confirmation. Their answer, when they gave me any, was always the same: "Forgive us our trespasses", but that is rather near the end. The reason, of course, was that this was the first thing they knew they wanted and knew they could only get from God. If they had been both hungry and hard up, I suppose they would have started with "daily bread". But our Lord says that when you come into the presence of God you should forget all about yourself and your needs, even your sins; you should be so filled with the thought of God that what you want above all things is that God's Name may be hallowed – reverenced – throughout the world. You are to ask for that first, because you ought to want it the most, and next that He may be effectively King of the world He has made, so that all men obey His law; and then that His whole purpose of love shall be carried out unspoiled by the selfishness of men.

We have got into a habit of saying, "God's will be done" in a mood of resignation. That is blasphemous. It means that, having found we cannot have our own way, we are ready to put up with His as second best. It will not do. We ought to say "Thy will be done" in ungovernable hope, knowing it to be so much better than our own. Then you ask for freedom from anxiety, "daily bread", to see your way one day ahead; that is little enough. Then, for the sense of His favour, without which you cannot serve Him with a full heart, and which you have so often forfeited; you must be forgiven if you are to serve Him wholeheartedly. Then there may be unnecessary difficulties, "Lead us not into temptation." And there is some evil that has actually got hold of us now, we want deliverance from that. And all this not because then we shall be good and happy, but because it is God's Kingdom, power and glory we are concerned about all the time.

It is the prayer you should want to offer if you loved God with all your heart, and you may learn to love Him with all your heart if you realise what this prayer means, and try to enter into it. Never let it become for you a formula.

From **The Art of Prayer:** An Orthodox Anthology

No unity with God is possible except by an exceedingly great love. This we can see from the story of the woman in the gospel, who is a sinner: God in His great mercy granted her the forgiveness of her sins and a firm union with Him, "for she loved much" (Lk 7:47). He loves those who love Him, He cleaves to those who cleave to Him, gives Himself to those who seek Him and abundantly grants fullness of joy to those who desire to enjoy His love.

To kindle in his heart such divine love, to unite with God in an inseparable union of love, it is necessary for a man to pray often, raising the mind to Him. For as a flame increases when it is constantly fed, so prayer made often, with the mind dwelling ever more deeply in God, arouses divine love in the heart.

And the heart, set on fire, will warm all the inner man, will enlighten and teach him, revealing to him all its unknown and hidden wisdom, and making him like a flaming seraph, always standing before God within his spirit, always looking at Him within his mind, and drawing from this vision the sweetness of spiritual joy . . .

The principle thing is to stand with the mind in the heart before God, and to go on standing before Him unceasingly day and night, until the end of life.

From **Markings** *by* Dag Hammarskjöld

> *Thou who art over us,*
> *Thou who art one of us,*
> *Thou who art –*
> *Also within us,*
> *May all see Thee – in me also,*
> *May I prepare the way for Thee.*
> *May I thank Thee for all that shall fall to my lot,*
> *May I also not forget the needs of others.*

Keep me in Thy love
As Thou wouldst that all should be kept in mine.
May everything in this my being be directed to Thy glory
And may I never despair.
For I am under Thy hand,
And in Thee in all power and goodness.

Give me a pure heart – that I may see Thee,
A humble heart – that I may hear Thee,
A heart of love – that I may serve Thee,
A heart of faith – that I may abide in Thee.

From **Readings from St John's Gospel** *by* William Temple

The essence of prayer is to seek how we may share our Lord's sacrifice. It finds its fullest expression in the Eucharist when we offer ourselves to Christ that he may unite us with Himself in His perfect self-offering to the Father – that self-offering to which He dedicated Himself in His great High Priestly prayer.

John 17

JESUS'S PRAYER FOR HIS CONTEMPORARY AND FUTURE DISCIPLES

When Jesus had said these words, he raised his eyes to Heaven and said, "Father, the hour has come. Glorify your Son now so that he may bring glory to you, for you have given him authority over all men to give eternal life to all that you have given to him. And this is eternal life, to know you, the only true God, and him who you have sent – Jesus Christ.

I have brought you honour upon earth, I have completed the task which you gave me to do. Now, Father, honour me in your own presence with the glory that I knew with you before the world was made. I have shewn yourself to the men who you gave me from the world. They were your men and you gave them to me, and they have accepted your word. Now they realise that all that you have given me comes from you – and that every message that you gave me I have given them. They have accepted it all and have come to know in their hearts that I did come from you – they are convinced that you sent me.

I am praying to you for them: I am not praying for the world but for the men whom you gave me, for they are yours – everything that is mine is yours and yours mine – and they have done me honour. Now I am no longer in the world, but they are in the world and I am returning to you. Holy Father, keep the men you gave me by your power that they may be one, as we are one. As long as I was with them, I kept them by the power that you gave me; I guarded them and not one of them was destroyed, except the son of destruction – that the scripture might come true.

And now I come to you and I say these things in the world that these men may find my joy completed in themselves. I have given them your word, and the world has hated them, for they are no more sons of the world than I am. I am not praying that you will take them out of the world but that you will keep them from the evil one. They are no more sons of the world than I am – make them holy by the truth; for your word is the truth. I have sent them to the world just as you sent me to the world and I consecrate myself for their sakes that they may be made holy by the truth.

I am not praying only for these men but for all those who will believe in me through their message, that they may all be one. Just as you, Father, live in me and I live in you, I am asking that they may live in us, that the world may believe that you did send me. I have given them the honour that you gave me, that they may be one, as we are one – I in them and you in me, that they may grow complete into one – so that the world may realise that you sent me and have loved them as you loved me. Father I want those whom you have given me to be with me where I am; I want them to see the glory which you have made mine – for you loved me before the world began. Father of goodness and truth, the world has not known you, but I have known you and these men now know that you have sent me. I have made your self known to them and I will continue to do so that the love which you have had for me may be in their hearts – and that I may be there also."

Valdivielso *from* St Theresa of Jesus *by* E. Allison Peers

> Since Thou art God of love, Oh make me love Thee;
> Receive me in Thyself, now Thou hast found me,
> Fain would I have Thee bound – do Thou then bind me;
> And with love's arrows that Thou holdest, wound me;
> O fire of love, in love's strong furnace prove me;
> Unite me with Thyself, Whose love's around me.
> Pierced is Thy breast; within it do Thou take me;
> Unmake in me the man; God do Thou make me.

From The Journey Inwards *by* F. C. Happold

THE OBLATION AND CONSECRATION OF THE WORLD

This spiritual exercise was inspired by Father Teilhard's Mass on the World included in *Hymn of the Universe*:

Let my mind be still, emptied of all thought of self, that in quietness and humility I may bring before You, my Lord, the totality of the life of the earth.

May my heart, cleansed by Your transforming fire, be a pure altar on which I may offer to You all the labour and sorrow of mankind.

On the paten of my heart I would place, O my Lord, the purposeful action of men, their aspirations, their achievements, their work. Into my chalice I would pour their sorrows, the failings and the pain of every living being.

Into this oblation of the whole world I would gather, first, those closest to me, those whose lives are bound up with my own personal life, those known to me, especially those whom I love, those with whom I work.

With these may I unite those more distant and unreal to me, the whole anonymous mass of humankind, scattered in every corner of the globe. In imagination I would unite myself with the ceaseless pilgrimage of mankind, with its joys and sorrows, its hopes and fears, its successes and failures, that I may be one with it all.

Let every sentient being be placed upon the altar of my heart, that I may raise them all up to You.

And not only the living would I gather into this oblation, but also the dead, that they too may be incorporated into the material of my sacrifice.

It is not enough. I would draw into it every form of life, animals and birds, reptiles and insects, trees, flowers, and all the kindly fruits of the earth. Let those too be laid upon this inner altar, that they too may be offered to You.

And yet the oblation is incomplete. Into it I would draw the very fabric of the earth itself, the material substance of which it is composed, that I may present nothing less than everything to You who are the All-in-All.

Creative power, shining, deathless Spirit, wherein lay hidden the earth and all its creatures, so infuse this Your world with Your attraction that it may more and more be led back into You from whence it sprang.

Timeless Word, outpouring of the essence of the mysterious, ineffable One, made flesh for us in the Lord Jesus. You are ever moulding this manifold, phenomenal world so as to incorporate it more and more into Your divine life. You are ever plunging Yourself into its depth and totality so as to touch us through everything within and without us, breathe into it now Your transforming might; You are our life and giver of life.

May all life, past, present, future, that which was, that which is, and that which is to come, be now elevated at the altar of my heart, that in and through You, O eternal, cosmic Christ, it may be presented, a holy sacrifice, in the secret place of the Most High, that all may be hallowed and consecrated unto that great Day of the final redemption of the whole creation, when this corruption shall put on incorruption and this mortal shall put on immortality, and all things shall, in and through You, be brought back into One from whence they came.

Now over the whole earthly pilgrimage of mankind pronounce Your revealing, consubstantial words, words of consecration, and also the annunciation of the ultimate mystery of the universe and of ourselves:

This Is My Body
This is My Blood.

From **The Journey Inwards** *by* F. C. Happold

PRAYER IS A SOURCE OF INNER POWER

Through real prayer a vast energy is generated which transforms, enriches and illuminates, for through it we are linking ourselves with that power which is the inexhaustible motive force which spins the universe.

Prayer is also one way, though only one way – the way of the scientist is another – of exploring the nature of Reality; it has a noetic quality. True prayer, especially mystical prayer, by releasing and developing spiritual insight and vision, opens up aspects of reality which are beyond the reach of rational thought alone.

Further, prayer is an essential practice for one who would lead that active life which is the lot of most of us, in the best way. Through prayer action is transformed and redeemed by its being taken up into something higher than itself. When in prayer, one places every thought and word and deed in God, dedicating all to God, one is no longer imprisoned, as are so many in our age, in one's own activity. The one who does this is following the teaching of Jesus, who said: "Seek ye first the Kingdom of Heaven and all these things shall be added unto you."

Jesus was not the only spiritual teacher who gave this advice, it is given in that most beautiful of Hindu scriptures, The *Bhagavad Gita*: the world is imprisoned in its own activity, except when actions are performed in worship of God. Therefore you must perform every action sacramentally, and be free from all attachment to results.

Finally through prayer, one may come to a realisation of one's true self. The great insight of Hinduism was this realisation, that the ego, the self, of which one is chiefly conscious and which one regards as oneself, is not the true self at all. It is merely a phenomenal self, destined to disappear when the body dies. A man's true immortal self is a divine spark within him, the greater Self, which is of the same essence as the Supreme Self, the Godhead Itself. This belief is expressed in the Hindu formula of faith (Thou art that).

This teaching is not peculiar to Hinduism. It is found in the same essential form in the doctrine of the indwelling Christ of St Paul and in the Spiritual Marriage of John Ruysbroeck:

This essential union of our Spirit with God does not exist in itself, but it dwells in God, and it flows from God and it returns to God as to its Eternal Origin. And in this wise it has never been, nor ever shall be, separated from God, for this union is within us by our naked nature, and, were this nature to be separated from God, it would fall into pure nothingness.

If you have experienced an inner realisation of your real self as the Christ within you, and your phenomenal self as only the instrument used by this greater self, Christ, you will become very humble. You will no longer have any attachment to, still less claim any reward for, your deeds, however good, for you will know that they do not belong to you at all.

From **The School of Prayer** *by* Olive Wyon

Wherever life and prayer have been divorced, something is wrong; neither develops aright. The reason is that unity of God is intended by Him to be reflected in the unity of the whole life. To understand the place of prayer in life is to unify your personality, and therefore to strengthen the whole of your being.

In true prayer, prayer is the very breath and power of life, we fulfil the purpose for which we were created.

The Effect of Christ's Ascension *by* William Temple, *taken from* **A Treasury of the Kingdom**

In the days of His earthly ministry, only those could speak to Him who came where He was. If He was in Galilee, men could not find Him in Jerusalem: If He was in Jerusalem, men could not find Him in Galilee. But His ascension means that He is perfectly united with God; we are with Him wherever we are present to God; and that is everywhere and always. Because He is "in Heaven", He is everywhere on earth; because He is ascended, He is here now. Our devotion is not to hold us by the empty tomb; it must lift up our hearts to heaven so that we too, in heart and mind thither ascend and with Him continually dwell: it must send us forth into the world to do His will; and these are not two things but one.

From **Christ Our Priest** *by* C. R. Bryant, S.S.J.E.

1 Tim 2: 5–6: "There is one God and one mediator between God and men, Christ Jesus himself man, who sacrificed himself to win freedom for all mankind."

The Sacrifice of Christ was not intended as a substitute for our own commitment to God; rather it was its seed. Christ lived a fully human life in order to enable us to live up to our own human potential. The greatest obstacle to our living our lives to the full is undue fear. If you say that selfishness is a greater obstacle, then I must answer that undue fear is the chief cause of selfishness. Not selfishness but undue fear is the opposite of that faith which God asks of us. It is fear of God's demands that hinders me from being open to God; it is fear that others will take advantage of me that prevents me from being open to my fellows. So Christ faces the things we fear in order to infect us with his own courage. We all want success and dread failure; Christ underwent failure. We all want others to accept us and dread rejection; Christ was rejected. We like to be in a strong position, to be masters of our own fate, we hate being defenceless. Christ knew what it was to be strong: he could dominate crowds and have them hanging on his words; but he made himself vulnerable, he embraced weakness, helplessness. We all dislike being blamed especially when we are not guilty; Christ though innocent was condemned to death for sedition and executed between two criminals. We all dread intense physical pain and avoid it if we can; Christ faced the probability of the cross all through His ministry and in the end endured it in fact. He confronted the kind of fears that unman us in order to destroy their power over us. This is what being our mediator led Jesus to. This is how he sacrificed himself to God for our freedom. This is what identifying himself with us involved for him.

. . . The quality needed more than any other for the task of mediating, of drawing people together, is love. Jesus is our mediator because, as no one else, he loved the Father, and, as no one else, he loved his fellow men and faced unflinchingly the cost of loving like that in a world afraid to love. It is because we see in Christ, and particularly in his passion, the love of the Creator, reconciling mankind to himself, drawing them into unity, that we are led to affirm that in him we are face to face with our Maker; that through this man, our brother and our priest, God himself is at work, breaking down the fears and suspicions that divide man from man and establishing peace. Christ is our peace. He is our bridge-builder. He is the magnet, that can draw all men into one as he draws them into oneness with the Father, who is above all and through all and in all.

Lord Jesus Christ, You lived and died and live again to unite us with our Creator and Father. You have made yourself the Bridge across the abyss which estranges us from God. From our fellows and from our true selves. You are the Way through whom we approach the Father. You are the Son through whom we are made sons of God. Through You we rely on the Father's acceptance and forgiveness. Set us free to be bridge-builders and peace-makers in our divided world. Make us agents of Your reconciling love.

St Francis of Assisi, 1182–1226

> Lord, make me an instrument of Thy peace;
> Where there is hatred, let me sow love;
> Where there is injury, pardon;
> Where there is discord, union;
> Where there is doubt, faith;
> Where there is despair, hope;
> Where there is darkness, light;
> Where there is sadness, joy.

UNION WITHIN CHRISTIANITY

Thanksgiving for the Churches *from* **A Book of School Worship** *by* William Temple

For the Roman Catholic Church;
    its glorious traditions, its disciplines in holiness, its worship, rich with the passion of the centuries; its noble company of martyrs, doctors and saints;
    We thank Thee O Lord, and bless Thy Holy Name.

For the Eastern Orthodox Church;
    its treasure of mystic experience; its marvellous liturgy; its regard for the collective life and its common will as a source of authority;
    We thank Thee O Lord, and bless Thy Holy Name.

For the great Protestant Communions;
For the Congregationalist concern for the rightful independence of the soul and of the group;
    We thank Thee O Lord, and bless Thy Holy Name.

For the stress in the Baptist Churches upon personal regeneration and upon the conscious relation of the mature soul to its Lord;
    We thank Thee O Lord, and bless Thy Holy Name.

For the power of the Methodists to awaken the conscience of Christians to our social evils; and for their emphasis upon the witness of personal experience, and upon the power of the disciplined life;
    We thank Thee O Lord, and bless Thy Holy Name.

For the Presbyterian reverence for the sovereignty of God and their confidence in His faithfulness to His covenant; for their sense of the moral law, expressing itself in constitutional government;
    We thank Thee O Lord, and bless Thy Holy Name.

For the witness to the perpetual real presence of the inner light in every human soul borne by the Society of Friends and for their faithful continuance of a free prophetic ministry;
We thank Thee O Lord, and bless Thy Holy Name.

For the Lutheran Church; its devotion to the grace of God and the word of God, enshrined in the ministry of the word and sacraments;
We thank Thee O Lord, and bless Thy Holy Name.

For the Anglican Church; its reverent and temperate ways, through its Catholic heritage and its Protestant conscience; its yearning concern over the divisions of Christendom, its longing to be used as a house of reconciliation;
We thank Thee O Lord, and bless Thy Holy Name.

From **The Household of God** *by* Leslie Newbiggin

. . . The very essence of the Church's life is that she is pressing forward to the fulfilment of God's purpose and the final revelation of His glory, pressing forward both to the ends of the earth and to the end of the world, rejoicing in the hope of the glory of God. The treasure entrusted to her is not for herself, but for the doing of the Lord's will, not for hoarding but for trading. Her life is to be forever spent, to be cast into the ground like a corn of wheat, in the ever-new faith and hope of the resurrection harvest. Her life is precisely life under the sign of the Cross, which means that she desires to possess no life, no security, no righteousness of her own, but to live solely by His grace. When she becomes settled, when she becomes so much at home in this world that she is no longer content to be forever striking her tents and moving forward, above all when she forgets that she lives simply by God's mercy and begins to think that she has some claim on God's grace which the rest of the world has not, when in other words she thinks of her election in terms of spiritual privilege rather than missionary responsibility, then she comes under His merciful judgement as Israel did.

. . . The Church exists, and does not depend for its existence upon our definition of it. It exists wherever God in His sovereign freedom calls it into being by calling His own into the fellowship of His Son. And it exists solely by His mercy.

God shuts up and will shut up every way except the way of faith which simply accepts His mercy as mercy. To that end He is free to break off unbelieving branches, to graft in wild slips, and to call "no people His people". And if, at the end, those who have preserved through all the centuries the visible "marks" of the Church find themselves at the same board with some strange and uncouth latecomers on the ecclesiastical scene, may we not fancy that they will hear Him say – would it not be like Him to say – "It is my will to give unto this last even as unto thee?" Final judgement belongs to God and we have to beware of judging before the time. I think that if we refuse fellowship with Christ to any body of men and women who accept Jesus as Lord and show the fruits of His Spirit in their corporate life, we do so at our peril. With what judgement we judge we shall be judged. It behoves us therefore to receive one another as Christ has received us.

I know that this is just what most of us are unwilling to do. We feel that other Churches must accept, as the precondition of fellowship, such changes as will bring them into conformity with ourselves in matters which we regard as essential, and that failure to insist on this will involve compromise in regard to what is essential to the Church's being. But for precisely the same reason we cannot admit a demand from others for changes in ourselves which would seem to imply a denial that we already possess the *esse* of the Church. And even a proposal to make these concessions mutual and simultaneous does not solve the difficulty. It may appear to "save face", but at the cost of losing the integrity of faith.

All this way of thinking rests upon a static and non-temporal conception of the Church as something which possesses the fullness of being here and now. If the argument of these lectures is true we have to abandon this altogether, and to conceive of the Church in the perspective of a real *eschaton* for which we wait in faith and hope, still involved in this sinful age and yet living by the mercy of God. This acceptance of a real end means that the dimension of time is a reality within the life of the Church not only "What is it now?" but "what is it becoming?" To accept one another as we are does not mean leaving one another as we are. It is precisely the beginning of a process of mutual correction and of speaking truth in love to one another as brethren. For if the Church exists only *by* His mercy, it exists *for* the doing of His will. He has given us sufficient knowledge of what His will is. It is that we should be His witness to the uttermost parts of the earth, preaching the Gospel, doing the mighty works of the Kingdom, baptising the nations, and bringing all men into the one fellowship whose visible centre is the sacrament in which we are partakers of His risen life and show forth His death till He come. There is no body of Christians which does not depart in some or all these respects from His will. We have too long devoted our strength to mutual accusation and to self-defence, on the basis of what the Churches *are*. Surely it is time for us to meet one another in penitent acknowledgement of our common failure to be what the Church ought to be. On the basis of what we are none of us can be said to possess the *esse* of the Church. That is the real truth of our situation. There was a stage in the ecumenical debate at which the formula suggested for our mutual acceptance was: "All have won, and all shall have the prizes." Surely it is precisely the reverse of this that we must acknowledge. "They have all turned aside, they are together become unprofitable." The place of our meeting will not be the place where in our easy-going way, we can decide – after all – to let bygones be bygones. It will be none other than the mercy-seat where alone Christ meets with us, the place where we know we are sinners against God. Nothing that the Church is can provide us with our basis of assurance. Our only basis of assurance is the mercy of Christ who calls His Church to be His own glorious bride, without spot or wrinkle or any such thing. None of us has any standing save in that mercy. The mark of our calling will surely be looking forward and a hurrying forward which are a sort of echo of the grace of God who quickens the dead and calls the things that are not as though they were, a determination to cease judging one another for what we are, and to build one another up in faith and hope and love into what He had called us to be.

Prayer for Unity:

Pray for Unity such as Christ wills and by the means He chooses:
Grant that in Thee, who are perfect Charity, we may find the way that leads to Unity, in obedience to Thy Love and to Thy Truth.

Psalm 18:28

Thou also shall light my Candle; the Lord my God shall make my darkness light.

From **The School of Prayer** *by* Olive Wyon

PRAYER AND THE PURPOSE OF GOD

We believe that the Christian Faith alone can create permanent unity; thus "the fate of the world rests, in the last resort, on the existence of a nucleus of believers who are the bearers of the seed of unity".

This is a terrifying thought, the burden is too great for us, if we look at ourselves: our committees, our organisations, our "movements" will not of themselves, achieve anything lasting. With one voice the saints down the ages assure us that God alone can create, redeem, restore.

He alone can do this work through a "body" prepared by Him to do His will.

Thus we end where we began: with the will of God, but the stream has broadened out, and we realise with awe and delight that prayer means co-operation with the will of God for His purposes and thus our small human lives are filled with eternal meaning. The purpose of God is nothing less than the restoration of the whole created order to the end for which He made it.

As we co-operate with Him we know, by faith, that we are part of a great spiritual movement which is largely hidden from our present sight. But – by faith – we behold the city which hath foundations, whose Builder and Maker is God.

In the hidden spiritual movement, the life of prayer both of the individual Christian and of the Christian community is an integral and fundamental element.

This truth cannot be too strongly emphasised. Just as the body cannot live without water, so the soul cannot live without prayer.

Only through prayer do Christians "hold the world together". This is the testimony of all the saints.

From **The School of Prayer** *by* Olive Wyon

As our desire for unity within the Church of Christ increases, so also shall we be moved to an ever more urgent desire for the righting of human wrongs. For the love of Christ takes hold of us, and we see and feel that all the burden of misery due to human sin, selfishness, indifference, and hardness of heart, is – literally – "intolerable". Our prayer and our work alike will be moved by the conviction that – in the words of John Woolman – "to labour for a perfect redemption from the spirit of oppression is the great business of the whole family of Jesus Christ in this world."

We are called to pray, and to work, for a new social and international order, informed by the spiritual purpose, in which every human being shall have full freedom to use all his gifts and faculties in the service of God.

Frustration *from* **Daily Readings** *by* William Temple

The one complete cure for the sense of frustration and futility is to know and to do the will of God. Everyone to whom this becomes a reality is at once supplied with a purpose in life and one which covers the whole of life.

From **Readings from St John's Gospel** *by* William Temple

I AM THE DOOR OF THE SHEEP

The pastoral office, like all other offices in the Church, is a focalisation, so to speak, or function of the whole Church and all its members. We all exercise influence; that is a natural fact. If we are Christians, our influence is qualified by that consideration, and will draw men nearer to Christ or drive them further from Him, according to the balance of attractive or repellent qualities in ourselves. Our first question must be – How can we be sure that it draws men nearer? And the answer is that our entry to the lives of our neighbours must be *through the door*. But not only are we possessed by nature of the power of influence; we are responsible for exercising it to the uttermost. We are called to be Christ's witnesses. But by what right do we dare to attempt the direction of a neighbour's life, or even of a child's? And again the answer is that we approach him *through the door*.

I have no right to call men to adopt my tradition or to follow my manner of life. But I may call them to accept the Truth and to follow the Way which is Life. The ordinary way of saying this is to insist that we can only be the agents of God's work so far as God is Himself acting through us. But how are we to ensure this. We so easily assume that what seems to us good must be the will of God. We make our plans for the work of God, and ask Him to prosper them. But they may be seriously infected with our prejudice, ignorance and shortsightedness. In particular, we can never see in advance that the way to final success lies through immediate failure; yet God may know that this is so; it is the way of the Cross. How are we to avoid putting self as an obstacle in the way of God's purpose as we offer it to be the agency of that purpose? Again by coming *through the door*.

The meaning becomes clearer if we consider the alternatives. We may come to our pastoral work, the exercise of influence, through love of power and the satisfaction which we derive from guiding others; or through the love of fame and repute; or even through partisanship and the desire to win adherents for our own "school of thought". But none of these entitles us to exercise deliberate influence over another.

A man who attempts it is a "thief and a robber". He is merely an intruder; he is usurping functions to which he has no right. Nothing can give me warrant for the sacred responsibility of deliberately influencing a soul except that I approach that soul "through the door" which is Christ . . .

To come to it "through the door" means at least three things:
(1) to come to the task, and every part of it, in prayer;
(2) to refer all activities to the standard of the Mind of Christ;
(3) to accept what happens as nearer to the will of God than our own success would have been. It means putting Christ in the forefront of thought, and self, in all its forms, right out of the picture.

From **Readings from St John's Gospel** *by* William Temple

UNITY

Christ came "in the Father's name" as representing Him in the world, but this He could do only because He was one in character with the Father.

In that character of holy love the Father is prayed to watch over the disciples, holding them within the sphere of that love, so that it may possess their hearts – of which the proof will be their unity among themselves.

That they may be one. The Lord is going away. In the whole world His cause will be represented by this little handful of disciples. If they fall apart the cause is lost. What is most of all essential is that they be united. We see in the Acts of the Apostles in how many ways the infant Church was tempted to disunity – as for example in the doctrinal difference concerning the authority of the law for Gentile Christians, or the personal difference between Paul and Barnabas concerning John Mark. Such division at that stage would have been fatal; it has been sufficiently disastrous coming later, as it did. So the Lord's prayer was, and (we cannot doubt) still is, that His disciples may be one.

But the unity of the Church is precious not only for its utility in strengthening the Church as an evangelistic agent. It is itself in principle the consummation to which all history moves. The purpose of God in creation was, and is, to fashion a fellowship of free spirits knit together by a love in all its members which answers to the manifested love of God – or, as St Paul expresses it to "sum up all things in Christ". The agent of that purpose is the Church, which is therefore called the Body of Christ, through the activity and self-edifying of which Christ Himself is "fulfilled" (Ep 1:23) where we should read for "the fullness of Him that filleth all in all" – "the fullness of Him who, taking things all in all, is being fulfilled". For the fulfilling of Christ to the "measure of the stature of His completeness" is the meaning of universal history.

The unity of the Church is something much more than unity of ecclesiastical structure, though it cannot be complete without this. It is the love of God in Christ possessing the hearts of men so as to unite them in itself – as the Father and the Son are united in that love of Each for Each which is the Holy Spirit. The unity which the Lord prays that His disciples may enjoy is that which is eternally characteristic of the Triune God. It is therefore something much more than a means to any end – even though that end be the evangelisation of the world – it is the life of Heaven. For His prayer is not only that they may be one; it is that they may be one as we.

Before the loftiness of that hope and calling our little experience of unity and fellowship is humbled to the dust. Our friendships, our reconciliations, our unity of spirit in Church gatherings or in missionary conciliations, beautiful as they are, and sometimes even wonderful in comparison with our habitual life of sectional rivalries and tensions, yet how poor and petty they appear in the light of the Lord's longing. Let all of us who, concerned in Peace movements or Faith and Order conversations with fellow-

Christians of other denominations, take note of the judgement under which we stand by virtue of the gulf separating the level of our highest attainment and noblest enterprise, from the prize of the call upwards which God gives in Christ Jesus – that they may be one as we.

Prayer:

O God our Father, fill us with grace and truth, that in all our dealings one with another we may show forth our brotherhood in Thee.

We commend to Thee almighty God, the whole Christian Church throughout the World. May the grace and power of the Holy Spirit fill every member so that they may all be one in Thee, and may bear witness for Thee on the earth, to the glory of Thy Name. Amen.

From **The Household of God** *by* Leslie Newbiggin

MISSION AND UNITY

The Church, which is the extension to creatures of the life of God Himself, cannot be defined in merely functional terms. But neither can it be described apart from the mission in which it has its being. Our Lord's prayer on the night of His passion binds together indissolubly the Church's relation to God and its relation to the world: He prays for all who believe the apostolic preaching. "That they may all be one; even as thou, Father, art in me, and I in thee, that they also may be in us: that the world may believe that thou didst send me" (Jn 17:21). The Church's unity is the sign and the instrument of the salvation which Christ has wrought and whose final fruition is the summing-up of all things in Christ. In so far as the Church is disunited her life is a direct and public contradiction of the Gospel, and she is convicted of submitting some partial or sectional message for the good news of the one final and sufficient atoning act wrought in Christ for the whole human race.

There is one Lord, one faith, one atoning act, and one baptism, by which we are made participants in that atonement. In so far as we, who share that faith and that baptism, prove ourselves unwilling or unable to agree together in one fellowship, we publicly proclaim our disbelief in the sufficiency of that atonement. No one who has shared in the task of seeking to commend Christ to those of other faiths can escape the shame of that denial. It is because we have not truly faced the judgement of the Crucified; because we have not been willing to go down with Him into the place of utter dereliction where He went for us; because we have not allowed the Holy Spirit who is given only on the far side of Calvary, to have the real mastery of us; because we have clung stubbornly to what we had and have not been willing to cast everything at His feet as we must do when we face one another as fellow-Christians in living and open encounter; because – in short – we have not deeply accepted for ourselves that atonement through death, that we are unable to be made one. And therefore the world does not believe, because it does not see the signs of atonement so profound and complete that all mankind in all its infinite variety and contrariety can find there its lost unity. To say that the Church must be one in order that the world may believe is to summon one another to a return to the source of the Church's being in Christ Himself. As we confront one another, divided by our sundered traditions of speech and practice, yet drawn together by the work of the living Holy Spirit so that we cannot but recognise Christ in one another, we are forced through the crust of our traditions to a fresh contact with the living Christ. As we face the challenge which such encounter addresses to the things we hold most precious, we are compelled to face again the ultimate secret of the Church's being, which is life – through death – in Christ. And when we allow the living Christ to do His atoning work in us, to break down our divisions and knit us into one, we are by that very fact given a new power to go out to the world to invite all men to share in the atonement which is for all, and in the life of the family here on earth which is the fruit of that atonement, the instrument of its furtherance to all nations and all generations, and the sign of its consummation at the end of the world. We cannot be Christ's ambassadors, beseeching all men to be reconciled to God, except we ourselves be willing to be reconciled one to another.

One can only exhibit the connection between mission and unity by saying that missionary obedience puts the Church in a situation where its true nature is understood and disunity is seen for what it is. It is no accident that the modern movement for Christian reunion is a by-product of the modern missionary movement, and that its chief impetus has come from the areas where the Church has been formed by missionary expansion outside the frontiers of the old Christendom. This is more than a matter of perspective, though it is partly so. Evangelistic work places the Church in a situation in which the stark contrast between Christ and no-Christ is constantly being faced. In such a situation other matters necessarily fall into second place. The reality of what Christians have in common is seen to be of an importance far outweighing everything that divides Christians one from another. That profoundly important fact, which most Christians accept in theory, in practice drops out of sight when the missionary task drops out of sight. That is but one example of the corruption which infects a Church which ceases to be a mission. But as the last sentence indicates, this is more than a matter of proportion. It is a matter of the whole nature and being of the Church. When Christians are engaged in the task of missionary obedience they are in the situation in which the Church is truly the Church. They are actual participators in Christ's apostolate. They participate in His redeeming love for the world, the love which seeks to draw all men to Him. Their bearings are taken, so to say, upon the twin points of Christ's finished work of atonement in the drawing together of all men and all nations into one in Christ. In that situation the disunity, which is easily taken for granted among Churches which are not in a missionary situation, becomes literally intolerable. It is felt to contradict the whole nature of the apostolic mission at its heart. It is out of that situation of unbearable self-contradiction that the demand for reunion in the mission field has come.

I do not think that a resolute dealing with our divisions will come except in the context of a quite new acceptance on the part of all the Churches of the obligation to bring the Gospel to every creature; nor do I think that the world will believe that Gospel until it sees more evidence of its power to make us one. These two tasks – mission and unity – must be prosecuted together and in indissoluble relation with one another . . .

Our task is firstly, to call upon the whole Church to a new acceptance of the missionary obligation to bring the whole world to obedience to Christ; secondly, to do everything in our power to extend the area of co-operation between all Christians in the fulfilment of that task, by seeking to draw into the fellowship of the ecumenical movement those who at present stand outside it to the right and to the left; and thirdly, to press forward unswervingly with the task of reunion in every place, until all who in every place call upon the name of the Lord Jesus are visibly united in one fellowship, the sign and instrument of God's purpose to sum up all things in Christ, to whom with the Father and the Holy Spirit be all the glory.

Prayer *by* Queen Elizabeth I

REGARDING THE SACRAMENTS

His was the Word that spake it,
He took the Bread and brake it,
And what His word does make it
That I believe and take it.

In the Hope of the Resurrection, *a sermon preached by* Dr Eric Abbott *in Westminster Cathedral on 25th January 1971*

I am truly thankful to be with you this evening; thankful to God. In the north aisle of the Chapel of Henry VII in Westminster Abbey, Queen Elizabeth the First lies buried. Hers is a fine tomb, though not so splendid as that of Mary Queen of Scots, in the South Aisle of the same Chapel.

All too few people, however, realise that in the same tomb where

231

Elizabeth is buried lie the mortal remains of her half-sister Mary Tudor. And there is this inscription: "Consorts in the Kingdom and in the tomb here we rest, Elizabeth and Mary, Sisters in the hope of resurrection."

So many of the doctrinal and ecclesiastical issues which divide us still are summed up in the persons of these half-sisters, Elizabeth and Mary Tudor. But they were buried in the same tomb in the hope of resurrection.

Must we be for ever, in this world, prisoners of our own history? We know that the walls that divide us do not reach to heaven, but what about our unity in the Body of Christ in this present world, in this our "state of probation", in the Church Militant?

At the very least let me affirm our faith in the resurrection – the resurrection of our Lord and the resurrection of the Church *in Him*. The mystery of Christ and His Church is not exhausted. We believe in the resurrection of the Church. We believe in the resurrection of the Church even while some theologians bid us look into its grave. We may be experiencing in our own persons the grave and gate of death through which our faith is that *with* Christ and *in* Christ the Church *can* pass to its joyful resurrection.

Must we be for ever prisoners of our own history? We shall always be, to an inescapable extent, historically conditioned; but at the same time the Christ who died and was "raised from the dead by the glory of the Father" enables us to transcend our history.

This is precisely what God Himself enables us to do by the grace of Christian prayer. As men and women who are historically conditioned, and to a greater or less extent prisoners of our own Church history, we are enabled by prayer to transcend our history.

Some Suggestions

May I make some suggestions as to how I see us achieving this in God-given prayer? For let us remember this is a Week of Prayer for Christian Unity. It is not a week of debate about doctrine and dogma. We may indeed be very conscious of the crisis in the Church, and that crisis may be the background of the strenuous act of faith that we are making that the Church *is* Christ's Body (though we see it as a Body of His humiliation) and that the Holy Spirit is the very soul of the Church and that the gates of hell shall not prevail against it. The crisis may be very much in our minds and hearts and consciences. But, I repeat, this week is a week of Prayer, not of debate. Changes in the Liturgy, Priestly Celibacy, Validity of Orders, Apostolic Succession, Papacy, Collegiality, Episcopacy, the nature of Authority and where it resides, the responsibility of an enlightened conscience in rendering obedience and in offering penitence – these and many other burning issues fling us together in what we hope will be the loving clash of continual debate. But these tremendous matters, not a few of which may continue to divide us for years to come, lead us in this week not to debate (for which there will be plenty of opportunities) but to prayer.

My old friend Bishop Gordon Wheeler, with whom when he was Administrator of Westminster Cathedral I sallied forth in years past and stood side by side on the plinth of Nelson's Column in Trafalgar Square, asks in a fine article in the *Yorkshire Post* whether the Week of Prayer for Christian Unity has had its day. I am sure that it has not. But I am equally sure that we are tempted to think that the Week of Prayer for Christian Unity has now done its job and that the ecumenical task now lies in conferences, conversations, schemes – all of which may be good and necessary but all of which may also be decidedly Pelagian. The Week of Prayer for Christian Unity continues not only in order that all Christian ecumenism may be under-girded by prayer, but even more, to proclaim year by year that the Unity we pray for is the Gift of God – it is not man's invention, it is not man's contrivance.

Now I return to the suggestions I offer of the God-given prayer by the grace of which we prisoners of our own Church history may transcend that history.

My first suggestion is that, with all Christians in mind, we contemplate the wounds of Christ. What are these wounds? They are not merely the wounds He receives from a "wicked world". More poignantly, they are the wounds He received and receives "in the house of His friends". "What are these wounds in thy hands?" (Zc 13:6) "Those I received in the house of my friends." In silent prayer, look at the crucifix, contemplate the wounds, be penitent.

But then – those same wounds became scars in the Lord's resurrection body. The wounds-become-scars are the credentials of the risen Christ to doubting Thomas. There is a particular glory in these wounds changed to scars. "With what rapture gaze we on those glorious scars."

Secondly, we can silently contemplate the undivided Christ, as St John describes Him in the Passion narrative. In that narrative he tells how the soldier with a spear pierced the side of Jesus and he quotes :"they shall look on him whom they pierced". On the other hand, he tells how the legs of Jesus were not broken and quotes again "a bone of him shall not be broken". The Passover Lamb must be whole and unblemished. Even so, the Evangelist is saying though the body of Jesus is pierced on the Cross and in that sense He is broken He remains whole and entire, the undivided Christ.

Thirdly there is the prayer-action when we/you receive the blessed Sacrament. The Host which is received is, strictly speaking, a fragment. It is the result of the Fraction. But you do not receive fragmentation.

233

You may be experiencing fragmentation in both Church and world. But in the "Bread of Life" which is broken you receive the unity of the mystical Body of Christ.

> *Immortal love, for ever full,*
> *For ever flowing free,*
> *For ever shared, for ever whole,*
> *A never-ebbing sea..*

Fourthly, if we are allowed to attend the Eucharist in some other tradition than our own, we do not receive sacramentally if we observe the rules as they are. But spiritual communion is always open to us. By spiritual communion we receive through faith the virtue of the sacrament which we cannot yet receive with our mouth. It may be for some of us a most salutary and penitential exercise, in the words of Walter Frere, sometime Bishop of Truro, "to receive Thee spiritually in hope to receive Thee sacramentally in the restored Eucharist of Thy undivided Church".

The Heart of the Praying Christ

This leads me to a further suggestion for our unity prayer. It is that we should meet one another in the heart of the praying Christ – that is, that while acutely conscious of our divisions and while the debate – even the struggle (for Truth is at stake) – continues, we should and can, silently and by faith, meet at a deeper level than the divisions, in our Lord's praying Heart. For He is the eternally praying Christ and our vocation in this matter is to enter into His prayer. And if this brings us into darkness, or if entering into His prayer for our unity brings us sharp pain in the consciousness of our separation from one another, this must be expected by those who have any vocation to this kind of prayer. Let us, then, meet in the heart of the praying Christ. And if the Holy Spirit has brought us in our life of prayer into the unitive way, if in silence, in darkness – even in dereliction, in "unknowing" – we are resting in God the Blessed Trinity in Unity, then there is a real sense in which Unity prayer is being offered within us, all the time.

A Conclusion . . . Sanctification

I must bring these suggestions to an end. I finish with a brief answer to two questions. The first is this: "What are the separated Christians to pray for one another?" For myself, I try always to bear in mind the wise counsel of the Abbé Paul Couturier (to whom we owe so much), who advised that this prayer should be for the Unity which God wills and by the means that He wills. I think one might add, "and at the time that God wills", for people seem anxious to say that organic unity must come by such and such a year – this again, I am sure, is Pelagian and wrong. But the one great petition which Paul Couturier gave us to use for one another was sanctification. We are praying for one another in this special week of God-given effort, and this is gratefully remembered by the Church on 25th of January. "Sanctify them in Thy truth" is our Lord's prayer for us in the high-priestly prayer of St John, chapter 17.

You may think me wrong, but you pray for my sanctification. I may disagree with you on what still seem fundamental issues, but I pray for your sanctification. Have you noticed how the Saints of every Christian tradition, speak with one voice? Unity does not come by our talking of nothing but unity. Unity is the fruit of holiness and the fruit of holiness in the truth-sanctification.

And the last question is this: "What about the world?" What indeed! There is a great Catholic doctrine of "recapitulation": it was formulated by Irenaeus but it is there in St Paul in germ; the doctrine that Christ sums up, recapitulates, our human nature in its entirety. He is, in Luther's famous phrase, the Proper Man. Our Lord is not merely religious man. He is Man, He sums up mankind, of whom He is the Head. And therefore our Unity-prayer, while it still concentrates on the separated brethren who are fellow Christians, the baptised, finds itself in a divided world and the Church begins to see ever more clearly that she must be catholic and apostolic as never before if mankind is to be served and brought back into unity and peace.

As Gordon Wheeler says in the article which I have already mentioned: "Vigorous emphasis is (now) laid upon the conviction that all belong to a Church-for-others and that true ecumenism entails commitment to serving mankind."

"God so loved the world that He gave His only begotten Son" . . . Shall Christians love one another less than they love the world? As I said at the beginning, I know by faith that the Mystery of Christ and the Church is not exhausted, and I am sure that the Week of Prayer for Christian Unity has not "had its day", if only it can remain a Week of Prayer.

UNION WITH ALL MEN

From **The Household of God** *by* Leslie Newbiggin

The salvation of which the Gospel speaks and which is determinative of the nature and function of the Church is – as the very word itself should teach us – a making whole, a healing. It is the summing up of all things in Christ. It embraces within its scope the restoration of the harmony between man and God, between man and man and between man and nature for which all things were at the first created. It is the restoration to the whole creation of the perfect unity whose creative source and pattern is the unity of perfect love within the being of the Triune God. It is the very essence, universal and cosmic.

In using the word "universal" I do not intend to exclude the possibility that men may finally be – as the Apostle puts it – castaways. To exclude that possibility would obviously be to depart completely from the gravely realistic teaching of the New Testament, with its insistent reminders that there is a broad and easy way leading to destruction and that many go therein. What is intended in the use of the word "universal" is to emphasise firstly that the nature of the salvation is governed by its source which is a love that reaches out after all men, goes to all lengths to recover one lost sheep, and cares and must ever care for the rebel and the traitor with all the Passion of Calvary; secondly that there can therefore be no private "salvation", no perfection of joy and rest until the passion of that love is quenched, until He has seen the travail of His soul and is satisfied. It belongs to the very heart of salvation that we cannot have its fullness until all for whom it is intended have it together.

It is because this is the nature of salvation, that our experience of it now must have the character of a foretaste, an earnest longing; that we who have the first fruits must yet groan waiting for our adoption; that we cannot simply be quit of the old Adam and live wholly in the new Adam who is Christ; that we must live still in the flesh by faith, still involved in the old sinful order along with all humanity, while yet at the same time truly involved in the new order of righteousness with all our brethren, the new humanity in Christ; that we know in our own selves the warfare of flesh and spirit, of bondage and freedom. We cannot enjoy the fullness of salvation until we have it together in the fullness of His Body the Church. The new man into which we would fain grow up is a corporate humanity, wherein all the redeemed from every tribe and tongue are made one harmonious whole. Thus the tension which every Christian knows in his own experience between the new man and the old, between the Christ and the old Adam, is – in part at least – the tension of the uncompleted missionary task. We cannot "grow up in all things unto Him, which is the head" (Ep 4:15), except by going out into the world to make all men one with us in the fullness of His body. The eschatological tension cannot be understood apart from the tension of missionary obligation.

From **Prayers of Life** *by* Michel Quoist

> *I am not made of plaster, God says, nor stone nor of bronze.*
> *I am living flesh, throbbing, suffering.*
> *I am among men, and they have not recognised me . . .*

For I am everywhere that men are, God says.
Since the day when I slipped among them, on a mission to save them all;
Since the day when I definitely committed myself to trying to gather
    them together.
        Now I am rich and I am poor, a workman and a boss.
I am a union member and a non-union member, a striker and a strike-
    breaker for men, alas, make me do all kinds of things.
        I am on the side of the demonstrators and on the side of the police,
            for men, alas, transform me into a policeman.
        I am a leftist, a rightist and even in the centre.
        I am this side of the iron curtain and beyond.
        I am a German and a Frenchman, a Russian and an American,
        A Chinese from Vietnam and Vietminh.
        I am everywhere that men are, God says.

From **God & Sons** *by* Dewi Morgan

The great world religions are in a melting pot – and the metaphor is a good one. Each is coming into contact with every other in a way which has not previously been possible in the whole of human history and none is left unaffected. This is indeed the first time that Christianity has been brought into real encounter with other faiths, for never before has it been able to meet them with any degree of equality. We have already seen something of the way in which Christianity has become a worldwide faith. But hitherto it has been able to approach other religions only encapsulated in all the antipathies created by its relationship with a conquering West. The commonplace fallacy that Christian missions have expanded only because they have been able to ride in an imperial chariot has long since been exploded. But little as Christian expansion has really owed to colonial expansion, it has inescapably been associated in colonised minds with the coloniser; the missionary has had the same colour face as the administrator and the soldier and he went to the same schools and spoke of the same country as home. Today's Christian missionary may be of any race or country and he can travel free of any disadvantages of association with an overlord. He can and indeed must learn to go through the process of emptying himself of legal trappings as Paul told the Philippians his master did. He can and indeed must learn to go as one who serves not as one who dominates and in that, too, has a chance to imitate Christ. Above all, perhaps, he can go as one who wants to learn before he can teach, as one who will listen before he speaks. And that will mean the faith he carries is going to be changed and enriched as the insights of other men are brought to bear on its depths. Christianity in fact, is going to benefit from the resurgence of other faiths which with new confidence will offer their gold, frankincense and myrrh.

But Christianity at all its best moments has always known that it must learn from all men. The writer of the Epistle to the Hebrews was surely looking beyond the Old Testament when he said that at sundry times and in divers manners God had spoken in times past to the fathers. Paul was quite happy to pick up a quotation from a Greek poet and quote it with approval when he discoursed at Athens. John in his Gospel used a Greek term when he talked about the Logos, and Justin Martyr in the second century amplified his thought when he said "Christ is the Logos, in whom the whole human race has a portion, and all who have lived according to this Logos are Christians, even though like Socrates and Heraclitus among the Greeks they are accounted godless." No Christian thinker, however conservative, has condemned Clement of Alexandria for starting with what his hearers knew and expounding Christ through Greek myths. And Augustine, giant of Christian teachers, said that true religion had always existed and was only called Christian after the appearance of Christ. In the Middle Ages, Aristotle and Cicero enjoyed almost canonical authority.

The early Christians knew that Christ who was all truth had not come to destroy but to fulfil the law and the prophets and all that was true and good in any man's thought and culture. For the last couple of centuries, western Christians have been at a serious disadvantage in trying to remember this cardinal fact. They have been part of a conquering civilisation. They have been conditioned by a climate of thought in which the West seemed inevitably superior to anything the rest of the world could show in any sphere. They have slipped into habits of mind of accepting "the lesser breeds without the law" as heathen capable of nothing but bowing down to wood and stone – and who could expect to learn anything from such people? You cannot benefit from contact with another man if you allow no value of any sort for his convictions. You talk down to an inferior and cannot hope for any of the pleasure or enlightenment which conversation would bring.

The Christian faith is today out on the ocean of world religions and is subject to the same favourable trade winds and the same destructive gales as they are. Christianity is exposed to other religions... To quote Kraemer (*Religion and the Christian Faith*, p. 20), "For the first time since the Constantine victory in A.D. 312 and its consequences, the Christian Church is heading towards a real and spiritual encounter with the great non-Christian religions. Not only because the so-called younger churches, the fruits of the work of the modern missions, live in the midst of them, but also because the fast-growing interdependence of the whole world forces the existence and vitality of these religions upon us, and makes them a challenge to the Church to manifest in new terms its spiritual and intellectual integrity and value."

We are living in a new world and Christianity is but one among the religions . . .

I write as a Christian priest, and I deliberately make the statement that but for one thing, and one alone, Christianity is no more than one among the religions and indeed hardly deserves to be even that if it forgets its relationship with Christ. Indeed, one must put it more brutally. Christianity deserves to be forgotten and is best forgotten if it fails to forget itself and remembers only the Christ who is its cornerstone. Other religions have tenets of immense value, have a capacity for vast moral endeavour, have deep insights into the inner mysteries of life. But only Christianity has Christ. And Christ is all that Christianity has. It needs no more.

Prayer *from* The Accession Service *from* A Book of School Worship

O God, the Father of our Lord Jesus Christ, our only Saviour the Prince of Peace: Give us grace seriously to lay to heart the great dangers we are in from our unhappy divisions. Take away all hatred and prejudice, and whatsoever else may hinder us from godly union and concord; that as there is but one Body, and one Spirit, and one hope of our calling, one Lord, one faith, one baptism, one God and Father of us all, so we may henceforth be all of one heart and of one soul, united in one holy bond of truth and peace, of faith and charity, and may with one mind and one mouth glorify Thee; through Jesus Christ our Lord. Amen.

From The Household of God *by* Leslie Newbiggin

THE BODY OF CHRIST

In fact the Church has sinned and – in the new dispensation as in the old – God retains His freedom over His Church to chasten and correct, to call those who were no people His people, to raise up of the stones children of Abraham. He is faithful to His covenant even when men are unfaithful, but the whole purpose of His covenant is – as St Paul makes clear – that He may have mercy upon all, therefore there can be no room in it for any human claim upon God, for any thought that whereas those outside the covenant must depend simply on the free and uncovenanted mercy of God, those within it have – as it were – a *right* to His mercy. We have already pointed out that the complexity of St Paul's argument in Romans 9–11 arises from just this fact. There is a covenant and a covenant people, and God is faithful to His covenant. But the substance of that covenant is all pure mercy and grace. If men presume to claim for themselves upon the basis of the covenant some relationship with God other than that of the sinner needing God's grace, the covenant has been perverted.

And where that has happened God, in the sovereign freedom of His grace, destroys these pretensions, calls "No people" to be the people, breaks off branches and grafts in wild slips, filling them with life which is His own life imparted to men.

There is no law in His kingdom save the law of pure grace. That is why they come from east and west to sit down with Abraham and Isaac, while the sons of the Kingdom are cast out, for the sons of the Kingdom have no place there unless they are willing to sit down with all whom the Lord of the feast shall call, and to receive His mercy in exactly the same way as the publicans and sinners.

From **God & Sons** *by* Dewi Morgan

The frightening thing is the recurrent theme in the Bible that the world so often knows God better than His Chosen People do. It was "his own" who knew him not, when Christ came to them. And Jesus had cause to say: "I have not found such faith, no, not in Israel. But many shall come from the East and the West. The men of Nineveh will rise up at the judgement with this generation and condemn it." And Paul recalled Isaiah's words: "I have been found by those who did not seek me. I have shown myself to those who did not ask for me." The children of this world are in a strange way so often wiser than the children of light. Perhaps the other religions are having their resurgence precisely so that they may lead the Israel of the new covenant nearer to Christ the author of the covenant.

The one thing that makes Christianity different is its relationship with Christ. That it has failed to demonstrate this relationship is tragically true. "I would accept Christ were it not for my experience of Christians" is how one Indian summed it up. Christ promised that His Spirit would remain with the Church and would guide it into all truth. But he did not suggest that the Spirit would *force* the Church along the right path. Christians are subject to the gravitational pull that afflicts all men. Consequently the story of the Church has been marred by human follies even as it has been ennobled by its moments of human greatness. The follies have come when the Church forgot its Master. Its greatnesses have been when it has voluntarily yielded control to him.

How far can one assess whether or not the Church remembers its Master at this time? How far can one see in Christianity anything of the spirit of resurgence which is evident in other religions? The essence of the life of Christ was that, motivated by love, he was ready to lose his life

240

in order that men might be made whole. How far does the Christian body show a similar willingness today? The cynic who stands on the touchline will respond with a facile, "Not at all". The Christian who is sensitive to the deep inner surges in Christendom (which is no longer a geographical entity) will find himself much more optimistic. The second Vatican Council is a concrete example of resurgence within Christendom. Non-Roman Christians are no less active though their activities, being more diffuse, are less dramatic.

Best known of all the trends in contemporary Christianity seen as a whole is the ecumenical movement, the surge towards reunion. It is by no means showing smooth and steady progress but that can hardly be expected with a 2,000-year backlog to catch up on. And Christians, like other men, love old ways and old conservatisms. Yet here a little, there a little, one sees increasing evidence that each segment of the broken body of the Church is becoming more ready to die to its own idiosyncrasies and find new life in a greater whole.

Alongside today's ecumenical movement goes what is known as the liturgical movement, in its own way dynamic. Its concern is to ask how best men may worship God, how best men may turn from self-centred pre-occupation and fix a loving gaze upon their creator. And again the relevance to the death of self is visible.

No less significant in the contemporary Christian scene is all the thinking which, somewhat fortuitously, has become to be associated with the Bishop of Woolwich. It should be stated quite categorically that such thinkers are sincerely out to advance the Christian faith. Yet the man in the street is not far from the mark when he says that what such people want is to see the Christian faith *as it is at this moment*, fall into the ground and die.

Embracing all these and in significant ways influencing each present trend in Christianity is the relationship of the Christian faith with other faiths. Probably the most articulate single expression of this was in the Vatican Council. Having first accepted a share in the blame for the disunity of the Church (and this indeed meant the death of the Roman Church as it had come to be) the Council went on to outline a new charter for its future dealings with men of other creeds, especially Jews. The Council proclaimed its indissoluble unity with the ancient Israel of which the Jews are progeny and stated that even though the Jews rejected Jesus as Messiah they are no more accursed than other men. All manifestations of anti-Semitism, indeed all discrimination based on race, colour, class or religion were condemned and there went out a new call for co-operation with the Jews. No less important than new relationships with Judaism are the new relationships with other religions. All the peoples of the earth together with their various religions, it was affirmed, are one community. All religions attempt to answer the same vital question in different ways. Although the Church looks to Christ for the fullness of truth, she does not therefore deny anything which is true or holy in other religions. Christians should enter into dialogue with members of other faiths and recognise and acknowledge all their spiritual, moral and cultural values. The Church looks with respect on Hinduism, Buddhism and Islam. And the declaration closes with a statement of its belief in the brotherhood of all men under one Father.

Think for a moment of the Church which blessed Crusaders intent on destroying Islam, or the Church with elaborate Inquisitional processes to compel men into a tortured credal statement. We have travelled a long way and that Church is dead. Yet there is still far to go. To quote Cardinal Bea (the captain who piloted the declaration to port through many a storm) "The declaration in fact constitutes a highly important and promising beginning, but only a beginning, of a long and serious march towards the arduous goal of mankind in which all men will truly feel and behave as sons of the same Father who is in heaven." . . .

The Christian believes that Christ is the unique and perfect example of the truly and completely human. He believes that in Christ all men and all creation find their consummation. He believes that Christ was before the world began and in Him all things have their being. Christ was and is the Logos. That being the case, Christ is in some sense already in all men and all religions. The Christian will therefore approach all men and all religions with respect knowing that he can learn something of Christ in them even as he can show something of Christ to them.

To quote Canon Max Warren in his introduction to the magnificent Christian Presence series, "Our first task in approaching another people, another culture, another religion is to take off our shoes, for the place we approach is holy. Else we may find ourselves treading on men's dreams. More serious still we may forget that God was here before our arrival. We have then to ask what is the authentic religious content in the experience of the Muslim, the Hindu, the Buddhist, or whoever he may be. We may, if we have asked humbly and respectfully, still reach the conclusion that our brothers have started from a false premise and reached a faulty conclusion. But we must not arrive at our judgement from outside their religious situation. We have to try to sit where they sit, to enter sympathetically into the pains and griefs and joys of their history and see how these pains and griefs and joys have determined the premises of their argument. We have, in a word, to be 'present' with them."

To be "present". That is precisely the inner heart of the Incarnation. The Word became flesh. God became man. God with us. And never more, surely, than in this twentieth century as the God with all men becomes more visible as all men, by the logic of the world situation, become better known to each other.

From **The Times,** February 1971

THE SURVIVAL OF THE JEWISH FAITH

Judaism perhaps feels more acutely than the other monotheistic faiths Dietrich Bonhoeffer's problem of how to speak of God in an age of no religion. It is only now, some 25 years after the murder of six million Jews by the Nazis, that a pattern of thought is emerging in our response to the catastrophe which overwhelmed Jewry. Or rather, several patterns, because no two Jewish theologians would answer alike the question, "How do we think of God after the holocaust?"

The neo-orthodox continue to believe in God's all-powerful, all good attributes almost as if the holocaust had never happened, and there was no problem of theodicy. At the other extreme, the response has been a death-of-God philosophy. For them, the horrors of the concentration camps have severed the strand uniting God and Man, Heaven and Earth: we must make our own way in a silent, unfeeling, purposeless cosmos. Such thinkers wish to preserve the traditions and ethical obligations of Judaism, but they discard God as the cornerstone of Jewish belief. This surely renders meaningless most of those traditions and ethical obligations which they prize so highly. Less radical are the theologians who fashion a finite, limited God, a guarantor of ethics corresponding to the best impulses in man, so that the agonising question: "Where was God in Auschwitz?" does not arise.

In what follows I would like to explain what progressive Jews in this country believe about God and the future of Judaism: God, Torah, and the people Israel. Torah – God's teaching – is borne by Israel from God to all peoples, and stands by itself. Not so God and Israel who cannot exist without each other. They grow together, they suffer together. Above all they need each other. God is revealed through Israel, who is the symbol for ideal mankind, witnessing to him and his presence in a sceptical world. "If you are my witnesses, then I am your God, but if you are not my witnesses, then it is as if I am not God" runs the rabbinic comment to a verse in the book of Isaiah.

Given God's voluntary dependence on man, to regard God as perfect in power as he was perfect in vision at the beginning would be what William James calls "the monistic superstition". Likewise mankind symbolised by Israel, is not to be regarded as the perfected crown of God's creation. Man is an incomplete creature who must struggle through the hardships and sufferings of this world towards his goal of union with God. God and man, the father and his child, will come together at the end, when man has reached spiritual maturity. And then God will be fulfilled. "On that day the Lord shall be One, and his Name One", says the prophet. It is left to man to make or to mar that supreme integration.

This hope in a future when man will grow freely to choose God enables our faith to survive the holocaust of the concentration camps, just as it enabled that of the Jews of ancient Palestine to survive two destructions of the Temple and exile. We can keep faith without denying God, or despairing of the evil in the world. We are led onwards, understanding that it is the lot of witnesses to the truth to suffer hardships and persecution. According to the old rabbinic text, a question asked of every Jew before the judgement seat is, "In your lifetime, did you continue to hope for salvation?" The rabbis mean to teach by this that the Jew must never despair, no matter how tragic his history, for to despair would be the ultimate defeat of God, and the rejection not only of the six million victims of Hitler, but of those countless numbers in every age who lived and died as witnesses to God's name.

From **Johanna at Daybreak** *by* R. C. Hutchinson

SPOKEN BY A JEW

"You see," he said, "happiness – as I understand the word – depends on an attitude of mind; one has to start by supposing it as a possible state for oneself. And that's what none of us believes any longer, because we carry wounds of the spirit which can't be healed. To give you an instance – one which naturally comes to my own mind. When I was arrested – that was before the War – my wife Naomi was very ill. I asked the man who came for me – he came to my office, he was young, and very goodlooking, with a cultured voice – I asked him if he would take me to see my wife for just five minutes, to say farewell. He refused absolutely, he said my private worries were no affair of his. And to me that was like a final statement in philosophy, it seemed to tell me that in a world where the highest form of life – speaking biologically – could be so casual towards another creature's suffering the idea of happiness was just a romantic illusion. We here, I think we're all like that. We can't convince ourselves any more of people's goodness – when we look into a stranger's face we're asking all the time, What are this person's real intentions? What power has he to do me harm? It means that for us nothing is permanent, nothing certain. Today we're alive, we're not being molested, we're free to associate with those we're fond of. But we count on none of this,

244

we don't even expect that everything will be the same tomorrow. That's something which you – I speak with great respect, dear lady – cannot imagine or understand, the idea of spending one's whole life with a sense of desperate insecurity. Instinctively listening all the time for the loud knock and the rasping voice, waiting for a new torture of separation." He had not raised his scholarly voice, but a new intensity had made it more incisive . . .

"Then you count yourself among Schopenhauer's disciples?" "Schopenhauer", he answered with a certain weariness, "was one of those ill-starred creatures who fabricate synthetic philosophies to serve as a frame for their own abnormal mentality. Listen: if you will grant me a little more of your patience I should like to explain to you how I differ from that noxious pedagogue . . . No, honoured lady, you'd be wrong if you wrote me off as a pessimist – in truth I'm exactly the opposite. Experience may tell us that human beings are mostly cruel to the point of madness. But God who created them is not a madman. The very fact that we speak of cruelty as "unnatural", though we see it everywhere in nature (in ourselves as well), is enough to show that there's an entity outside us – greater than we are, less transient, calling for our obedience – one to whom cruelty is intolerable. How else can the mere idea of mercy have come to us, enclosed as we are in a system where mercilessness appears to be the principal of survival?" . . .

"Perhaps I may cite my own people", Herr Oestmann resumed, "as an illustration of what I've said. In our earlier history you find us guilty of appalling wickedness – greed, monstrous cruelties, constant religious infidelity. And for that we've been punished, again and again, by subjugation to tyrants, disasters of every kind. But that long record of depravity never extinguished our inborn knowledge of what is good and holy – there have always been voices from among ourselves to protest that we've betrayed our calling. In my belief that's why we've been allowed to survive – as a people, I mean – even when we're scattered round the globe. It's because we've produced in every age something greater than ourselves – a message, an oracle, insisting that righteousness is an entity independent of human kind, infinite in power exerting a unique authority. Our tortuous history – the suffering which has followed all our deviations and our blasphemies – it has served to offer the world that awe-inspiring lesson at a terrible cost to our selves. And if that's our tragedy, paradoxically it's our glory as well – the belief, the knowledge, that God so uses us to show mankind his power and his moral perfection. Forgive me: that is something – may I say – far greater than the 'happiness' which others regard as the prize of living."

From **The Path to Glory** *by* J. R. H. Moorman

The third incident is concerned with the unknown exorcist. The disciples may know that they are but men, and so be learning the lesson of dependence; they may know that they are not very wise and not very strong, and so be learning the lesson of lowliness. But though weak and foolish they are Christ's men. They have followed him and been accepted by him, and this must inevitably separate them from the world and put them in a class by themselves. Jesus must now teach them the third lesson in humility, that of tolerance and trust.

It was John who gave Jesus the opportunity of teaching them this lesson. He referred to a man "casting out devils in thy name" whom the Apostles had reproved. He had no authority, was not even a disciple. He had no right to use the name of Jesus, and his doing so could only cause confusion. They had therefore stopped him. But Jesus told them they had erred in so doing. The man, though not a Christian, was a man of devotion and discipline (for devils, as we know, come out only "by prayer and fasting"). Even though he was not in the fold at all, even though he was an outsider and a free-lance, out of the main stream of Christian life, untouched by the covenanted means of grace; even so he was doing the work of Christ.

"Other sheep I have which are not of this fold", the true fold, the Church and body of Christ. This is a very hard teaching for us to accept. It was the teaching which scandalised the Pharisees, for Jesus had to tell them that salvation was no longer connected with membership of the Church or observance of the Law, but was the free gift of God through Christ to all who would receive it, to the Gentile as well as to the most loyal of Jews. "The Kingdom of God shall be taken away from you and shall be given to a nation bringing forth the fruits thereof" (Mt 21:43). The same problem faces us today. What is the good of having a Church and a system of authority if those who decline to come into it are to be regarded as faithful servants of Christ, doing his work as much as those who submit themselves to the discipline of discipleship? But we have got to do what Christ tells us to do. After all who knows best – we or God? Thus the third lesson in humility which the disciples had to learn was to trust God and not try to prevent others from doing his work. "He that is not against you is for you."

From **The Journey Inwards** *by* F. C. Happold

"Before time was the Word (The Divine Logos) already was. The word was in God, and what God was, the Word was. The Word then was with God at the beginning, and through Him all things came to be; no single thing was created except through Him. All that came to be had its life in

His life and that Life was the Light of men . . . And the Word became flesh and dwelt among us, and we saw His glory."

The idea of the potency of the Word or Logos (which literally means a word) is an ancient one. It is found for instance, in the description of creation in the first chapter of the Book of Genesis, with its continuous reiteration of the phrase, "And God said . . . ." It is found, too, in the formulation of cosmic philosophy in the Chaldean Oracles: "The One spake and immediately the Three came forth and became the Many, the Many returned again through the Three into the One."

The idea of the Logos is found in that fusion of Greek philosophy with Jewish and Oriental ideas which was taking place with its centre in Alexandria, at the time of the birth of Jesus, and which spread through the Eastern Mediterranean world.

Here the Logos, the Thought of God, is pictured as the divine Energy through which the phenomenal world, the differentiated world of time and space, the Many, came into existence, as the Activity, the Coming-forth of the ineffable, attributeless One. Further the Logos was regarded not only as the Thought and Activity of the Godhead, but also as the Light which illumines every man, so that in the depths of his inner being man may have contact with and so know the unknowable Source of all being; and not only through the intuitive, perhaps formless "knowing" of the centre, spark or apex of the soul, but also, though only partially, through the divine faculty of reason. If the universe is conceived in its essential unity, everything in it is seen as the manifestation in space-time "forms" of one ultimate Reason; it is the expression of the Divine Thought, of the creative eternal Mind.

The Logos was also called the Son or the Wisdom of God and was regarded as the link and mediator between the eternal and the ephemeral. Thus the Logos doctrine expressed a principal of activity within The One and Perfect Godhead which made it possible for It to manifest Itself in and through the phenomenal world.

Now if the Logos, which ever was and ever will be, is the Light which illumines every man, every great spiritual teacher must have been inspired and illuminated by the same Divine Logos. Theologians of the early Christian Church, whose religion-philosophy was within the limits of their own age, a cosmic one, declared this. The second century Christian apologist, Justin Martyr, to whom "Christ was and is the Logos who dwells in every man" declared that, in that they were inspired by the Logos, Socrates and Plato, as well as Moses and Isaiah, though they had lived before Jesus walked this earth, were, "Christians". And perhaps we, whose world is so much bigger than that of Justin Martyr or those other Christian theologians, Clement and Origen, who developed the same idea, may be prepared to say that so were, for instance, the Buddha and the inspired writers of the Hindu Upanishads and the Bhagavad Gita.

Another great Father of the Church, St Augustine, wrote: "That which is called the Christian religion existed among the ancients, and never did not exist, from the beginning of the human race until Christ came in the flesh, at which time the true religion which already existed began to be called Christianity."

"And the Word became flesh and dwelt among us." Let our meditation move a step further. The Divine Logos, which was before time began, before the universe came into existence, and was and is God; which is both the Principle of Activity and Outpouring within the Unity of the Godhead and also the Inner Light which shines, and has ever shone, in every man, a divine "seed" or "spark", implanted in him which it is the task of each to realise in his own experience; at a particular point in time became incarnate in a man, Jesus of Nazareth, bone of our bone, flesh of our flesh, and yet the manifestation within the historical process of the timeless, creative outpouring of the One through the Three into the Many.

This is the central dogma of the Christian Faith. To understand its significance and splendour it is necessary to try to grasp its subtle meaning. Jesus of Nazareth is acknowledged as the Incarnation of the total, cosmic Christ, the Divine Logos, in time, and so named Jesus Christ. In that incarnation the divine and human essences are found in perfect union, so He is confessed as truly God and truly man.

"Jesus of Nazareth is the epiphany of Christ – I should prefer to say *the* Christ – in history."

So said Father Panikkar in the dialogue with Ian Stephens. He goes on, "The whole Christ is Alpha and Omega, the beginning and the end, first begotten of the Absolute. In other religions he may not be recognised as Jesus and yet the real and not only the nominal link to the transcendent is by this definition of the Christ . . . Christ is universal by definition. We could equally well call him say, Isvara (one of the Hindu deities), or by any other name pointing towards the same function, but historically this function has been performed by Jesus. So he plays a unique role in history, which does not exclude at all the functions of the different prophets . . .

In this pilgrimage in time something succeeded in and through Jesus of Nazareth. The Christian faith is that the Christ, the Alpha and Omega, the Panto Pantocreator, etc., appeared in Jesus."

Letter *from* the Dean of Westminster

Sir, – May I beg the hospitality of your columns to give to your readers some information about the "service of silence" which is to be held in Westminster Abbey on Saturday, December 10th, at 6 p.m.

The holding of this service was agreed in Chapter from the beginning of our planning of the Abbey's nine-hundredth anniversary year. It has been discussed at length, and we are undertaking it in full consciousness of our allegiance to our Lord and of our responsibility to the Church.

As your readers will be well aware, we have gathered much of our thinking and praying during this anniversary year around the "One People" theme. It is necessary for the fullness of the proclamation of this theme that we should open our doors wide and generously, on one significant occasion, not only to all Christians but to all men.

What we have said all along when announcing our programme for the anniversary year we still say – that there will be one occasion when we invite our brethren of other faiths, and indeed all men of goodwill, to come and share this period of silent meditation with us. To do so on this particular occasion does not mean that we have turned away from the "scandal of particularity" which is inherent in the gospel. It does not mean that we have turned to a universalism which would gloss over all differences. Nor will the service be an essay in syncretism.

The service will take place in the nave, traditionally a place of concourse. It will last for exactly one hour. In accordance with its title, it will be largely a time of silence. I shall myself introduce the service and give the first reading. This will be followed by five minutes silence, after which, at intervals of ten minutes, members of the Jewish, Muslim, Hindu, and Buddhist faiths will read their chosen passage.

Each time the reading is over, the congregation will enter into a deep silence, which we trust will grow profounder as the hour goes by. I shall close the service in the same manner in which I opened it. There will be music before and after the service, but no music in the course of it. There will be no spoken prayers, only the readings, the meditation, the silence.

We have chosen December 10th because it is Human Rights Day, and 6 p.m. so that our Jewish friends can join us if they are so minded. Human rights – what profound unity is still waiting to be fully realised and implemented, what moral resolution is waiting to be stirred?

Gathered together in the nave of the Abbey ("My house shall be called a house of prayer for *all* nations"), we shall realise our common humanity and contemplate in prayer and resolution our common predicament. As Christians we shall do this in the name of him who took our humanity upon him, whom we believe is the Eternal Word and the Light that lighteneth every man.

Eric Abbott

Unity *by* Carolyn Scott, *taken from* **One**

> *A gulf bridged makes a cross;*
> *A split defeated is a cross.*

(Laurence Van Der Post)

In the Meditation Room at the United Nations Building in New York, a shaft of light cuts across the altar of iron ore. The shaft streams from an unknown source.

It represents a unity between men.

That shaft of light in the silence is all things to all men, of whatever race, nation or faith. To one it is the purpose, to another, the reality.

It takes the name of the Light of the Mind, and the name of the Presence of God. It represents the depths of each man's mind; the reason for each man's being; the meaning of life.

It is only here, at the basis of life, in the iron and the light and the mind of man, that universal unity has been found. For the rest, the search goes on. A statue marks a success; a fiery cross on a doorway, a concentration camp in Greece, hunger and narrow minds mark the failures.

But the statues stand. The symbols remain. The communion that has begun, continues, and these things speak of unity.

Below the white peaks of the Andes, between the Atlantic and the Pacific Oceans, stands the statue of Christ the Redeemer, the Christ of the Andes. It marks the end of a sixty year long dispute. Carved into the stone are the words:

"Sooner shall these mountains crumble into dust than the peoples of Argentine and Chile break the peace which they have sworn to maintain at the feet of Christ the Redeemer."

In Coventry Cathedral, on the high altar, stands a cross of nails. Another stands before an altar in Dresden. In the Cathedral bookshop on a cross of nails postcard, are the words:

"The Cross of Nails is a relic that grew out of the destruction of the cathedral in 1940. As the roof burnt, 14th century hand-forged nails which had fastened together its beams, littered the sanctuary. The following morning, the inspiration came to shape three of the nails into the form of a cross. The cross has become the symbol of Coventry Cathedral's ministry of international reconciliation."

A cross of nails stands on an altar in the race-rioting state of Alabama. Young people from Coventry helped to rebuild a hospital in Dresden. Young Germans helped to build the international youth centre at Coventry. And the statue of Christ the Redeemer has stood for 64 years. These things represent a unity between nations.

250

The Iron Curtain remains; the Wall between East and West Germany stands; Americans and Asians die in Vietnam. But a Chinese child and an English child can play hopscotch across chalk marks in a playground, because they understand without words. A child in Greece searches for the same fun as a child in England, because they are both embarking on the same adventure. An old woman freezing in one room in London in the winter because she cannot afford fuel, and an old man sitting and waiting to die in the heat of India, ask themselves the same question.

There is a unity between the old and a unity between the young, that has nothing to do with nationality.

An infrequent ferry boat takes pilgrims and tourists across from the Scottish mainland to the island of Iona. Standing in the shadows of the Abbey cloisters, the home of the Iona Community, is a bronze sculpture called the Descent of the Spirit. It was created by Jacob Lipchitz, a practising Jew. There are two identical statues, one in a secular American community, another in a Dominican Church in France. They were given by an American woman in recognition of three places that practise true community. The sculpture represents the Virgin Mary. On it are the words: "Jacob Lipchitz, faithful to the religion of his ancestors, has made this Virgin for the better understanding of men on earth that the Spirit may reign."

This represents a unity of faith.

At London Airport a chapel of St George is being built underground to serve the twelve million people who pass through the airport everyday, and the thirty-five thousand who work there. It will be a single chapel for the use of Roman Catholics, Anglicans and Free Churchmen. At Churchill College, Cambridge, the new chapel is completely ecumenical – so much so that it has been neither dedicated nor consecrated. In East Germany, Lutherans share their churches with Roman Catholic refugees from Czechoslovakia. Muslims, Hindus, Jews and Christians search for common ground and try to find a common God.

But in India, Hindu and Muslim are opposed. In Israel, Arab and Jew live on the edge of war. In England, a man will believe that to call the Lord's table an altar is heresy; in Scotland, walls are chalked with "no popery"; and in Ireland bitter religious feuds drag on.

Unity is one thing: uniformity another. Tolerance is one thing: compromise another. Unity fights poor housing conditions, educates, feeds the hungry. Tolerance disowns the narrow-minded bigotry that splits and divides. Uniformity obliterates individuality. It can result in Red Guards and mass media advertising. Uniformity irons out a man's mind for him, watering down the glory, without strengthening the weaknesses. Religious unity, like any unity, is a coat of many colours. The weaving is intricate, and threads fine.

"Here," say Lutheran ministers in East Germany, "the churches are strong because times are difficult." And in Russia, where the great bells of the Kremlin no longer toll to celebrate Easter Day, where the guns are silent and the incense gone, there are still vast, silent crowds that gather at the midnight of Easter to pass on the whispered greeting: "Christ is Risen! – He is risen indeed!"

Faiths are held together by a unity of purpose. When men lose sight of the purpose, faiths split and fall apart. But the true men of faith are tied by no denominational bonds. A court of law sent a girl who had been on drugs back from prison to the Church that had been trying to help her. In the prison they had wanted to know about this place that meant so much to her. They asked about the people there.

"It was hard to tell them," she said. "They kept asking your name, and we just call you Christian."

In Johannesburg at Easter time, Africans borrow a painting from the Cathedral to hang in the churches in the African reserves. The painting is called Simon of Cyrene. It shows a black man carrying a cross. It was painted by a white European: the English artist, Delmar Banner. He painted it to show the sharing of the Negro in the burden of the cross, and the sharing of Christ in the burden of the Negro.

This is unity between the black and the white man. In a Birmingham play-group, black and white children play together. But when they leave school, equality ends. In Vietnam, black and white Americans fight side by side; at home snipers shoot, homes are burned, and black and white only unite to loot the gutted stores. In South Africa, a child may be forced to prove her colour before a court of law and to live apart from her parents. Black Power rears up, and white supremacy clings to the reins. In the shanty town settlements of Jamaica, in the joint ventures around London, where people are attacking the problem together, there are successes, and there will be more. But men fear a new world, and they fear the uneasy unity that is called half-caste.

Jesus lifted up his eyes to heaven and prayed, "That they all may be one; as thou Father, art in me, and I in thee, that they also may be one in us; that the world may believe that thou hast sent me".

Unity has become a parochial word. Its catholic intensity has been narrowed, and the breadth of its call cramped. But unity is of the universal. It does not belong to nationality or race or faith alone. Unity belongs to all mankind.

"There is neither Jew nor Greek, there is neither bond nor free, there is neither male nor female: for ye are all one in Jesus Christ."

For a moment, beauty holds man together: the Pietà, a Brandenburg concerto, the first light of dawn. But beauty, like the iron and light, strikes at the hidden things in man's mind. Day by day, it is the failures that are obvious. Peace treaties are broken, and truces are kept only for strategy. States secede, commonwealths crumble, and political parties are broken apart. Men fight, they starve and they pray in separate buildings to different gods. Men are divided within themselves. But there are landmarks of unity. The words that last, the communities that stand, the friendships that are unbroken, the links that remain strong. There are the basic unities, the iron and the light and the beauty that endure. Because there is in all men something that is the same.

From The Book of Prayer for Students

Father of men, grant that men everywhere may come to realise that the one solution of international rivalries and the one guarantee of abiding peace is in obedience to thy Will and in following the mind of Christ.

From Worship and Witness (Quaker publication) No. 20 *in the series* Study in Fellowship

THE SEARCH FOR GOD

One of the most attractive episodes in the history of the Christian Church is that of the conversion of the pagans of northern England to Christianity. The story we owe to Bede who tells us that Edwin, being almost convinced of the truth of Christianity but wishing to test it by the opinion of his countrymen, summoned his elders to a council meeting and invited Paulinus to put his case. Edwin then asked each one individually for his opinion. From one whose name has not been preserved came the answer:

"The present life of man, O King, seems to me, in comparison of that time which is unknown to us, like to the swift flight of a sparrow through the room wherein you sit at supper in the winter, with your commander and ministers, and a good fire in the midst, while storms of rain and snow prevail abroad: the sparrow . . . flying in at one door and immediately out at another, whilst he is safe within, he is safe from the wintry storm; but he immediately vanishes out of sight into the dark winter from which he had emerged. So this life of man appears for a short space, but of what went before, or of what is to follow, we are utterly ignorant. If therefore, this new doctrine contains something more certain, it seems justly to deserve to be followed." (*Ecclesiastical History of England:* Bk II, Chap. 13)

The reply has a timeless quality about it. It echoes with the long sadness of the race as it reflects on the fragility of human life and the ultimate fear that, coming from the unknown, going into the unknown, it may ultimately prove to be a delusion.

To move from Edwin sitting with his council in seventh century England to Tolstoy sitting in his study in nineteenth century Russia is to move not only a distance of twelve centuries but from one culture to another totally different. And yet the same sadness remains: "Why should I live?" says Tolstoy at the age of fifty the height of his fame and in a mood of the deepest depression. "Why should I do anything? Is there in life any purpose which the inevitable death which awaits me does not undo and destroy? . . . I sought like a man who is lost and who seeks to save himself – and I found nothing. I became convinced that all those who had sought before me . . . . have recognised that the very thing which was leading me to despair – the meaningless absurdity of life – is the only incontestable knowledge accessible to man." (*Confessions*)

And finally, to Sadhu Sundar Singh, the son of a devout Hindu family who having learnt from his mother that there was a peace of soul which was the greatest treasure that anyone could possess sought it with increasing urgency for several years until finally, "a wild resolution seemed to possess him that he would either find out the truth that was behind this agonising conflict, or else put an end to himself." (*Sadhu Sundar Singh*: C. F. Andrews)

A pagan tribesman, a sophisticated Russian novelist, a passionate Indian boy; different countries, different centuries, different cultures – but one and the same search! A search for a simple, authoritative answer, an answer satisfying at once to mind, will and feeling. Grounded in the enduring problems of man-made evil and of physical suffering, answered in one generation, asked afresh in the next, the demand is not only for an assurance about the purpose of man's life; more often it is a demand for an assurance about the purpose of God's planning – if indeed there be a God.

To the anxious, forthright and often hostile demands, whether of seventh century or twentieth century pagan, the answer does not lie in creeds and theologies. These are, at best, the embodiment of experience rather than experience itself: they can make no more response than the table makes to the pounding fist. The answer comes – when it comes – in what lies behind all these, in the ear that has caught the echo of truth and knows that although the sound has been struck in a centre inaccessible to logical enquiry, the note is, nevertheless, a true bell-note. It is the answer of life to life: for the Christian the discovery that he who was seeking was himself being sought.

THE CHALLENGE TO THE CHRISTIAN

The Good Pagan

. . . But what has all this to do with Christianity? The seeking either in solitude or in company with others is not alone peculiar to the Christian church, nor has the answer always been found by those within, or escaped those outside its bounds. And in this last lies the problem which besets any honest Christian, Quaker or non-Quaker. It is to put it shortly, the problem posed implicitly by the good man who is not a Christian.

How does it come about that one who belongs to another religion – or to none at all – may be so far as human judgement can tell every bit as good as a good Christian? Does this mean that neither any specific form of religion nor religion itself is essential to a life which is, by common consent "good"?

To the Quaker the problem is in one way probably less perplexing and yet more challenging than to any other branch of the Christian church. For from the beginning, Friends have declared that "the light that lighteth every man" is not a prerogative only of those called Christians. Barclay, writing in the early years of the Society says: "There may be members of this Catholic church both among the heathens, Turks and Jews, and all the several sorts of Christians, men and women of integrity and simplicity of heart, who . . . are by the secret touches of this holy light in their souls, enlivened and quickened."

The belief itself, however, combined with the unprogrammed nature of the Quaker Meeting for Worship based on silence creates its own dilemma. It is often argued that Quaker and Hindu for example can together sit down in silence and, in spite of their differences join in common worship – the more easily because Friends meeting to worship God, demand no more of one another than sincerity, and yet this very sincerity is the foundation of all religious worship. Thus, it is said, Christian and Hindu and humanist meeting together in sincerity within a Quaker meeting may find a unity which transcends the barrier of formal belief or affiliation. So many have testified to the truth of this that as a statement of fact it must be accepted (we have after all to accept a great deal that we do not understand, that we think perhaps ought to be otherwise!). Nevertheless, to leave the argument here is to go only half-way with Barclay. It is to overlook the fact that while he and his colleagues perceived that the light of Christ was not restricted to any one race or nation, in much the same way that Paul perceived that the response to his Gospel would come from Jew and Gentile alike – yet neither Paul nor Barclay considered themselves absolved from the task of preaching their Christian message. On the contrary, the fact that "There may be members of this Catholic church both among the heathens, Turks and Jews . . ." (and we may add, "among Communists, humanists and militant atheists") was to them all the more reason for declaring to them the message which would bring a fuller understanding of that which they already partly understood.

255

The Christian Failure

But if the achievements of the non-Christian saint are what come home most poignantly to the Christian propagandist, it is the failings of the Christians themselves which most often barb the anti-Christian's attack on the Church. To those in Africa and Asia who see Christianity from the outside, it is the religion of the white man who has for so long used his superior power to dominate, to exploit and often to destroy – in short the creed of the conqueror. The western pagan, on the other hand, may admit the nobility of the life of Christ and of some of his followers. He may admit, too, the immense liberation of man's spirit which has resulted from the influence of western protestantism. Nevertheless, he points out, Christianity despite its high ideals has failed to eradicate and done little to modify the brutality of man to man. Paschendael, Hiroshima, French terrorism in Algeria – all these, too, are part of the Christian heritage along with the emancipation of women, the devotion of Father Damien and the beauties of the King James Bible.

The Comfortably Indifferent

And finally, after the actively hostile and the merely cynical, there are the indifferent – those who ask no more of life than that it shall give them the possessions they want, a husband or a baby, a television set or more ski-ing trips . . . provided that life continues in its not-too-uncomfortable way, provided that they have enough to eat, to keep themselves warm at night and enough to grumble about, they ask for little more, and stories drawn from a time and a world remote from their own make decidedly less appeal than the cartoon page of the Daily Mirror – or of the New York Herald Tribune.

THE ANSWER

In the face of so much hostility, as of so much apathy, the reply of the Christian never has been simple – it is a complex one made with his whole life, actions and words both public and private. And always with the recollection that the workings of a man's mind are not as open to inspection as the workings of a motor car – or an electronic computer – that they are often dimly understood by the man himself. The most unpromising material often yields the most surprising results – one of the most remarkable features of the Sower is not only that the good ground yielded a hundredfold but that even the shallow ground produced a crop.

For despite the increasing success with which they are eliminating the discomfort from life, human beings remain human beings and pre-occupied as it may be with accounting procedure, with serving meals or with "case work" the human mind remains still a human mind subject to longing and disappointment, to jealousy and love – in short to all the ills that the spirit is heir to. To these passions race, class, income, political allegiance can make very little difference. Before them the human being stands with only such protection as his own insight and spiritual strength affords and it is when, underneath the neat city suit or worn tweed jacket, these are being tested to the limits, that the understanding word or sympathetic gesture can make the difference.

> The desert is not remote in southern tropics,
> The desert is not only around the corner,
> The desert is squeezed in the tube train next to you,
> The desert is in the heart of your brother . . .
>
> *Choruses from the Rock:* T. S. Eliot

At times, the mind, unable to take the strain, cracks and splinters; at times it survives, but is badly warped. But there are some men and women who have not merely "taken the strain" of what life can do to them, not merely "lived through it" but have, in the process of so doing, won through to a calmer, clearer spirit. Death, the death of the spirit, if not of the body, has passed near to them and they have found that it had no power to touch that within them which truly lived, and from the day of that discovery forward they have – though often without words – borne witness to the truth of John's declaration:

"In him was life: and the life was the light of men."

Prayer *by* W. E. Orchard *from* **The Book of Prayer for Students**

UT OMNES UNUM SINT

O God, who hast made of one blood all the nations of mankind, so that all are children and members one of another, how is it that we are so slow to trace the family likeness, so reluctant to claim our common kinship? We pray thee, O our God, to make the peoples one.

We pray for the Church of Christ, so broken, scattered and dismembered, that none would think we followed all one Lord and held a common faith. Purge away the vanity, intolerance and unforgiving spirit which has kept us far apart. May the seamless robe not be utterly rent nor the body any longer broken.

We pray that since men's need is one, we all may find the one way to thee, the one God. Forbid that in our highest things we should find fellowship impossible. May the spirit of Christ break down all barriers and answer the desire of all nations.

We pray for union so deep and universal that it shall gather all within one fold; those who pray and those who cannot; those whose faith is firm and those whose doubt is slow to clear. May we never be content with aught that excludes another from the fullness of thy grace, a single soul from the welcome of thy heart.

Christt in Woolworth's *by* Teresa Hooley, *taken from* **Let there be God,** an anthology of religious poetry *compiled by* T. H. Parker *and* F. J. Teskey

> *I did not think to find you there –*
> *Crucifixes, large and small,*
> *Sixpence and threepence, on a tray,*
> *Among the artificial pearls,*
> *Paste rings, tin watches, beads of glass.*
> *It seemed so strange to find you there*
> *Fingered by people coarse and crass,*
> *Who had no reverence at all.*
> *Yet – What is it you would say?*
> *"For these I hang upon my cross,*
> *For these the agony and loss,*
> *Though heedlessly they pass Me by."*
> *Dear Lord forgive such fools as I*
> *Who thought it strange to find you there*
> *When you are with us everywhere.*

From **Genesis 28**

And Jacob came to a certain place, and stayed there that night, because the sun had set. Taking one of the stones of the place, he put it under his head and lay down in that place to sleep.

And he dreamed that there was a ladder set up on earth, and the top of it reached to heaven; and behold, the angels of God were ascending and descending on it! And behold the Lord stood above it and said, "I am the Lord, the God of Abraham, your father and the God of Isaac . . . . Behold I am with you and will keep you wherever you go, and will bring you back to this land; for I will not leave you until I have done that which I have spoken to you." Then Jacob awoke from his sleep and said, "Surely the Lord is in this place and I did not know it." And he was afraid, and said, "How awesome is this place! This is none other than the house of God, and this is the gate of heaven."

Editorial *by* C. R. Bryant, S.S.J.E., *from* **New Fire**

. . . The time is long past when we could think of all those outside the Church as simple heathen. Long ago the fourth gospel declared that the Word, who became man in Jesus, is the light of all men. In other words

God addresses all men, not only those who confess Christ or have heard the name of Jesus. Further, men grow to maturity, they come to recognise what is true and do what is right, as they respond to the culture in which they grow up. If then the light of God's Word illuminates Muslims, Hindus and Buddhists, as St John asserts that it does, it will shine through Muslim, Hindu and Buddhist culture. We need not suppose that all religions are of equal value (a supposition as improbable as that all men are equally wise) nor that ignorance, error and sheer hard-heartedness have not distorted what God is saying through these religious cultures and muffled the divine voice. After all, these distorting factors are manifestly at work in the partly Christian culture of modern England. We believe too that God has spoken uniquely in Jesus and that his revelation of himself in Christ must be the criterion of the truth and value of all religious cultures, including that of our own country. But without any weakening of his ultimate loyalty to Christ the modern Christian can learn some important lessons from the great non-Christian world religions.

The serious and sensitive approach of a religious Hindu or Muslim can help to free a Christian from a certain narrowness and provincialism. Foreign travel broadens the mind. The boy or girl who goes abroad for the first time to stay for three or four weeks in a French or German home will have many of his ideas shaken: ideas about meals, about polite manners, about the proper clothes to wear. Things that he had taken for granted he now sees to be just English customs; not laws of the universe but local bye-laws. He loses a little of his provincialism. He will not probably love his own country less, but he will love it with a new discrimination. In the same way the Westerner meeting the devout adherent of some non-Christian faith realises that there can be a genuine spiritual character which owes nothing to Mattins and Evensong or even the New Testament. This approach must be serious and sensitive, otherwise he may misunderstand what he sees and be repelled by what seems to him strange and meaningless. In a similar way some English travellers react against everything foreign; they seem to feel it a threat to their English identity and they return from their holiday abroad more obstinately English than before.

The Buddhist, the Hindu and the Moslem may further bring home to the modern Christian forgotten elements in his own tradition. The immanence of God, the greatness of the human spirit, the need for a man to undergo training if his spiritual capacities are to be realised, are ancient Christian truths, though neglected today. When he meets men of alien faith expressing these truths, not by talking about them but by taking them for granted and expressing them in their lives, the Christian is sent back in search of his own hidden treasure. Again the thoroughness, the reverence, the discipline of the Moslem prayer-rite will make many modern Christians uncomfortable at the fitfulness and superficiality of much so-called prayer among Christians.

We repeat, nothing to be learnt from other religions is a substitute for the knowledge of God in Jesus Christ. But other religions may help modern Western man and woman, thrown off balance by the new wealth that up-to-date technology has made available, to appreciate that knowledge afresh. They may help Christianity to become, in fact as well as in principle, a universal, world-embracing and world-uniting faith. There are many signs of spiritual hunger in the West. The hippies witness to a deep dissatisfaction with the civilisation that has nurtured them and on which they depend. Outbreaks of irrational violence, which is the child of fear, also point to a spiritual vacuum, the unsatisfied need for a worth-while purpose in life . . . We believe that some kind of religion is bound to fill the space waiting for it in the soul of Western man. We believe, further, that a Christianity freed from some of its Western trappings and enriched by the wisdom of the East could be the religion of the twenty-first century.

13

The New Thing

"Behold I am doing a new thing"

From **One,** *a sermon preached by* Eric Abbott, Dean of Westminster, *at the closing service of the 900th Anniversary Year,* 28th December 1966

I begin my sermon as I began a year ago. Let us look to the future which belongs to God . . .

May we all join together now in looking to the future which belongs to God. The first thing which this means is that we must have a strategy.

It is not enough to say "go forward". To that exhortation given without any qualification the Gadarene Swine might respond "and so say all of us".

It is sometimes better to stand still and wait. It is sometimes better to make a withdrawal that later on we may advance more surely.

We must go forward . . . we are to reach forth unto those that are before, we are to press toward the mark – but we are to go forward with a strategy. Without a strategy we drift or wander or stumble. We *must* go forward with a strategy.

Each of us must have his or her personal strategy; and here at the Abbey

261

on this our 901st birthday we need a corporate strategy, realistic, wise, courageous, imaginative, and arising from what we have learned in this last wonderful year.

Whether we think of the Christian strategy of a single individual or of the corporate strategy of a Collegiate Body like ours at Westminster, the strategy belongs to the life of faith. True it is not, in the ordinary sense of the phrase, an "age of faith" in which we live. But in faith we must go forward. If there is something which I personally believe with all my heart it is, in Richard Baxter's words, that "Christ leads me through no darker rooms than He went through before". Forward then in faith.

I was glad to see that Bishop Mervyn Stockwood in a recent symposium of articles by six thinkers on God in the Scientific age, quoted these lines which were written by J. J. Balfour:

> Our highest truths are but half-truths.
> Think not to settle down forever in any truth.
> Make use of it as a tent in which to pass a summer's night,
> But build no house of it, or it will be your tomb.
> When you first have an inkling of its insufficiency
> And begin to descry a dim counter-truth looming up beyond,
> Then weep not, but give thanks,
> It is the Lord's voice whispering: "Take up thy bed and walk."

Forward in faith; take up thy bed and walk. This does not mean that I jettison the Creeds, for they are patient of limitless exploration, being rooted in history, made by a believing and worshipping community, a series of symbols and signposts, speaking of the ineffable mystery of God the Creator, the Redeemer, the Sanctifier, of our human destiny in Christ and of our spiritual home here and hereafter.

And therefore I can say "Forward in faith" because I believe not only that there is an *ens realissimum* but that this Ultimate Reality or Purposeful Mind is truly named as the God and Father of our Lord Jesus Christ. In Him I believe as the Alpha and Omega of the universe and of us creatures. I do not forget the galaxies, but neither do I fear them. And if God revealed in Christ is the Beginning and the End, I believe, indeed I know by faith, that Christ is with us at every stage of our journey. Therefore forward in faith means forward to greet the Christ of tomorrow.

And therefore again, the individual strategy must centre upon Christ ... Our individual strategy is memorably described by St Paul and declared with absolute plainness. It is going to be a life in which we know Jesus more and more (and are known by Him), in which we know the power of His resurrection (which means that He holds for us the secret of constant renewal which includes effective forgiveness and genuine absolution); it is going to be a life in which we know the fellowship of His sufferings (and there will come a number not of our choosing but of His). It is going to be a life which we do not count ourselves to have apprehended – we never say proudly or complacently that we have "arrived" and are now "perfect".

But – and who could define our "forward in faith" better than this? – we are to forget those things which are behind, even in our case the peculiar satisfaction of a 900th anniversary year. We are to reach forth unto those which are before, we are to press toward the mark for the prize of the high calling of God in Jesus Christ.

There is our individual strategy which each of us must interpret realistically in terms of our own life and circumstances, remembering that the Church's life and Christ's cause are maintained in a multitude of men and women, the vast majority of whom are lay folk not clerics, in a multitude of avocations in the secular world which is God's though we call it secular ... Corporately we at the Abbey shall have our strategy ... We shall seek, under God, to make this house of God more and more a house of prayer; we shall seek under God, a true contemporary spirituality; we shall give ourselves to the ministry of the Word believing in the prophetic task of the Church; we shall seek to strengthen and nerve to her special vocation our dear mother the Church of England; we shall serve by all proper means the ecumenical cause; we shall never forget that we are called to set forward the unity of mankind; we shall be like Father Willie Doyle, Jesuit Padre in the first World War, who, as he stooped over a wounded soldier in the No Man's Land between the British and German trenches, was rebuffed by the soldier with the words: "I don't belong to your Church." "No," said Willie Doyle, "but you belong to my God."

The Abbey therefore goes forward to be Anglican, Catholic, Ecumenical, and Christianly Humanist, and at the heart of these things it will cling to the evangelical facts, Bethlehem and Calvary, the birth, the life, the death, the saving sacrifice, the mighty resurrection, and the glorious ascension of Jesus Christ, in whose name we go forward in faith; and when it is hard, as it will be in all sorts of ways, this life of faith, remember that you have a strategy; remember too that "Christ leads me through no darker rooms then He went through before".

By M. Louise Haskins, *quoted in a Christmas broadcast* by George VI

I said to the man who stood at the gate of the year: "Give me a light that I may tread safely into the unknown." And he replied, "Go out into the darkness and put thine hand into the hand of God. That shall be to thee better than a light and safer than a known way."

From **The True Wilderness** *by* H. A. Williams

Often we shall have to change the direction of our thinking and our wishing and our striving – that is what repentance means – taking our bearings afresh and trying a new road.

Prayer:

Dear God give us serenity to face those things in life which cannot be changed and the courage to strive to change those things which should be changed, and in both to put our whole trust in Thee. Amen.

From **The Shaking of the Foundations** *by* Paul Tillich

ISAIAH 43:16, 18–19

> *Thus says the Lord*
> *Who made a way through the sea,*
> *A path through the mighty waters.*
> *"Remember not the former things,*
> *Neither consider the things of old;*
> *Behold I am doing a new thing,*
> *Even now it is springing to light.*
> *Do you not perceive it?*
> *A way will I make in the wilderness*
> *And rivers in the desert."*

... "Remember not the former things, neither consider the things of old" says the prophet. That is the second thing we must say about the new: it must break the power of the old, not only in reality, but also in memory; and one is not possible without the other. Let me say a few words about this most sublime point in the prophetic text and in the experience of every religion. We cannot be born anew if the power of the old is not broken within us; and it is not broken so long as it puts the burden of guilt upon us. Therefore religion, prophetic as well as apostolic, pronounces above all, forgiveness. Forgiveness means that the old is thrown into the past because the new has come. "Remember not" in the prophetic words does not mean to forget easily. If it meant that, forgiveness would not be necessary. Forgiveness means a throwing out of the old, as remembered and real at the same time, by the strength of the new which could never be the saving new if it did not carry with it the authority of forgiveness.

I believe that the situation is the same in our social and historical existence. A new which is not able to throw the old into the past, in remembrance as well as in reality, is not the really new. The really new is able to break the power of old conflicts between man and man, between group and group, in memory and reality. It is able to break the old curses, the result of former guilt, inherited by one generation from another, the guilt between nations, between races, between classes, on old and new continents these curses by which the guilt of one group, in reality and memory, permanently produces guilt in another group. What power of the new will be great and saving enough to break the curses which have laid waste half of our world? What new thing will have the saving power to break the curse brought by the German nation upon herself before our eyes? "Remember not the former things", says the prophet. That is the second thing which must be said about the new.

"Behold I am doing a new thing." "I" points to the source of the really new, to that which is always old and always new, the Eternal. That is the third thing which must be said about the new: it bears the mark of its eternal origin in its face, as it did when Moses came from the mountains with the tablets of the law, opening a new period of history. The really new is that which has in itself eternal power and eternal light. New things arise in every moment, at every place. Nothing is today as it was yesterday. But this kind of new is old almost as soon as it appears. It falls under the judgement of the Preacher: "There is no new thing under the sun." Yet sometimes a new thing appears which does not age so easily, which makes life possible again, in both our personal and our historical existence, a saving new, which has the power to appear when we least expect it, and which has the power to throw into the past what is old and burdened with guilt and curse. Its saving power is the power of the Eternal within it. It is new, really new, in the degree to which it is beyond old and new, in the degree to which it is eternal. And it remains new so long as the eternal power of the Eternal is manifest within it, so long as the light of the Eternal shines through it. For that power may become weaker; that light may become darker; and that which was truly a new thing may become old itself. That is the tragedy of human greatness in which something eternal appears.

When the Apostles say that Jesus is the Christ, they mean that in Him the new eon which cannot become old is present. Christianity lives through the faith that within it there is the new which is not just another new thing but rather the principle and representation of all the really new in man and history. But it can affirm this only because the Christ deprived Himself of everything which can become old, of all individual and social standing and greatness, experience and power. He surrendered all these in His death and showed in His self-surrender the only thing which is eternally new: love. "Love never ends," says His greatest apostle. Love is the power of the new in every man and in all history. It cannot age; it removes guilt and curse. It is working even today toward new creation. It is hidden in the darkness of our souls and of our history. But it is not completely hidden to those who are grasped by its reality. "Do you not perceive it?" asks the prophet. Do we not perceive it?

From **The Journey Inwards** by F. C. Happold

A wind has blown across the world
And tremors shake its frame;
New things are struggling to their birth
And naught shall be the same.
The earth is weary of its past,
Of folly, hate and fear;
Beyond a dark and stormy sky
The dawn of God is near.

A wind is blowing through the earth,
A tempest fierce and strong;
The trumpets of the Christ the King,
Thunder the skies along;
The summons to a high crusade
Calling the brave and true
To find a new Jerusalem
And make the world anew.

The Transfiguration by Edwin Muir

So from the ground we felt that virtue branch
Through all our veins till we were whole, our wrists
As fresh and pure as water from a well,
Our hands made new to handle holy things,
The source of all our seeing rinsed and cleansed
Till earth and light and water entering there
Gave back to us the clear unfallen world.
We would have thrown our clothes away for lightness,
But that even they, though sour and travel stained,
Seemed, like our flesh, made of immortal substance,
And the soiled flax and wool lay light upon us
Like friendly wonders, flower and flock entwined
As in a morning field. Was it a vision?
Or did we see that day the unseeable
One glory of the everlasting world
Perpetually at work, though never seen
Since Eden locked the gate that's everywhere

And nowhere? Was the change in us alone,
And the enormous earth still left forlorn,
An exile or a prisoner? Yet the world
We saw that day made this unreal, for all
Was in its place. The painted animals
Assembled there in gentle congregations,
Or sought apart their leafy oratories,
Or walked in peace, the wild and tame together,
As if, also for them, the day had come.
The shepherds' hovels shone, for underneath
The soot we saw the stone clean at the heart
As on the starting-day. The refuse heaps
Were grained with that fine dust that made the world;
For he had said, 'To the pure all things are pure.'
And when we went into the town, he with us,
The lurkers under doorways, murderers,
With rags tied round their feet for silence, came
Out of themselves to us and were with us,
And those who hide within the labyrinth
Of their own loneliness and greatness came,
And those entangled in their own devices,
The silent and the garrulous liars, all
Stepped out of their own dungeons and were free.
Reality or vision, this we have seen.
If it had lasted but another moment
It might have held for ever! But the world
Rolled back into its place, and we are here,
And all that radiant kingdom lies forlorn,
As if it had never stirred; no human voice
Is heard among its meadows, but it speaks
To itself alone, alone it flowers and shines
And blossoms for itself while time runs on.
But he will come again, it's said, though not
Unwanted and unsummoned; for all things,
Beasts of the field, and woods, and rocks, and seas,
And all mankind from end to end of the earth
Will call him with one voice. In our own time,
Some say, or at a time when time is ripe.
Then he will come, Christ the uncrucified,
Christ the discrucified, his death undone,
His agony unmade, his cross dismantled –
Glad to be so – and the tormented wood

Will cure its hurt and grow into a tree
In a green springing corner of young Eden,
And Judas damned take his long journey backward
From darkness into light and be a child
Beside his mother's knee, and the betrayal
Be quite undone and never more be done.

Prayer:

Do Thou give us, O Holy Spirit of God, a new mind to comprehend Thy loving purposes, a new heart to rejoice in them, and a new perseverance upon the paths of Thy will, now and ever.

———

To Thee, O Lord.
For Thee, O Lord.
With Thee, O Lord.
In Thee, O Lord.

Acknowledgements

THE COMPILER acknowledges with gratitude the courtesy of the following companies and individuals in permitting the use of copyright material: The Longman Group Ltd for *The Fruits of the Spirit, Abba* and *Light of Christ* all by Evelyn Underhill; J. M. Dent and Sons Ltd for *Immanence* and *Theophanies* both by Evelyn Underhill; Penguin Books Ltd for *The Religious Life* by Sister Edna Mary; The Lutterworth Press and Dr Leslie Weatherhead for *Time for God*; The Religious Education Press, T. H. Parker and F. J. Teskey for *Let there be God* (1968); A. R. Mowbray Ltd for *In the Silence* by Father Andrew, *Our Daily Prayers* by W. J. Carey; Christopher Bryant S.S.J.E. for *The Psychology of Prayer* and for editorial material from *New Fire* (32a Marston Street, Oxford); Methodist Publishing House for *Five for Sorrow, Ten for Joy* and *The Use of Praying* by Neville Ward; Miss Carolyn Scott for *One*; The National Council of Churches for *The Revised Standard Version Bible*; Punch for *The Green Veil*; Constable and Co. Ltd for *The True Wilderness* by H. A. Williams C.R.; James Nisbet and Co. Ltd for *Worship* by Evelyn Underhill; The Faith Press Ltd for *The Life of the Spirit* by Herbert Waddams and *Christian Spirituality Today* edited by Archbishop Michael Ramsey; Associated Book Publishers Ltd for *Concerning the Inner Life* by Evelyn Underhill; Search Press Ltd for *In Time of Temptation* by Ladislaus Boros; Gill and Macmillan Ltd for *Prayers of Life* by Michel Quoist; Alfred A. Knopf, Inc. for *The Prophet* (copyright 1923 by Kahlil Gibran; renewal copyright 1951 by Administrators C.T.A. of Kahlil Gibran Estate and Mary G. Gibran) and for *Jesus, Son of Man* (copyright 1928 and renewed 1956 by Mary G. Gibran and William Saxe, Ad. C.T.A. of the Kahlil Gibran Estate); SCM Press Ltd for *Spirituality for Today* edited by Alan Ecclestone, *The Honest to God Debate* by J. A. T. Robinson and David L. Edwards, *The School of Prayer* by Olive Wyon, *Life Together* by Dietrich Bonhoeffer, *Household of God* by Leslie Newbiggin, *Honest to God* by J. A. T. Robinson and *The Shaking of the Foundations* by Paul Tillich; Macmillan and Co. Ltd for *Readings from St John's Gospel, Palm Sunday to Easter, A Book of School Worship* and *Lent with William Temple* all by Archbishop William Temple;

Index of Authors